More about
The Cultivate Project

The book you hold in your hands is the anchor for a best-in-class generational mentoring initiative that infuses life-on-life relationships into the DNA of a school. Designed specifically with the busy teacher in mind, *The Cultivate Project* helps teachers:

- *transform* the student interactions they already have into life-shaping "mentoring moments,"
- *connect* with this new, mysterious Millennial generation in a way that inspires spiritual growth, and
- *engage* the hearts of students mired in a purposeless, relativistic, and apathetic culture.

In addition to this 280 page paperback, *The Cultivate Project* consists of:

The Cultivate Project Professional Development Training Course. A 14-session DVD course (worth 2 CEUs and 1 optional graduate credit) featuring fast-paced dialogue between leading Christian teacher-mentors on tough mentoring questions, complete with implementation guide.

The Cultivate Community. A groundbreaking online resource that enables teachers to assess their mentoring style, get further training, download topic-specific mentoring plans, and track mentorees' progress.

The Cultivate Project launches teachers into a whole new way of understanding their calling and relating to their students. Here's what educators are saying:

- "Just the shot in the arm we needed." School Head
- "This is *the* catalyst we need to move our school to the next level of ministry effectiveness." Administrator
- "Exactly the right tool at exactly the right time." Principal
- "Restores the joy of teaching." Student Activities Coordinator

Check out www.TheCultivateProject.org for more information.

CULTIVATE:

Forming the Emerging Generation through
Life-on-life Mentoring

cul·ti·vate (kŭl'tə-vāt')

to nurture, foster;
to seek the goodwill of;
to improve, tend;
to promote the growth of;
to form, refine;
to prepare to bear fruit.

JEFF MYERS, Ph.D.
WITH PAUL AND PAIGE GUTACKER

PASSING THE BATON INTERNATIONAL, INC.
P.O. Box 7
Dayton, TN 37321
www.TheCultivateProject.org
423-570-1000

First published in the United States of America by Passing the Baton International, Inc.

THE LIBRARY OF CONGRESS HAS CATALOGED THIS EDITION OF THE BOOK AS FOL-
LOWS:

Myers, Jeffrey
Cultivate: Forming the Emerging Generation through Life-On-Life Mentoring
p. cm.
Includes biographical references.
ISBN-13: 978-0-9815049-2-6
ISBN-10: 0-9815049-2-2
Library of Congress Control Number: 2010906486
Mentoring. 2. Discipleship—Christianity. 3. Education—Christian.

Foreword

By Josh & Sean McDowell

It's our pleasure to introduce and recommend *Cultivate* – a book that echoes our passion to see a generation of young people find the Christian faith to be relevant, reliable, and relational. That's what we've written about in our new book, *The Unshakable Truth*, and it's what we've devoted our lives to.

[Josh:] *For decades, the mission of the Josh McDowell Ministry has been to serve others until the whole world hears the truth of the gospel. This is the focus of everything we do. Each of our legacies depends upon passing the baton of godly faithfulness to the next generation.*

[Sean:] I've spent years as a Christian educator, and Jeff Myers and his team at Passing the Baton International have profoundly changed the way I think about influencing young adults. I've come to firmly believe that worldview training through personal, life-on-life mentoring is the key that unlocks genuine influence.

The hearts of young adults are our treasure, and *Cultivate* is the treasure map.

[Sean:] The next generation is primed and ready for relationship with you. Yes, you. Their hearts are open. There's never been a better time.

[Josh:] *And it's simpler than you think; Cultivate will show you precisely how to begin reaching them, step by step, through numerous "here's-how-you-could-say-it" conversational examples. This is the practical piece of the puzzle many parents, youth pastors, teachers, and other caring adults are missing.*

Like us, the authors of *Cultivate* are members of two different generations; Jeff Myers is a Gen Xer and Paul and Paige Gutacker are both

Millennials. As we've experienced in our own ministry, this combination of perspectives adds depth and richness to the discussion. We're convinced that *Cultivate* holds something significant and fresh for mentoring novices and veterans alike.

[Sean:] You've made an excellent choice in picking up this book. You're joining a movement of hundreds of thousands of people who are rediscovering the ancient art of mentoring.

[Josh:] *Your influence can be tremendous and eternal. Blessings on you as you begin forming the emerging generation through life-on-life mentoring!*

Josh & Sean McDowell

Thanks to:

We'd like to thank our loving and supportive families, our community, our dear friends – old and new, and the dozens of caring adults who mentored us and gave shape to our souls. Thank you for allowing God to use you in our cultivation.

We're humbled by the feedback, insight, encouragement and financial support that brought *The Cultivate Project* to reality. May thousands upon thousands in the emerging generation come alive as a result of your touch. We would like to specifically thank the following people:

Jim Van Eerden, Paul Stanley, Tim Krupa, and the Thompson and Drake families for their vision for this project and their dedication in bringing it to life.

John Cook, JR Kerr, Paul Stanley and Christie Woodson for helping guide PTBI to reach its potential.

Matt Benson, Sean Bevier, Andy Crumpler, Dan Egeler, Roger Erdvig, JR Kerr, Juergen Kneifel, Sean McDowell, Wolfgang Seibler, Paul Stanley, Tony Stoltzfus, John Stonestreet, Mary Verstraete, and Bonnie-Marie Yager for letting us pick your brains and glean from your evaluated experience.

David Austin, Kris Berger, Sean Bevier, Terry Broberg, Gail Ratzlaff, Ben Williams, Kim Woody, Matt Benson and Bonnie-Marie Yager. We loved the discussions with you, we are humbled by your editing prowess, and we will always be grateful for the insightful feedback that made this a much better book.

Rob Carter, Marla Crisman, Antoinette Duran, Roger Erdvig, Spencer Folmar, Sean McDowell, Koyah Rivera, Tammy Skinner and Patrick Winfield for participating in *The Cultivate Project* DVD. Let's keep the dialogue going!

John Craig, Steve Dill, Brian Dougherty, Robin Hom, George Hornickel, and Wendell Meadows for being vision-driven early adopters. May many thousands follow in your wake.

– Jeff Myers, Paul Gutacker and Paige Gutacker

Quick Look:

Contents:

Introduction

Who We Are

Throughout *Cultivate*, we'll be using the collective pronoun "we" to describe the authors of this volume. Thank you for giving us the opportunity to introduce ourselves. We are the staff of Passing the Baton International, Inc. (PTBI), a non-profit organization with a mission of mobilizing adults to personally and intentionally mentor, coach, and disciple the emerging generation to be culture-shaping leaders. Dr. Jeff Myers, the lead author, founded PTBI in 2006, after 15 years of training young leaders as a college professor, curriculum developer, and speaker. Paul and Paige Gutacker serve as researchers and writers for PTBI. At the time of this writing, Paul is working on his masters in spiritual theology and Paige is becoming certified as a professional life coach.

In some ways we didn't know what we were getting into when we started PTBI. The last four years have been a whirlwind, with PTBI trainers addressing more than 125,000 people in keynote addresses and delivering an intensive, live training workshop to more than 20,000 people, in an average group size of 100 participants. As of this writing, 1,000 Christian schools and churches are now using the training in DVD form. Trainers are offering our training course in five languages in ten countries. Our first group of trainers has already equipped other trainers, and these folks are now enthusiastically preparing Christian adults to pass the baton in hard-to-reach places in Asia and Africa.

As we watch God work, we have absolutely no doubt that there is a global movement of God in our time, calling the church back to the kinds of incarnational relationships that Jesus demonstrated during His time on earth. This movement of living life-on-life involves an enthusiastic embrace of one-on-one and small group relationships, hospitality, encouragement, challenge, inspiration, and even correction. It reflects a hunger and thirst to not just survive, but to discover what it means to develop genuine, transgenerational community. This movement is in step with the African proverb which states, "If you want to go fast, go alone. If you want to go far, go together."

How To Read This Book

Cultivate is laid out in a three part movement: *Gardening Tools, Growing Seasons,* and *Greenhouse Conditions.*

Part One: Gardening Tools starts the book with a simple, fresh idea: mentoring is like cultivating a garden. Gardeners must know what they are cultivating, so Part One asks the question: "What is the emerging generation like?" The answers may surprise you – and they will certainly set you up to engage meaningfully with this generation of young adults. Then, the book provides the cultivating tools you need by developing a new model for mentoring based on six relational gestures. When mentors employ all six of these gestures, the end result is a relationship which provides the ideal space for growth to take place.

Part Two: Growing Seasons suggests that just as there are natural seasons during which certain crops grow best – there are certain seasons during which young adults need answers to three important life questions: "What is the purpose of my life?", "What is true?", and "What difference do I make?" The imagery of the growing season suggests that you have to *know* your mentoree in order to discern what God is doing in that person's life during that growing season. Walking alongside the emerging generation as they wrestle with these questions and focusing on these three areas of flourishing is the direction we believe life-on-life mentoring should take.

Part Three: Greenhouse Conditions erects the scaffolding of good mentoring relationships. People often associate the word "greenhouse" with "greenhouse gases," which carries a negative connotation. In reality, a greenhouse is a strategically designed growth-accelerator. In Part Three we'll show how to build a mentoring greenhouse that is an ideal environment in which young adults can grow. You'll learn how to get started as a mentor, to find a mentoree, to deepen the relationship with your mentoree, to evaluate and close a mentoring relationship, to protect yourself and your mentoree, and to be cultivated as a mentor yourself. If you are looking for a quick start, begin with this section. However, we've put it as the third section of the three because we feel strongly that the ideas in the first two sections will inform how you interact with the ideas in the third.

Throughout the book we've made special room for stories from those who have been mentored by caring teachers. These stories come from faithful readers of Jeff's weekly leadership email newsletter, and you'll find them sprinkled throughout (set in shaded boxes).

We hope you enjoy *Cultivate*.

– Jeff Myers, Paul Gutacker and Paige Gutacker

PART ONE:
GARDENING TOOLS

Picking Up the Skills to Cultivate Young Adults

What You'll Find In Part One
- How to cultivate people through personal, life-on-life relationships.
- A pivotal discussion on generational differences which highlights twelve distinctives of the emerging generation alongside practical, thought-provoking conversational approaches.
- A new paradigm of mentoring that helps people expand their repertoire of relational gestures (modeling, friendship, advising, coaching, teaching, and sponsoring).
- Powerful, actionable training on employing the gesture of coaching.

CHAPTER 1:
How People Grow

What To Expect
- The mystery of how one man influenced dozens of America's founding fathers and shaped history.
- Buddies and bosses: why most people miss the mark when it comes to intergenerational relationships.
- God's pattern for relationships – and what happens when the church abandons it.
- The emerging generation: a wide-open opportunity to get relationships right.

How a Teacher at a Tiny, Rural School Changed the World

In 1768 a 45-year-old Scottish preacher took charge of a tiny, poor, rural school for teenage boys. He found the boys to be unprepared and unruly and the conditions of the school's only building to be deplorable. Because there were so few students, the preacher had to do all of the teaching himself until he was able to convince some tutors to help him. Yet, in faithfully mentoring his few charges, this preacher started down a path that changed the world.

The preacher's name was John Witherspoon. The small, dilapidated school he took charge of is now Princeton University. And what happened to the 450 students he trained during his 26 years as college president is one of the most astounding facts in American history:

- 114 became ministers
- 49 became U.S. Representatives
- 28 became U.S. Senators
- 26 became state judges
- 17 became members of their state constitutional conventions
- 14 became delegates to the state conventions that ratified the Constitution
- 12 became members of the Continental Congress
- 8 became U.S. district judges
- 5 became delegates to the Constitutional Convention
- 3 became U. S. Supreme Court justices
- 3 became Attorney Generals
- 2 became foreign ministers
- 1 became Secretary of State
- Aaron Burr, Jr. became Vice-President
- James Madison became President[1]

If you're like us when we first saw this list, you're thinking, "Wow! One person really *can* make a difference!" And the truly remarkable thing is that Witherspoon didn't make a difference as a public official or a captain of industry – he changed the world as a *teacher*.

What was it about Witherspoon that influenced those young men to become America's founding fathers? We commonly get three answers to this question.

Some say: "It was Witherspoon's biblical worldview." Yes, Witherspoon reasoned from scripture and taught his students to do the same. This is foundational, but it's not enough to explain Witherspoon's influence. There are many preachers and teachers who teach the truth and yet fail to move their hearers to action. Certainly something about Witherspoon's approach went beyond content.

For more on what a biblical worldview is, see p. 114.

Others say: "It was Witherspoon's intelligence." No doubt John Witherspoon was a smart guy. He wrote and spoke a lot. But was it the force of his ideas that carried the day? It doesn't seem so. Historian Mark A. Noll says, "neither was he an intellectual giant or a particularly consistent thinker."[2]

Still others say: "It was Witherspoon's leadership gifts." Well, not really. Although Princeton prospered under Witherspoon's influence, it did not prosper as much as one would expect during a 26-year term of leadership. The average graduating class between 1768 and 1794 seems to have been about 17 students, and in the years surrounding the American War for Independence the college produced as few as five graduates a year.[3] On the radar of influence such a small, impoverished college would barely register as a blip.

Small numbers don't mean small influence. See p. 128 for what Jesus did to equip twelve world changers.

Worldview, intelligence and leadership are each important. But the thing that edged Witherspoon into culture-shaping influence is what he called "true religion" – the way in which one's faith is communicated from the inside out. The matters of the heart overflow into one's life, and it is this passion that causes genuine influence to bloom:

How can you cultivate "true religion" in your life? See p. 218.

> True religion will give unspeakable force to what a minister says. There is a piercing and a penetrating heat in that which flows from the heart, which distinguishes it both from the coldness of indifference, and the false fire of enthusiasm and vain-glory. We see that a man truly pious, has often esteem, influence and success, though his parts may be much inferior to others, who are more capable, but less conscientious.[4]

"Example is more intelligible than precept," he continued, noting that "a holy life immediately reaches, and takes possession of the heart."[5] God had transformed Witherspoon's interior life in a manner that overflowed naturally into the very way he interacted with people. One of Witherspoon's students, Ashbel Green, said that Witherspoon's cultivation of personal influence gave him *presence* in greater quantity than anyone he had ever met except George Washington.[6]

One name for this kind of influence is modeling. See p. 63 for more.

Witherspoon became one of the most influential men in history because he lived true religion in such a way as to influence a generation of young men who became America's founding fathers. Who are the John Witherspoons of today? Who will invest in the emerging generation of political, business, community and religious leaders? Who will prepare the teachers, moms and dads, film-makers and cutting-edge scientists? Who will build and nurture the church of tomorrow? Who will shape the future?

Our future leaders need more than TV personalities, heroes or superstars; they need to see God's transforming work in your life.

The answer is: *you*. You have the opportunity to prepare the emerging generation. You *must* prepare them because they will shape the future of people, organizations, and countries. Our future leaders need more than TV personalities, heroes, or superstars; they need to see God's transforming work in your life and experience that kind of transformation themselves.

Buddies and Bosses: How *Not* to Relate to the Emerging Generation

Every adult senses at some level the need to reach out to the emerging generation. That reaching out usually takes one of two forms: the "buddy" or the "boss."

Friendship is a vital part of mentoring. See p. 65 for more.

The buddy mentality's highest goal is to be *with* someone. The relationship itself is the point. An example of buddy mentality is a well-meaning youth worker who wants teenagers to think he's cool and to hang out with him like a friend.

Of course, being a buddy is not, in itself, a bad thing. God created us in His image, which gives us dignity and value. He made us for relationship with Him and with each other. Being in relationship with others is an amazing and essential part of being an image-bearer.

However, the buddy mentality doesn't take in the whole picture. By itself, it fails to account for the reality of human depravity. Human beings are broken, sinful, and in need of transformation. Young adults, like all of us, have sin, pain, immaturity, weaknesses, and blind spots. The buddy won't address these issues because that wouldn't be 'cool.' If the primary goal of an intergenerational relationship is to be buddies, it's easy for the young adult to miss what the relationship can bring: life transformation. And that's a big miss, because that is what God is all about – transforming His people to become like Christ and do His kingdom work.

What does a more complete picture of humanity look like? See p. 119.

The boss mentality, on the other hand, sees relationships as being *for* something else – as a means to an end, if you will. In the business world, bosses typically build relationships with employees so they'll be more productive. In the same way, many Christian adults form relationships with young adults as a means to something else, such as getting them to join the church or make some sort of spiritual commitment.

Of course, there is a place for teaching and advising. See pp. 67 and 69.

Of course, there is something good at the heart of the boss mentality. It recognizes that the Fall actually happened and that human depravity is part of our current reality. Young adults are broken, and the desire to guide them down a better path is a good thing.

But something is also missing from the boss mentality: a recognition of dignity. As fellow image-bearers of God, young adults are people, not projects – they are valuable and worth being in relationship with, for relationship's sake. Because it tries to control the outcome, the boss mentality misses how transformation actually works: from the inside out, not the outside in. Bosses try to measure success by surface changes, such as praying a prayer of commitment, admitting sin, reading the Bible more, or swearing less. Unfortunately, in only measuring these outward signs, a person with the boss mentality can miss what God is really after – not well-behaved moralists, but rather people who love Him with all of their hearts, souls, and minds.

We recognize that we are only talking about two extreme categories here, and that most relationships are fairly nuanced. Our point, though, is that adults should go deeper with young adults than being a buddy or a

As fellow image-bearers of God, young adults are people, not projects – they are valuable and worth being in relationship with, for relationship's sake.

boss. For those of us who have struggled with being buddies or bosses when it comes to relating to the next generation, here is a message of freedom: you don't have to try to be the coolest person to hang out with, nor do you have to have all the answers. There's another way to relate.

In fact, giving answers might actually inhibit growth. See p. 77.

Mentoring: The Key to Transformational Relationships

To discover the right approach to intergenerational relationships, we must start with the right assumptions. Young adults have dignity; God is active in their lives and they have great value. Young adults also suffer from depravity; they are not fine just the way they are, and God wants to mold them ever more into the likeness of Christ. Intergenerational relationships should transcend mere *withness* and simultaneously be cherished as having value beyond what they can be used *for*. We call this kind of relationship "mentoring." Fully recognizing that we are employing an overused word, let us paint a picture of mentoring that will infuse it with fresh meaning.

Mentoring is like cultivating a garden. The word "cultivate" means:
- to nurture, foster;
- to seek the goodwill of;
- to improve, tend;
- to promote the growth of;
- to form, refine;
- to prepare to bear fruit.

Obviously, cultivation only happens when the gardener is *with* the garden. It would be silly to try to garden from afar, hands-off from the soil, giving verbal commands to the seedlings. Also, the gardener cannot ultimately control what the seeds grow into; it's absurd to demand that the seedlings produce the kind of fruit he wants, on his time frame. A "boss" can't be a good gardener if he neglects the cultivation process by trying to skip straight to the harvest.

Young adults are often stunted by the cultural expectation of adolescence. See p. 96.

Cultivation also only happens when the gardener is *for* fruit. A gardener would be silly to be content with stunted seedlings and not offer them the nourishment and even pruning that would result in them shooting up into mature plants. It's pointless to garden with no intention to see flourishing or harvest fruit. A "buddy" can't be a good gardener if he neglects the cultivation process by not expecting the harvest.

Mentoring is the cultivation of young adults, the tender caring for and nurturing of them so that they will grow, flourish, and be fruitful.

The gardener can water, fertilize, tend, and prune – but only God causes the plant to flourish and bear fruit. Likewise the mentor can cultivate a young adult, but it is God who brings growth and transformation. The answer to the question "Is it up to me, or is it up to God?" is "Yes." God brings the results, and He does so through His people. In fact, this is what God has done for a long time.

For more on trusting God with the results, see p. 178.

God's Normative Pattern: Personal, Small, Influential

God is telling a story in which people are formed through relationships. In this story God infuses seemingly ordinary human relationships with His grace, making them powerfully transformational as a key part of His kingdom plan. God can use any means that He chooses to accomplish His purposes, but He most often uses personal relationships. We see this throughout scripture:

Moses brought a massive group of people out of Egypt, but he didn't treat them as a mass. He divided them into units of 1,000, 100, 50, and 10. He also commanded the children of Israel to share God's law with those they were in relationship with: their families and those they interacted with outside the home (Exodus 18; Deuteronomy 6:6-8).

In 2 Timothy 2:2 Paul urged Timothy to pass truth to other men that he knew were faithful – a vital task for the rapidly growing New Testament church. Also, in a letter to Titus at the end of his life, Paul outlined the importance of relationships between older and younger believers for the keeping of sound doctrine (Titus 2).

The greatest leadership successions in scripture were those where leaders walked with the next generation: Abraham/Isaac, Moses/Joshua, Naomi/Ruth, Elijah/Elisha, Jesus/John the Apostle, Paul/Timothy.

Mentoring is the cultivation of young adults, the tender caring for and nurturing of them so that they will grow, flourish, and be fruitful.

What made
the difference
for these
spiritually
mature
young
adults?
They had
mentors.

The greatest leadership failures in scripture were those where leaders failed in their responsibilities to the next generation: Adam/sons, David/ Solomon, Hezekiah/Manasseh, Eli/sons.

These examples, and many others, show that God uses relationships, as iron sharpening iron, to mold His people into who He wants them to be.

Not surprisingly, new research is confirming what scripture has already shown us about the significance of life-on-life relationships. In his recently completed doctoral dissertation at Talbot School of Theology, Jason Lanker demonstrated that adolescents who had natural mentors ("relationships with non-parental adults from whom high school students received support and guidance without the help of a formalized program") more deeply experienced God's presence, connected to God in times of suffering, felt realistically accepted by God and were secure in their relationships with Him.[7]

Sponsoring a
mentoree to an
additional mentor
is a great idea.
See p. 71.

What made the difference for these spiritually mature young adults? The study showed that it was not how long they had been Christians or how well their parents had modeled the Christian faith. Rather, it was the fact that they had mentors. And apparently, the more mentors they had, the higher their score was on Lanker's spiritual life assessment.[8]

Mentoring leads to other types of flourishing as well. As teachers become more skilled at mentoring, they develop a new approach to their students – one that mixes high expectations with an attitude of warmth, caring, support and acceptance. As it turns out, these skills are conclusively and overwhelmingly related to student success. Consider just a few insights from the volumes of academic research on the subject:

- Students' sense of being liked, respected and valued by a teacher predicted whether they would value the subject matter and expect success.[9]
- Students who believed their teacher cared for them believed they learned more.[10]
- Students' feelings of being accepted by teachers were significantly related to emotional, cognitive and behavioral engagement in class.[11]

- Teachers who expressed greater warmth tended to develop greater confidence in students.[12]
- Teachers' nurturing behaviors were related to students' adoption and internalization of teachers' goals and values.[13]
- Teachers' interpersonal relationship skills were significantly associated with students' achievement motivation and self-esteem.[14]
- Mentoring increased teachers' sensitivity to at-risk children and to children as individuals, and it improved the teachers' ability to cope with difficult situations.[15]
- Programs targeting bullying and other anti-social behavior in school have had mixed results at best, but a program in which at-risk students were mentored by adults in the school context resulted in significantly fewer reports of bullying behavior and lower feelings of depression.[16]

The Consequences of Abandoning God's Pattern

Tragically, although life-on-life relationships are God's pattern for transformation, they have been significantly neglected in the church – to the detriment of the emerging generation. Young adults have found the church to be an unfriendly place of shallow relationships and pat answers. Well-intentioned church workers may dispute this conclusion, but the emerging generation is voting with its feet. Those born in the 1980s and 90s have walked out on church: their level of church attendance is the lowest of any generation in American history.[17] Even among those who attended church in high school, only 20% maintain a similar level of commitment in their twenties.[18] This is especially alarming when we consider Norm Willis' strong warning: "In the light of generational transfer, Christianity is always one generation from extinction."[19]

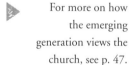

For more on how the emerging generation views the church, see p. 47.

Alarm leads to panic, and, in their panic, many Christians have let go of the very lifesaving ring that would lead to their rescue. Time and time again, well-meaning Christian leaders opt for big, splashy programs – ad campaigns, perfectly orchestrated stadium events, large-scale growth charts, and finely-tuned lectures for a huge audience – under the illusion that they can

The Powerful Impact of a Caring Teacher

It was 1965, and I was in the fourth grade in a new school. Mrs. V. was an encouraging teacher who took the time to get to know each student individually. I remember when she called me to her desk and expressed her amazement and pleasure that I had scored 100% on every math paper. She praised me and encouraged me to keep up the excellent work. I felt special.

Mrs. V. also passed her love of reading on to her students. Every day after lunch, she would read us a story, getting us so involved in the plot that we would beg her to read one more chapter. I credit her with my life-long love of reading.

In the 60s there were very few students from divorced homes living with grandparents and going to a new school. I was one of them. Mrs. V. became my protector and took care of me as I adjusted. She demonstrated the caring heart of a devoted teacher to me. On the last day of the year, I was one of the last students to leave. When my grandfather came to pick me up, Mrs. V. hugged me and cried. It wasn't until years later when I was a teacher that I understood why. Her friendship had a profound impact on me at such an impressionable age.

– Yvonne T.

manufacture growth through mass means. When it comes to people growth, the assumption has been that bigger is better. But that assumption is wrong. People grow better through cultivation rather than through mass production. Flourishing happens when gardeners dig their hands into the dirt and personally nurture a plant or two, not through a mechanical assembly line.

God seems to be a gardener. He starts some of His biggest moves small: a man and woman in a garden, a baby in a manger. He changes people from the inside out, and the change is usually quiet and subtle rather than flashy or spectacular. And, of course, Jesus' way is the same: he often turned away from large, eager crowds to invest time in 12 men of seemingly lackluster potential.

More on Jesus and the twelve ordinary men on p. 128.

It's a recipe for failure to embrace Jesus' *message* and simultaneously abandon his *method* of delivering it. Human plans do not improve on God's plans when it comes to achieving God's results. Bigger is not better; more *personal* is better – especially when it comes to the emerging generation's spiritual growth. Cultivation, not mass production, is what every generation needs.

The Desperate Need – and Huge Opportunity – of the Emerging Generation

Sadly, the emerging generation is largely going uncultivated. This generation of American parents has the unfortunate distinction of being the first generation in history to not concern itself with successfully bringing its young to maturity. As a result, America's young people are really hurting. Tonight, more than one-third of American kids will go to bed in a home where their biological father is not present.[20] It shouldn't be surprising that the National Research Council has stated that, sadly, "one out of every four adolescents in the U.S. is currently at serious risk of not achieving productive adulthood."[21]

Parents are neglecting their responsibility, and, despite the great need, other adults are not standing in the gap. A few years ago the Department of Justice and the National Network of Youth Ministries began a mentoring partnership called mentoryouth.com. We spoke with the director, Lynn Ziegenfuss, who had compiled a nationwide list of organizations working with youth who were open to having mentors. According to Lynn, the number of young people who remained unmatched with mentors numbered 600,000.[22] Education writer Jamie Littlefield says that, regardless of the overwhelming evidence that life-on-life mentoring works, there are still 14.6 million at-risk children in America, each of whom needs a mentor.[23]

The irony is that a surprising number of those in the emerging generation actually *want* mentors. Kara Powell and her colleagues at Fuller Theological Seminary recently discovered this through a survey of college-bound students. One of the questions posed to these young adults, who were regular church-goers, was why they had attended youth group. Of the 22 reasons listed, the respondents ranked "Safe to talk to adults about doubts and questions" 16th and "Adults take time to really listen" 18th. And yet, when asked for the top changes they desired for their youth group, three of

▶ Unsurprisingly, research shows that young adults are lonely. See p. 57.

*It's a recipe for failure to embrace Jesus' **message** and simultaneously abandon his **method** of delivering it.*

Want to become an expert at accountability? See p. 191.

the top five responses were: time for deep conversations, accountability and one-on-one time with leaders.[24] Bottom line: *the very thing young adults are most hoping to receive is the very thing they are least likely to get.*

Ironically, the emerging generation has been given everything except what it really wants: significant life-on-life relationships that cultivate their growth. And that's your cue.

Preparing to Cultivate the Emerging Generation

The very thing young adults are most hoping to receive is the very thing they are least likely to get.

We've laid out our case. The emerging generation is leaving the church in droves, and young people are often being neglected by parents and other adults. This leaves young adults starved for life-on-life relationship with someone besides their peers, all of which provides an incredible opportunity for teachers just like you. You have been designed by God to cultivate the emerging generation as He forms and grows them.

Our goal in *Cultivate* is to jump-start you into mentoring. With that in mind, we've designed the book with three distinct sections. The first part, *Gardening Tools*, provides the foundation for mentors by looking into the 12 major distinctives of the emerging generation and introducing a new paradigm for intergenerational relationships. You'll pick up the skills to cultivate young adults, including how to understand them and reach them at the heart level. The second part, *Growing Seasons,* suggests that there are three areas of flourishing on which to focus while cultivating young adults: design, wisdom, and leadership. The third part, *Greenhouse Conditions,* provides the how-to details for creating a growth-accelerating mentoring greenhouse. You'll learn from mentoring experts how to structure, safeguard, and deepen a mentoring relationship while getting clear, actionable answers to the most commonly asked questions about mentoring.

If you have to choose between reading this book cover to cover and putting it down and beginning to mentor, we hope you'll choose the latter. That's why we've composed the book in a way that allows you to flip to the section or chapter that is most relevant to your mentoring needs at this time. For instance, if you're seeking insight on choosing a mentoree, you may want to jump ahead to Chapter Nine.

If your experience is similar to ours, you'll find that the more you focus on life-on-life mentoring, the more you'll be filled with joy. It's not always easy, of course, but we believe you'll come to count the personal relationships you develop as some of the greatest blessings of your life.

And the potential impact is simply enormous. Imagine what would happen if Christians began to cultivate as John Witherspoon did. Even if we each had just a fraction of his success, the change would be so massive, and so undeniably miraculous, that the whole world would see God's power at work. This is something worth giving our lives to. What an immense privilege to bring the blessing of life-on-life relationships to the world!

CHAPTER 2:
Understanding the Emerging Generation

What To Expect
- Abandoning the five faulty approaches to the emerging generation (condemnation, regulation, accommodation, agreement, and imitation) and choosing the approach of understanding.
- The viewpoints of the four distinct generations in America today.
- Twelve key distinctives of the emerging generation and how they affect the way they think, what they believe, how they live, and how they relate.
- Clear examples for conversing with young adults in ways that engage their hearts and minds.

The Generations are Different – and That's a Good Thing

*The lack of
sameness
is good;
differences
are the
fragrance
of vibrant
relationships.*

An entire industry has sprung up around understanding generational trends. Polls, studies, corporate workshops, and books all proclaim insight that can be gained by drawing a circle around a vast number of people – tens of millions – and explaining them as a discrete group rather than a continuous flow of people being born and growing up. There is a persistent tendency for each generation to see itself as different from – and as better than – the others. British novelist George Orwell once wrote, tongue-in-cheek: "Each generation imagines itself to be more intelligent than the one that went before it, and wiser than the one that comes after it."[25]

Orwell's humorous observation hits the nail on the head. As we researched generational differences, we read our fair share of melancholy "Can-you-believe-how-far-down-we've-gone?" articles. We were surprised, though, to find a number of hyped-up, pollyannaish "The-future-is-peachy-with-these-young'uns-in-charge." prognoses as well. In *Cultivate*, we aren't particularly interested in a "better than/worse than" analysis. Rather, we want to understand what sets each generation apart from the others so we can better relate to them and encourage them in living God-glorifying lives.

Great commonality
is shared in
the imago Dei.
See p. 119.

In taking this approach, we've been surprised at the countless similarities between the generations. We share a common humanity. We share recent experiences. We face similar cultural pressures. We have much more in common than not; yet, we are not the same. Understanding is called for.

The lack of sameness is good; differences are the fragrance of vibrant relationships. Similarities bring us together, but differences keep us interested. For example, if you live in Phoenix, you don't talk about the weather with other locals – it's always hot and dry, so what's the point? Or, if you're a New York Yankees fan, you don't try to convince other Yankees fans that the team is great – they already believe it. In contrast to these examples, it's the areas of disagreement that usually create the best conversations: which TV show is most worth watching, which restaurant is the best in town, or which lure is most likely to catch a large mouth bass.

Four Generations – Four Views of the World

There are four commonly used categories in the literature on generations: Traditionalists, Baby Boomers, Generation Xers, and Millennials.[26] Let's take a look at each one.

- **Traditionalists** are those born between 1925 and 1945. Currently about 38 million are still alive in the U.S. Sometimes called "the greatest generation" for their survival of the great depression and feats of bravery as young service members in World War II and Korea, this generation is generally thought of as patriotic, conservative, hard-working and opinionated.

- **Baby Boomers** are those born between 1946 and 1964, comprising 78 million people in the U.S. population. This is the generation of Woodstock and Vietnam. Baby boomers grew up with social unrest, racial conflict and massive, rapid technological change. They are thought of as idealistic and competitive, yet they are also materialistic and focused on personal fulfillment.

- **Gen Xers** are those born between 1965 and 1979. They number about 62 million. They remember the fall of communism more than the terror of nuclear blackmail. They appreciate the advances brought to them by previous generations, but corporate and political scandals, the AIDS epidemic, etc., have made them leery about the so-called "progress" of modern society. They are seen as cynical and distrustful, but also entrepreneurial and self-reliant.

- **Millennials** are those born between 1980 and 2001. At 92 million, it is a significantly larger generation than the Gen X generation that preceded it. Millennials have grown up in a time of unparalleled prosperity and innovation, yet they've also become conditioned by the 24-hour news cycle to believe that bad news is the norm. Most of them have never known life without the internet and don't know how to look for information without Google. Millennials are viewed as entitled and impatient, but also as team-minded and focused on work-life balance.

To simplify the conversation about generational differences, we're focusing primarily on the distinctions between two broader categories: the established generation (adults) and the emerging generation (young adults, age 12 to early 20's). Those in the established generation include Traditionalists, Baby Boomers, Generation Xers, and some older Millennials. The vast majority of those in the emerging generation are Millennials.

Admittedly, these artificial age distinctions can be awkward as there's overlap as well as difference. An example that comes to mind is a twenty-something teacher who has more in common generationally with high school students than she does with a fifty-something teacher. But our thought is that if you're in authority, you're an influencer and are automatically viewed as an elder by young adults – no matter how much older you are. (Think back to your own childhood – do you recall which of your teachers were in their 20's, 30's, or 40's? Probably not. You likely just viewed them as *older*, lumping them in the same category of "adults" regardless of their decade of birth). That's why, for the purposes of this book, we'll be doing a broad sweep of adults into the established generation and dividing only between it and the typically much younger emerging generation. It's not a perfect system, but we're hoping it explains the generational differences that are relevant to mentoring Millennials.

Growing Up in a Different World

We are all shaped by our experiences, so what we have or have not lived through explains much about how we see the world. Because this is so, Beloit College puts out a "Mindset List" every fall to help college professors across the country understand the life experiences of the incoming freshmen. Here are some excerpts from the Mindset List for the Class of 2013 (those born in 1991, in the middle of the Millennial generation)[27]:

- Carter and Reagan are as distant to them as Truman and Eisenhower were to their parents.
- Everyone has always known what the evening news was before the Evening News came on.
- They have never used a card catalog to find a book.

- There has always been a Cartoon Network.
- Condoms have always been advertised on television.
- Migration of once independent media like radio, TV, videos and compact discs to the computer has never amazed them.

Does this list make you feel old? If so, welcome to the generational shift! While the "Mindset List" is intended to be both eye-opening and humorous, it makes the point that the cultural phenomena and life experiences of the generations are quite different, which results in different ways of thinking, communicating, and relating.

It is often the case that disconcerting generational differences leave an established adult feeling dismayed and even upset at emerging young adults. However, it's imperative to keep in mind that how we view the world is very much shaped by cultural norms and trends. Although cultural influence is always a two-way street, much of the way the emerging generation sees the world can be laid at the feet of a culture it did not create. We point this out not to induce guilt in the established generation or to remove responsibility from the shoulders of the emerging generation. Straight talk about these issues can build bridges of understanding, bridges which we must cross to pass the baton of godly faithfulness to the next generation.

Choosing the Approach of Understanding

We come to this generational discussion with one big question: how exactly should we respond to the emerging generation? In looking at the popular books and articles on generational differences, several common approaches emerge:

- Condemnation ("Nothing about your way is good.")
- Regulation ("I accept you to the degree that you change to be more like me.")
- Accommodation ("I endorse the way you are.")
- Agreement ("I think you're right.")
- Imitation ("I am like you.")

As Diana West points out in *The Death of the Grown Up*, the most prominent cultural response is imitation – trying to be like the emerging

The cultural phenomena and life experiences of the generations are quite different, which results in different ways of thinking, communicating, and relating.

For more on the cultural worship of adolescence, see p. 96.

generation in fashion, attitude and level of maturity. But frankly – that's creepy. It's odd to see middle aged women wearing youth fashions, senior citizens sporting nose rings, or forty-somethings mimicking teen jargon. It's embarrassing to hear adults try to curry favor with the emerging generation by excusing its excesses or imitating its style. Not only is it embarrassing, but it rings hollow to a generation that craves authenticity and thus wants adults to be adults, not knock-off versions of themselves.

Understanding is the heart of relationship. See p. 181.

All five of the above approaches fall short. But there's a sixth approach – and that's *understanding*. This approach says: "I can see where you're coming from, and I believe that we can both grow by sharing our experiences with one another." This isn't just fluff. Openness to share our stories and learn from one another makes for engaging, authentic conversations.

Being teachable doesn't mean giving up your convictions, though. The goal of understanding is acknowledging that differences exist and that each generation has various life experiences that must be meaningfully shared. People committed to understanding seek to listen well and ask questions, but don't downplay the value of sharing their own life experiences. Orwell articulately makes this point:

People committed to understanding seek to listen well and ask questions, but don't downplay the value of sharing their own life experiences.

> [O]ne ought also to stick to one's own world-view, even at the price of seeming old-fashioned: for that world-view springs out of experiences that the younger generation has not had, and to abandon it is to kill one's intellectual roots.[28]

Twelve Distinctives of the Emerging Generation

With the goal of building bridges of understanding, let's explore four areas of distinctiveness in the emerging generation: how they think, what they believe, how they relate, and how they live. For each of the twelve distinctives that follow, you'll find that we've created a few conversation-starting questions and a few response questions to illustrate how you might engage your mentoree in conversation around that topic. These questions are simply examples of what you could say to build your relationship while challenging your mentoree to think deeply and pursue positive change. As you read about these distinctives for the first time, however, you may just want to skim over the conversation examples so you don't get too bogged down. That's fine – our hope is that they'll make a great reference for you to come back to should those topics arise with your mentoree. In fact, we would suggest that as you read the distinctives, you take the time to jot notes in the sidebars on how you see them demonstrated in the lives of your students – and perhaps even in your life!

[How the Emerging Generation Thinks]

1. The emerging generation lives in complexity.

David Kinnaman and Gabe Lyons, authors of the groundbreaking book, *unChristian: What a New Generation Really Thinks about Christianity*, point out that those in the emerging generation "relish mystery, uncertainty, ambiguity. They are not bothered by contradictions."[30] When faced with a paradox or questions, they don't feel the need to rush to find answers. In fact, the Millennials' willingness to withhold judgment can drive the established generation crazy, for reasons that Bill Perry, founder of the Recon generational college ministry model, explains: "The established generation is more interested in the bottom line (truth, biblical worldview, right answers, etc.) and in getting there as quickly as possible. Not so with the emerging generation. For them, it's as much the journey as the destination."

What the mentor can do: avoid overly-simplistic answers or suggestions. Acknowledge ambiguities and complexities that are real, and be humble about what you don't understand or can't explain. Invite a conversation about mystery in the following ways:

- "Let's talk about what we can know and what we can't know. Why do you think we have uncertainty in some areas? What are some things you are certain of?"
- "One of the great things about a life of faith is that it is adventurous – it is a mystery. What are some things about your faith that you can't wrap your mind around? What are some mysteries of your faith?"

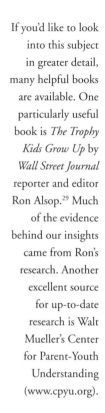

If you'd like to look into this subject in greater detail, many helpful books are available. One particularly useful book is *The Trophy Kids Grow Up* by *Wall Street Journal* reporter and editor Ron Alsop.[29] Much of the evidence behind our insights came from Ron's research. Another excellent source for up-to-date research is Walt Mueller's Center for Parent-Youth Understanding (www.cpyu.org).

For more on sharing truth with complexity-loving young adults, see p. 110.

- "Sometimes life just doesn't add up. Are there experiences or things you've been through that just don't make sense to you? What about them feels contradictory to what you would expect?"

Responding to a difficult issue can be tricky with the emerging generation. Here are some suggestions on how to respond clearly without over-simplifying complex issues:

- "Your question is a tough one and I don't want to brush it off with a simplistic answer. Can you give me some time to think it over and get back to you?"

Is it ever okay to say there are ideas you are willing to die for? Yes! See p. 113.

- "Here's what I think, but this isn't an issue I would take a bullet over."
- "I've spent a lot of time thinking about that myself. Let me tell you some of the thoughts I had along the way, and what I ultimately ended up concluding."

2. The emerging generation is overly self-confident.

Millennials have rarely been denied or told "no," they have always felt special, and they have inflated expectations of their own potential.[31] Since they have been cushioned from failure, Millennials may be overly optimistic about their level of skill and intelligence. They may even assume that they are just lucky, because they haven't had to work that hard for their success.

How can you give a young adult confidence in the right things? See p. 128.

What the mentor can do: give them perspective on their hopes and goals, offer wisdom to them, and encourage endurance. Initiate a conversation about self-confidence in one of these ways:

- "I've found that self-evaluating my strengths and weaknesses has been really helpful. Would you be interested in talking through that with me? It might give you a sense of what you're good at and where you can grow, which is essential to maturing and realizing your full potential."
- "Tell me about a time you attempted something you weren't sure you would succeed at. What was the result? What did you learn from the experience?"

- "What would it look like to take a risk this year? To really stretch yourself?"

If your mentoree has over-inflated expectations or unwarranted confidence, try one of these responses to create dialogue:

- "Pride is the age-old sin, and I don't think any of us are immune from it. What are some ways you see pride showing up in your life? Who might be someone you could share your struggle with and be accountable to concerning this pride?"
- "Sometimes we have blind spots when it comes to our lives. Who are some people you respect who know you well enough to give you honest feedback? What are some ways you could ask for their feedback?"
- "A lot of people show great potential when they're young, but when things get tough they give up. What really gets our respect, though, is people who stick with something, who show tenacity. What would it look like to develop endurance and tenacity? What are some things you want to stick with in the long haul? What are some areas in which you can stick it out now and practice persistence?"

3. The emerging generation wants to change the world.

Over 60% of 13-25 year-olds surveyed say they feel personally responsible for making a difference in the world.[32] This encouraging fact gives mentors a wide opening for discussing what it means to be a leader and how to be a blessing in the world. Curiously, some of this sense of responsibility may derive from their generation's sense of being special. Yes, it's good to want to make a difference, but if it's good because it "makes me feel good about myself" or because "it will cause other people to think well of me," then it feeds narcissism and can actually do long-term harm (both for the server and for those being served).

For more on what narcissism looks like, see p. 93.

What the mentor can do: speak in world-changing language and focus on opportunities they have to make a difference as a function of what God has designed them to do (rather than for the benefits those opportunities provide). Initiate conversations about making a difference in these ways:

Can students change a culture? Absolutely. See p. 135.

- "If you had all the time and money in the world to make a difference, what would you do?"
- "God designed us to be caretakers, to take care of this world and each other. This is our identity. Who have you seen live this identity out well? When people fail to live out their identity well, what does that look like? What are some things you care about that you think might come from this identity?"
- "When we read the end of the story that God is telling, we see in Revelation a world that is beautifully reconciled and restored. What do you long to see restored in the world? What do you long to see restored in yourself?"

Many young people already feel drawn toward certain causes or ministries. How do you encourage them while offering pushback against self-centered motives for service? Respond with one of these:

- "Some students seem to get involved in a cause because it's the trendy thing to do. What does it look like to genuinely care for something – even if it's not cool?"
- "I think it's awesome that you care about others and are involved in things that matter. I'd like to talk about what motivates you to do what you do. Could I have your permission to probe for a minute? What are some good motivations that should be developed? What are some bad motivations behind what you do that should be repented of?"
- "I know that you care about some really important causes. What could be holding you back from making a difference in your spheres of influence right now? How can I help you overcome those barriers?"

[What the Emerging Generation Believes]

4. The emerging generation has a negative view of church.

Kinnaman and Lyons studied young people ages 16-29 who have not had significant interaction with the church. As "outsiders," they view the church as anti-homosexual, judgmental, and hypocritical, and they see evangelicals and born-again Christians in a very negative light.[33]

This is critical. Remember how twenty-somethings are leaving the church in droves? See p. 31.

What the mentor can do: understand that the Millennials you're working with and/or their peers have this perspective, and be willing to talk about it. Express humility for failures of the church while gently offering another perspective. Consider these ways of bringing up the "church issue" in conversation:

- "Church can be a confusing, messy thing sometimes. What are some of your questions about the church? What are some ways you could potentially find answers?"
- "I know your generation is pretty skeptical about the church. This is understandable. What do you think are some of the reasons for this skepticism? Which are legitimate? Which are unfair?"
- "Scripture says the church is a body, and you are a member. Where do you see yourself fitting in the body? What is your role? What might the body lack if you aren't fully participating?"

Odds are, your mentoree and his or her friends will have some serious doubts about the church. You might even have doubts of your own. How do you respond in an honest and hopeful way?

- "I know it's easy to see flaws in the church today. You might be tempted to give up on it entirely. What does God say about the church in scripture? How might what He says affect your attitude towards the church today?"
- "Have you been personally hurt or let down by the church? If so, how?"
- "I understand your doubts about the church. There are some very real flaws and brokenness in it – and yet we know that we can't abandon it. What would it look like to explore what the church does

Express humility for failures of the church while gently offering another perspective.

47

well? Would you be willing to do some research this week and see if you could find five things that the church is doing/has done really well around the world? What about five things *your* church has done really well?"

5. The emerging generation wants what works.

Millennials are driven by pragmatism much more than their parents were.[34] There is an upside and a downside to this. On the positive side, they are focused on generating results rather than just reproducing the processes given to them by previous generations (for example, if they can make enough money working 30 hours a week, they don't feel as guilty about not working 40 or 50). On the negative side, the drive toward pragmatism fosters an "ends justifies the means" approach; it can lead some to justify cheating, lying or stealing, because, they rationalize, those activities "don't personally hurt others." Much of this pragmatism may be tied to an isolation from consequences, and is strongly connected to the next distinctive – moral relativism.

Some of this pragmatism may be tied to a shallow understanding of spiritual truth. See p. 115.

What the mentor can do: be practical and focus on outcomes, and yet simultaneously offer pushback against pragmatism as the key to the good life. Initiate some conversations in these ways:

- "We all like finding better ways to get something done – ways that just work better. Tell me about a time when you were able to do that. What was good about that experience?" (Celebrate this with your mentoree.)
- "Quite a few people think that whatever works in a situation (in business, in the classroom, with relationships) is what's right. What do you think about this pragmatic way of looking at life? What are some ways this perspective can be helpful? What are some ways it can be destructive?"
- "Cheating is viewed as more and more acceptable these days. What is lost when a person 'cheats because it works?' What does he or she miss out on? When is the process as important as the outcome?"

How do you respond when your mentoree is taking a shortcut that might be harmful or even sinful? Try these:

- "What you're talking about seems like it might work, but it strikes me as being ethically shady. What are your thoughts?"
- "It seems like you're taking the shortcut here. What might you miss out on by not going the harder way?"
- "What is it that you value most in this situation? What other values should be considered as you decide what to do?"

6. The emerging generation embraces moral relativism.

This is especially true in the realm of personal morality. This generation is twice as likely as Boomers to have had multiple sex partners by age 18,[35] and substance abuse and cheating are common.[36]

What the mentor can do: recognize that even if your mentoree is not dealing with these issues, his or her friends certainly are. Don't assume naivety or purity, even in young students. Because there is familiarity with these issues, they're probably not too taboo to discuss. But remember – this is an extremely important place for boundaries. See Chapters Ten and Twelve for clear guidance on how to set boundaries for proper self-disclosure. Initiate conversations in these ways:

- "These days, more and more people think that sex before marriage is okay. What do you think? What's the basis for your thoughts? Who agrees with you? Who disagrees with you?"
- "Life is complicated, and not all things or issues are clear. On the other hand, the Bible is straightforward about a lot of moral issues. What are some moral issues that are right or wrong for all people at all times? What are some issues that you think are more relative? Let's talk about that."
- "A lot of pop culture these days says that everything is relative – there is no right and wrong for everybody, there are no absolutes. What do you think about that? What are some possible results of people believing that?"

Keep in mind that the goal is not to make good little moralists. See p. 225.

This generation is twice as likely as Boomers to have had multiple sex partners by age 18.

Sharing truth is not enough. Young adults need to know that they know truth. See p. 115.

Either your mentoree or your mentoree's peers will make relativistic choices. How do you respond well? Consider these conversations:

- "I heard that _____ got involved with _____. What do you think about that? What do you think his or her reasons were for making that choice? What should inform us on whether that was wrong or not? Let's talk about it."

For more on having hard conversations with your mentoree, see p. 189.

- "You said that what you did wasn't wrong because it didn't hurt anybody. What do you base that definition of wrongness on? Who are some people that might have been hurt by your actions? What if one of those people is you?"

- "I'm glad you recognize that your friend made a wrong choice. What are some ways you can respond well to her? What do you think it looks like to be a true friend to her? How does her choice influence how you might handle a similar situation in the future?"

[How the Emerging Generation Lives]

7. The emerging generation multitasks.

Nearly one-third of 8 to 18 year-olds say they multitask "most of the time" by doing homework, watching TV, sending instant messages, talking on the phone, surfing the Web, or listening to music – simultaneously.[37] Not only can multitasking be physically dangerous, as in the case of texting while driving, it can also be relationally damaging, such as when a pattern develops of texting while in the presence of others.[38]

What the mentor can do: recognize that lots of thoughts unrelated to your mentoring time are going on in the mind of your mentoree. Feel free to initiate conversations about multitasking and the use of media and its effects.

- "Few things build relationships like great conversations. What do you think makes up a great conversation? What hinders one? In what ways does listening well make a difference?"

With more mature mentorees, you may want to have a conversation about the value of being present. See p. 149.

- "These days, it's easy to be a hundred places at once – physically in one place, yet texting friends elsewhere, maybe planning for tomorrow, thinking about dinner, and watching TV or listening to music. What are some times when this could really shortchange you, and what would you miss out on? When is it better to be fully present where you are?"

- "Multitasking lets us accomplish multiple things at the same time. What is good about that? What might be bad?"

When you see your mentoree's multitasking is unhealthy, here are some ways to respond:

- "I've noticed that you often check your phone during our time together. Tell me about that. What does that pattern communicate? What would it look like to unplug for a day?"
- "I know it's fun to stay connected with friends through texting or chatting. However, it can be quite distracting from whatever else is going on. When is it just not worth it to be distracted?"
- "You're pretty skilled at multitasking. I thought you'd be interested to know that research shows that when you multitask your brain diverts resources away from memory and learning so that you can focus on two things at once. What do you think about that?"

8. The emerging generation is slow to make decisions.

There is a strong tendency in the emerging generation to explore all of the possibilities before committing. This tendency to delay makes it harder for them to grow up, and it means that they may doubt their own judgments and rely on authority figures to tell them what to do.[39]

What the mentor can do: when it comes to making commitments, encourage good experimentation while discouraging reticence. Be careful to not promote a dependence on your approval; use the coaching gesture to get them to think for themselves and decide on a course of action. Here's how to talk about it:

Coaching is a great way to develop stronger commitment. See p. 86.

- "What's the hardest decision you've ever had to make? What made it so difficult? What voices in your life influenced the path you chose?"
- "Sometimes it's good to keep your options open, but sometimes you have to commit to one thing (and turn down others) in order to succeed. What do you think makes the difference? Which one

Nearly half say they are stressed out (twice the level of Boomers).

do you lean towards? Have you ever been afraid of closing off your options by choosing one thing? Tell me about that."

- "What is the next big decision coming down the road for you? When will you have to make the decision? What are some ways you could prepare to make the decision a good one?"

When your mentoree is slow to make a decision or commitment, respond in these ways:

- "I really appreciate how you respect my opinion on decisions you have to make. It's great to ask for wisdom. On the flip side, practicing decision-making develops confidence and responsibility, and that's a process I think you'll really benefit from. So, on this issue of _____, I'd like to coach you by listening and asking questions rather than giving you my opinion."

- "May I tell you something I've observed? It seems like you've made a series of 'safe' decisions and are settling for the status quo. It might be time to stir the pot. Take a risk. I'd love to see you put yourself out there and try something new and big. How can I support you in that?"

- "Decisions like this can be really tough to make. However, sometimes we have all the information we need and simply have to decide. I think it might be time for you to commit one way or the other. What would help you arrive at a choice?"

9. The emerging generation is overwhelmingly stressed out.

One-fourth of Millennials feel unfulfilled in life, and nearly half say they are stressed out (twice the level of Boomers). They feel exceptional pressure in areas that affect others' views of them, such as in getting good grades.[40] Alarmingly, new research is showing that parents are largely in the dark about how stressed their teenagers actually are – and how that stress is negatively impacting them.[41]

What the mentor can do: find ways to be a de-stressor in their life rather than a stressor. You may also need to work with them on practical

Perhaps your mentoree simply needs some time to relax and recreate. See p. 241 for some great ideas.

life issues such as developing healthy habits of eating, sleeping, exercise, and pace. Consider talking about it in these ways:

- "On a scale of 1-10, one being 'Not at all' and 10 being 'Oh my gosh, please help me,' how stressed do you feel on an average day? What are some of the reasons you can pinpoint?"
- "You're in a great time of life to experiment with different hobbies, activities, and interests. Pursuing too many at once, however, may be overwhelming and may make daily life stressful. It may be best to try various extra-curricular activities one or two at a time – each for a season. What do you think would be helpful about that? What would you like to make room for in this next season?"
- "One of the great things about the Christian life is that we believe God is in control – it's not all up to us. God designed things to reflect that truth by creating the Sabbath, a day to rest, recreate, and remember who He is. What would a day of rest look like for you? What do you think the benefits would be? In what ways might taking a day of rest honor God?"

How should you respond to a mentoree who is stressed out? Try these:

- "I know that you're involved in a lot of good things. But the stress of being so busy suggests that you need to make some changes. What are some things you need to stop doing in order to make room for things that are more important? What is something you could let slide?"
- "You don't want to let anything go even though your overloaded life is stressing you out. What is keeping you from making a change? What would be the worst possible outcome if you did let something go? If you didn't?"
- "God doesn't want you to live a stressed out life. How does being so stressed affect your quality of life? Your relationships with friends? Family? God?

Caring for the Outcasts

My family moved four times when I was a teenager, which meant that I went to a new school every year of high school. My junior year I had a teacher who really cared. She would talk to me before and after class, asking simple questions about how I was doing. In that same class were a few other girls who were also new and having a hard time adjusting, and our little group of outcasts banded together and formed friendships based on our mutual lack of belonging.

One Saturday afternoon we planned to go to the local ice skating rink. We were trying our best to skate around in circles without falling down. Out of the blue, something caught my eye. Across the rink, in the bleachers, sat my teacher! Clinging onto the sides, I made my way over to the bleachers. She called me by name and chatted with me and my group for a few minutes. She was all warmly bundled up, and it dawned on us that she had come out to the rink to be with us. We all basked in the glow of being important enough for her to come and simply watch us skate. We spent the rest of the afternoon taking a spin around the rink, then skating over to chat with our teacher.

I can't tell you what an impact she made on me that day. It was very clear to me that she was there on her own time, simply because she considered us important enough to hang out with. I am now a middle school teacher, and I make sure I spend time outside of school with my students.

- Allegra L.

[How the Emerging Generation Relates]

10. The emerging generation is extremely connected.

Millennials are enthusiastic about their connections to family and friends, are highly connected via social networking sites such as Facebook, and value teamwork – even to the point of showing groupthink.[42] Peer-to-peer relationships are extremely important to them.

What the mentor can do: recognize that the emerging generation desperately wants to be connected to you – they just might not be sure how. Also, they value their friendships so highly that if you criticize their friends, they may take the offense personally and disqualify your advice. Kim Woody, a friend of ours who teaches at a Christian school, is a Millennial, and she recognizes this in her own generation: "In the wake of divorce (which has affected my generation more than any), Millennials have created 'tribes.' We have created our own families."[43] Here's how to talk about the issue:

- "I know that your generation is really connected through all sorts of electronic means – cell phones, Facebook, etc. What do you like about that? In what ways do those connections help your relationships? In what ways, if any, do they hurt your relationships?"
- "Most people really value what their friends think. What are some things that are important to you that many of your friends value as well? What are some things that are important to you that your friends don't really care about?"
- "You know, for centuries the church has considered solitude and silence to be spiritual disciplines – activities that nourish us spiritually and give us space to connect with God. Sometimes it's really hard to be alone and be quiet when there is media, noise, and communication all around us 24/7. What would you think about each of us disconnecting from media and each spending a day by ourselves one Saturday? What would be hard about that? What could we learn about ourselves, our relationships, and God?"

You may see the negative side of your mentoree being so connected: signs of groupthink, going with the flow, and addiction to electronic communication. How do you respond without criticizing their all-important valuing of relationships?

- "It's tough to be that one person who stands alone on an issue. Yet sometimes the crowd is wrong. What are some things or situations that you would take a stand on even if your friends disagreed?"
- "I've noticed that you spend a lot of time chatting or texting. Tell me about that."
- "I know you've got a lot of friends online that you keep in touch with. I'm curious to know about how you view friendship. If I were an alien who just landed on the earth and didn't know what

friendship was, what would you tell me? What would you say are the qualities of a true friend?"

11. The emerging generation is uninhibited.

Millennials are much more likely than previous generations to be open about the intimate details of their lives and to be casual about personal matters, even going so far as to post them online in an exhibitionist, for-all-the-world-to-see manner.[44] They are often oblivious to boundaries and show minimal discretion, a lack of propriety, and a disrespect for privacy.[45] That doesn't mean they are incapable of embarrassment, though.

What the mentor can do: be ready for more information than you might expect. Yet, because they are used to relating online, they may not be uninhibited in person – it will most likely take time to connect with them face-to-face. However, if they are uninhibited, be gracious and don't over-react. At the same time, resist the temptation to over-divulge information about your own personal life. Here are some suggestions for talking about the merits and disadvantages of inhibition:

- "I know a lot of students put very personal details about their lives online. What do you think are some of the reasons a young person would do that? What is good about that trend? What might be bad about it?"
- "These days, it's really easy to know a lot about other people through Facebook, etc. Proverbs 11:13 says that a gossip betrays a confidence but a trustworthy man keeps a secret. What are some ways that scripture applies to how you and your friends communicate?"
- "All of us want to be known and understood. Who are some people who really know you well? Who are some people who really understand you? Tell me more about that."

When do you need to share something you've heard or read with parents, counselors, or even the police? See. p. 214.

Odds are, as your relationship with your mentoree deepens, you'll see the dark side of being uninhibited. How do you respond in a helpful way that affirms their desire to be known while gently showing them a better way to relate?

- "I noticed that you posted about _____ online. That was a deeply personal thing to share. What compelled you to share that online? In what ways, if any, could posting that be harmful? What things would you consider better to share with a few close friends than broadcast for anyone to see?"
- "Sometimes I've noticed that your status updates on Facebook or IM are vague remarks about something being wrong. It's impossible for anybody reading to discern what's really going on. Instead, I'm wondering if it'd be helpful for you, and for others, if you talked with someone you trust about what is specifically going on. What do you think?"
- "I noticed that you post updates fairly often about what you do day-to-day. What do you enjoy about being able to post those? Do you ever find yourself doing something just so you can post about it? What are your thoughts on that?"

12. The emerging generation is lonely.

This may seem to directly contradict the point above about connectivity, but both are simultaneously true. Sean McDowell, author of *Apologetics for a New Generation*, calls Millennials the "loneliest generation" because their relationships are mostly on the surface and don't meet the deepest needs of the heart.[46] Pastor and cultural critic Shane Hipps goes further to say that, growing up as "digital natives," Millennials are so accustomed to mediated interaction that they find face-to-face interaction increasingly intolerable and undesirable – especially when discussing a conflict.[47] In other words, they want intimacy and relationship, but are trying to meet those needs through technology. They don't yet realize this is impossible.

What the mentor can do: make sure your mentoree understands that your relationship isn't conditional. In a world where a friend can "delete" them from an online list, young adults greatly fear abandonment and short-term, shallow relationships. Let them know that you are here to stay, but also set good boundaries early on so that the mentoree doesn't become co-dependent or rely on the relationship for something it's not. Let him or her

Millennials want intimacy and relationship, but are trying to meet those needs through technology. They don't yet realize this is impossible.

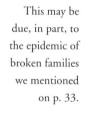

This may be due, in part, to the epidemic of broken families we mentioned on p. 33.

know when it is appropriate to contact you and when it isn't, and so forth. Consider these conversation starters:

- "I know the world seems pretty focused on shallow relationships, but I want you to know that I'm not going to abandon you." (If you say this, you had better follow through or you'll cause all sorts of long-term damage.)
- "I'd like to meet once a _____. You're free to text me or call at other times but keep in mind that I will be working during the day and with my family in the evening, so I may not respond to you right away – or even at all. I'll trust you to not abandon me in the silences if you'll trust me, too."
- "I know that you're well connected – but sometimes it's possible to be lonely at the same time. Who are some people you feel really know you – know who you are and what is going on in your life? Who are some people you would like to be able to confide in? What are some ways you could connect with them?"

For more on handling an over-dependent mentoree, see p. 198.

How do you respond to a mentoree who is lonely, or afraid of abandonment, or over-dependent?

- "It's really hard when you don't feel close to anyone. When do you feel most lonely? Tell me about that. How can I support you in deepening some friendships or finding some true friends?"
- "On Facebook, you and I are just one of hundreds of 'friends.' Honestly, mediated friendships are no replacement for being face-to-face with someone. Who are some people you can spend more time with in person?"
- "I'm really glad that we've connected so well. I think, though, that I'm seeing a trend of you being over-dependent on our relationship. That can be harmful for both of us, and because I want our relationship to continue and to be healthy, I think it'd be helpful to set up a few limits: _____, _____, _____."

The Emerging Generation Craves Relationship – With You

After going through hundreds of pages of data on the emerging generation, we have to admit that we were quite overwhelmed by some of its characteristics. We kept reminding ourselves, though, that God is not wringing his hands over this. What's happening with the emerging generation is not somehow a wrench in God's plan to build His kingdom. Nor is He concerned that our awkward efforts to pass the baton will ruin His plans. He has called us for such a time as this (Esther 4:14) and is equipping us to will and to do his good pleasure (Philippians 2:13).

And there is one especially bright spot in everything we've learned. When Millennials are approached from the standpoint of understanding, they respond with a strong desire to form relationships. *You* are someone they'd like to know and be known by. Curiously, what you represent is actually cooler for them in some ways than what their own generation has produced. As a quick example, a recent article on CNN's website pointed out that 81% of respondents between the ages of 16 and 29 said they liked the Beatles, whereas only 39% of respondents liked one of the most popular rock bands of recent times, Coldplay. The article says, "To put this in perspective: Try imagining young adults back in the 1960s putting the big jazz bands of the roaring '20s at the top of their list of favorites. Not very likely."[48] Retro is hip, and you're retro.

All this to say: the emerging generation wants to know *you*. They want to know what *you* think. They want to hear *your* story. They want to be challenged and encouraged by *you*. And they want *you* to know them. This is a tremendous opportunity made possible by a unique cultural window that may not be open forever.

CHAPTER 3:
Relational Gestures
– A New Paradigm of Life-on-Life Mentoring

What To Expect
- A definition of life-on-life mentoring based on what Jesus did with his disciples.
- A discussion of how mentors should practice six relational gestures: modeling, friendship, advising, coaching, teaching and sponsoring.
- How connecting, not expounding, is the hinge on which teaching ought to swing.
- Thoughts on relational flexibility: just as athletes must stretch and condition to avoid injury, teachers must develop relational flexibility to relate naturally with students.

How Jesus Related To His Disciples

At Passing the Baton International we love the idea of mentoring. We do academic research on relationality. We try to hone our coaching skills. But the most important thing we strive to do is to build all of our thoughts about human connectedness on a biblical foundation. For us, this means studying the life of Christ to understand what it means to be His disciples and to disciple others.

It was in the course of one of these studies that we noticed a passage in the gospel of Mark that neatly summarizes three parts of the relational ministry of Jesus:

> And he went up on the mountain and called to him those whom he desired, and they came to him. And he appointed twelve (whom he also named apostles) so that they might be with him and he might send them out to preach and have authority to cast out demons. (Mark 3:13-15)

We'll get into more detail about this passage in Chapter Seven, but it's important to note at this point that Jesus did three things:
- He called to him those whom he desired.
- He appointed 12 to be with him.
- He sent them out to preach and have authority over the spiritual realm.

These three points merge to form our understanding of what life-on-life influence is all about. Life-on-life is a journey in which both mentor and mentoree are growing more like Christ. It is about people doing life together, learning interdependence, and seeking the Lord. It is an expression of the church – the body of Christ.

Mentoring is a particular kind of life-on-life influence in which an adult mentor employs certain relational gestures to bring a young adult to understand and live out a God-given life purpose, to a greater understanding of the truth, and to the desire to exert a positive influence. We call the object of these efforts the "mentoree."

At PTBI, we have come to acknowledge the existence of six primary types of actions that compose the mentoring relationship. We call these six actions "relational gestures" and use the acrostic "M-FACTS" to make them easier to remember:

- **M = Modeling** shows a mentoree what successful living looks like in a particular area of life.
- **F = Friendship** offers companionship and builds a mentoree's confidence.
- **A = Advising** provides direction when a mentoree is at a loss for what to do.
- **C = Coaching** supports a mentoree who is willing to grow toward greater levels of success.
- **T = Teaching** helps a mentoree gain a right understanding of truth.
- **S = Sponsoring** paves the way for a mentoree to intentionally move toward greater influence.

Each of these six relational gestures has been used throughout the ages with astounding results. On its own, however, each gesture is incomplete. If any one gesture tends to dominate your relationships, you might be missing opportunities for personal growth and short-circuiting the process of really being with students in a life-on-life fashion. In combination with other relational gestures, though, each of the six adds to the fullness of the mentoring relationship. Let's take a more detailed look at each one.

Modeling: Influencing Someone through Your Life's Example

The well-known dictum that "actions speak louder than words" is actually backed up with research. Psychologist Albert Mehrabian found that 55% of our communication is through our posture and facial expressions, 38% is through our tone of voice, and only 7% is through our words.[49] If there is a contradiction between what you *say* and what you *do*, students will tend to trust your actions as the most reliable guide for what you truly believe.

Modeling isn't about putting on a spiritual show. Rather, it's an invitation to a student to walk alongside and learn from your life. Jean E. Rhodes,

If any one gesture tends to dominate your relationships, you might be missing opportunities for growth.

cul·ti·vate
to nurture, foster

How a Compelling Example Can Lead to Faith

My senior year in high school I took a physics class from Mr. L. He was a favorite among students – not because he was easy, but because he clearly explained difficult concepts. He would even offer to personally tutor anyone who needed it. We knew that he cared about us and as a result most of us put in extra effort.

That spring Mr. L. asked me to babysit for his children when he and his wife went out for a date. After hanging out with his family I respected him even more. I saw that he honored and cared for his wife, and his children were well behaved–they even asked me to pray with them before they went to bed. This was at a time when I didn't yet know God's call on my life.

Mr. L. and his family kept in touch even after I graduated high school. They invited me to dinner when I was a freshman in college and I remember them sharing their faith with me. Shortly after this, I acknowledged Jesus Christ as my Lord and Savior. I have no doubt that God used Mr. L.'s friendship and example to bring me to faith in Him.

- Donna H.

Invite a young leader to walk alongside you. See p. 132.

a leading researcher on mentoring, explains that young people will "adapt their behaviors and adopt new ones" after observing their mentor's life – and comparing it to their own.[50] In other words, they're watching you for how to live. Paul Gutacker tells the story of the man who, through the gesture of modeling, most shaped his walk with Christ:

It's hard for me to imagine someone who exemplifies the gesture of modeling better than my father: Jim Gutacker. Looking back over my growing up years, I can see three specific ways that he influenced me.

First, my dad spoke of truth with me. In addition to our nightly family devotions, he also brought truth into other everyday moments, such as memorizing scripture with me when we went backpacking – literally having the words of God on our lips as we "walked along the way" (Deuteronomy 6:7).

Second, my dad lived out what it meant to seek to know Christ. I would often come downstairs early in the morning and find him on his knees in the living room, praying for our family.

Third, my dad encouraged me to put my faith into action. As a 15 year-old, he apprenticed me in his ministry, giving me significant responsibilities and leadership opportunities, and often asking for my opinion on various matters. When I had innovative ideas for the ministry, he not only encouraged me to run with them, he also invested his own time and energy in supporting them.

Through speaking, living out, and encouraging, my father shaped my faith in profound ways I'm now deeply thankful for.

Modeling is a great relational gesture. Paul's dad didn't have a curriculum or checklist. Rather than focusing on "how to help Paul grow," his approach involved living out the truth and inviting Paul into his own personal process of spiritual growth. Note that modeling requires togetherness. Modeling would have been much less as effective if they had not been around one another (hiking, doing ministry together, etc.). Also note that modeling assumes you have something to model. Paul's dad had an active spiritual life which he invited Paul into (memorizing scripture, praying in the living room, and doing ministry). Modeling, our first relational gesture in the M-FACTS paradigm, requires you to take a look at your own life and evaluate if you, personally, are growing or are stagnant. For more on self-evaluation and personal growth, see Chapter Thirteen.

This is what John Witherspoon did. See p. 25.

cul·ti·vate
to seek the goodwill of

Friendship: Being a Faithful Confidant and Trusted Companion

Real friendship goes beyond simply "hanging out." A friend is a person with whom you express mutual caring – someone who is a confidant by choice. In his best-selling book, *The Friendship Factor*, Alan Loy McGinnis says that "friendship is the springboard to every other love."[51] Yet this powerful relational gesture is on the wane today. According to a recent study by Miller McPherson, Lynn Smith-Lovin and Matthew Brashears, the number of Americans who said they have no one with whom to discuss important matters has tripled since 1985.[52]

This is true of the emerging generation. See p. 57.

Seeds of trust, compassion, and community are all watered within the rich soil of the relational gesture of friendship. Paul remembers an illustrative friendship with one of his professors at Bryan College:

> Few people have demonstrated life-on-life influence to me like Michael Palmer. I loved how he taught with both humor and wisdom. One day he approached me about getting coffee so we could to talk about a paper I'd written. We grabbed breakfast and he asked me question after question about my story, my family, and my new college life. "Breakfast with Palmer" became a tradition that would last for the next three years.

> Every time I bumped into him on campus he would smile, shake his head, and teasingly say, "Unbelievable." Then he'd look me straight in the eye and ask how I was – and I knew he really wanted to know. It was as if every time we met he had been hoping to run into me.

> A few weeks before graduation, Michael told me: "Until now, you've been a student and I've been your professor, but now we will be friends – we will be peers." In this way, I was welcomed into adulthood by a man I deeply respected – a man who now calls me his friend.

This story illustrates the deep connection and influence that intergenerational friendship brings. Friendship can also be an excellent gateway to other relational gestures. Unfortunately, people often treat friendship as if it is the sole relational gesture. Jeff Myers recalls an experience which demonstrates how an overdependence on friendship might short-circuit other life-on-life opportunities:

> I once served as the retreat speaker for a church's youth group ski trip (free skiing!). As I debriefed with the small group leaders one evening, a college-aged chaperone said, "It's really going well. I think the guys in my group are really starting to like me." I was conflicted: I was happy for his relational success, but I also realized that his focus on being "buddies" to the guys might prevent him from speaking truth to them.

Friendship is an essential relational gesture, but it should never be used as a way to avoid influence or saying hard things when they need to be said.

It is natural for mentoring relationships to become friendships over time, as occurred with Paul and his professor. It is also a great idea to begin a mentoring relationship in the context of friendship.

Friendship can often fall into the "buddy mentality" mentioned on p. 26.

Advising: Guiding Someone through Your Experience and Wisdom

The relational gesture of advising is ideal for providing direction when a young adult has no idea what to do. It involves bringing your collected experience and wisdom to bear on their situation. Sometimes advising looks like sharing your story with a young person so that they can glean lessons for their own life situation ("When I was your age…"). Other times it can be passing along your thoughtful opinions. Jeff was the student government president of Washburn University many moons ago. Once elected, he realized that he didn't have the leadership skills necessary to cope with the in-fighting and chaos that often typify student leadership efforts. Fortunately for Jeff, an advisor rode to the rescue – though not in the way he had expected. Jeff tells the story in more detail in his book *Handoff*, but here's a summary of what happened:

cul·ti·vate
to improve,
tend

> The first thing I remember Dr. Mary Rowland saying to me was, "This could be the best year of your life or the worst year of your life, depending on whether you listen to me." As you might expect, I found her maternal bossiness unnerving. Dr. Rowland was Vice President for Student Life, and making sure the student government didn't go haywire was one of her responsibilities.
>
> Dr. Rowland started by helping me rehabilitate our disgustingly shabby student government offices. The effect was immediate; the refurbished offices instantly raised my credibility. Dr. Rowland tilted things in my favor through a simple act, and this made me even more willing to listen. She helped me put together a successful strategic planning retreat, make peace between various student groups, and turn that year of student government into a great success.
>
> Dr. Rowland helped me until I became the leader I was meant to be. Sadly, she died just one year later, but the lessons she taught me in our times together stay with me to this day.[53]

Advising is an important relational gesture. Dr. Rowland advised Jeff based on her leadership experience. She was quite direct and had strong opinions, but that was exactly what Jeff needed in that stage of his leadership journey. Unfortunately, adults often consider advising to be the gesture of choice when it comes to intergenerational relationships. When advising is employed exclusively, it stifles young adults' self-leadership and development, encouraging dependence rather than maturity.

When is it good to withhold advice? See p. 77.

Coaching: Listening and Asking Powerful Questions to Support Someone's Success

Coaching is the relational gesture of asking questions, listening, and supporting the mentoree in setting and achieving worthy goals. It is a conversational approach that focuses on the growth and forward motion of the mentoree. The coaching gesture promotes personal responsibility, thereby fostering development instead of dependence. When done well, coaching is shown to increase the likelihood that mentorees will actually apply what they are learning, rather than simply assent intellectually. Throughout this book you'll learn dozens – no, hundreds – of questions that you can use within this powerful support-expressing gesture, and Chapter Four will specifically train you in the essentials of the coaching gesture.

For a detailed introduction to coaching, see Chapter 4.

Paige Gutacker shares about a professor at Bryan College who naturally acted out the coaching gesture:

cul·ti·vate

to promote the growth of

> I met Matt Benson, the Vice President of Spiritual Formation at Bryan College, on a class retreat shortly after learning of the sudden death of a fellow student. In the midst of deciding whether or not to conclude the retreat early, Matt turned to me and unexpectedly brought me into the decision-making process: "What do you think?" As a freshman student, I was shocked to be included in such a significant decision. Five years later, I realize that the tone of that initial meeting characterizes much about the nature of my relationship with Matt, who invested in my life over the following years and used countless questions to help me think and grow.

Matt saw my potential in ways I often did not. He helped me real-ize that potential by stretching me beyond my self-perceived limits by asking open-ended questions such as: "Tell me about such-and-such." "What are your thoughts on _____?" "How did _____ go?" "What are some ways that _____?" and "What is God doing in your life?"

It was evident that Matt cared about the *process* of my development – not just the outcome. The way Matt used the coaching gesture increased my confidence and sense of responsibility for my own deci-sions, developed my trust and respect for when he did give advice, and provided a greenhouse for growth that has impacted me tremendously.

Coaching is a powerful relational gesture. Paige's description of Matt's influencing style illustrates the important values of listening and asking questions, while trusting God for guidance. Keep in mind, however, that coaching is not the ultimate gesture. There are certainly times when input is necessary, such as through teaching and advising.

Teaching: Explaining Truth in an Understandable and Compelling Fashion

As the old saying goes, "A good teacher is like a candle; it consumes itself to light the way for others." Teaching lights the way for students, help-ing them grow in a right understanding of the truth. It is focused on seeing students identify and apply truth in a meaningful way.

In most Christian gatherings around the world, a special elevation is given to a certain kind of teaching (what is commonly called *preaching*), as the primary means by which spiritual truth is transmitted. The justification for this is summarized by the Apostle Paul in Romans 10:14 – "And how are they to hear without someone preaching?"

The Greek word used for "preaching" in this passage is *kerusso*, which refers to an official herald expounding on important news with authority. "Expound" comes from the same root word as "expose," and the skill of mining the biblical text for spiritual truth is called "expository preaching." Since the word *preaching* has fallen out of fashion, however, the skill of ex-pounding on scripture is now called *Bible teaching*, and those who are good

"A good teacher is like a candle; it consumes itself to light the way for others."

For six reasons coaching is a great relational gesture, see p. 78.

cul·ti·vate
to form, refine

69

at it are widely celebrated. Millions flock to their churches and stadium events, listen to their programs on the radio, download their podcasts, and read their books.

Much of the educational environment is arranged to harness the authority that is bestowed upon such teachers. When it comes to explaining truth in an understandable and compelling fashion, it's more common than not to see one person facing the group, while everyone else remains quiet and listens (or is supposed to). Lectures, chapels, convocations, and special speakers follow this format.

A careful re-reading of the gospels, though, reveals that exposition is not the dominant way Jesus taught. Jesus occasionally addressed the crowds, but mostly he walked and talked, discussed, asked and answered questions, told stories, engaged in debates, and liberally used outdoor activities to get his point across.

Based on the example of Jesus in scripture, it seems that *connecting*, not expounding, is the hinge upon which teaching ought to swing. Teacher and author, Parker Palmer, explains it this way:

> I argue that there is one thing that all good teachers have in common: They all have a "capacity for connectedness." They all connect their selfhood with their students and their subject. Good teachers weave a fabric of connectedness between all three, and the loom on which they do the weaving is their own heart.[54]

As we talked over how to move the teaching gesture away from an overemphasis on *expounding*, Paige called to mind a teacher who was highly influential in her own life because of her capacity for connectedness:

> Beverly Bradley, my music teacher for nine years from childhood through my teens, influenced my life in ways I may never be able to calculate.

> Ms. Beverly taught the subject matter very well (she's a great musician!) and believed in me enough to stretch me and serve as my champion in all creative endeavors. I vividly remember how she praised my first

poem and displayed it on her piano, sharing it with others. Later, she gently led me through the process of recording my first original composition – with constant words of support. Over the years, she built my confidence as much as she built my musical skills.

Ms. Beverly really understood the value of personal relationships to successful teaching. She took an interest in my life and carefully listened to my youthful thoughts, ideas, and dreams. Her great sense of humor made it fun and easy to be with her. Her joy overflowed into our times together; I cannot count the times she sincerely exclaimed "Praise the Lord!" accompanied by a strong laugh – right in the middle of our lessons. I knew that she (an adult!) valued me as a person, and I couldn't escape knowing we were friends.

Ms. Beverly taught me the material – for which I'm grateful – and simultaneously taught me life – for which I'm immeasurably grateful.

Teaching is a significant relational gesture. As Paige's story makes clear, Ms. Beverly taught in a way that clarified the subject's connection to her students' lives. Out of the overflow of a life spent joyfully following Christ, Ms. Beverly invested personally in Paige's life – encouraging and championing her efforts. By doing so, Ms. Beverly fostered a lifelong love of music in Paige's heart. Teaching is of vital importance, but it doesn't stand alone. As Ms. Beverly's example illustrates, implementing multiple relational gestures paints a full picture and creates a strong environment for growth.

Teaching can often fall into the "boss mentality" mentioned on p. 26.

Sponsoring: Using Your Reputation to Advance the Opportunities of Another

Writing recommendations is probably the most common form of sponsorship, but we define sponsoring more broadly as intentionally advancing others into positions where they can grow in influence.

Jeff has been speaking on the national stage now for many years, and his very first speeches came because a sponsor enthusiastically advanced his career. Here's how Jeff describes it:

cul·ti·vate
to prepare
to bear fruit

71

I recall the first speech I was ever paid to give (at least they paid my travel expenses). To me, it was a complete disaster – but there was one man in the room who thought I had potential. Roger Norrie was at that time the Assistant Director of the Northwest Region of the Association of Christian Schools International. Later, he called to ask if I would speak at a student leadership conference.

Embarrassed about my earlier speech, I said, "Let me see if my boss is able to do it." Roger replied, "I would like for you *personally* to be the speaker." Roger encouraged me through the whole process and fed me invitations to other events. At one point, a last-minute cancellation left Roger without a keynote speaker for a large teacher convention. He asked me to fill in. It was the first time in my life I had ever spoken to 3,000 people, and not just once, but three times.

Then Roger began to share with his colleagues in other regions that I had "hit a homerun" as a keynote speaker at his event, and since that time I've addressed more than 40,000 Christian school teachers and 10,000 Christian school students, all because Roger sponsored me into a position of influence in the Christian education movement.

Sponsoring is an excellent relational gesture. Roger expressed belief in Jeff's skill as a communicator. More than that, though, he became a champion for Jeff, using the trust he had developed with others to help Jeff gain a significantly larger platform for his message. Something to watch out for: sponsoring is a great relational gesture, but take pains to ensure that the relationship is valued for its own sake, not just for the networks it opens up.

Don't Get Stuck in One Relational Gesture

In our experience, people typically find it easy to take the one gesture they're most comfortable with and employ it to the exclusion of all the other gestures. Some teachers, for instance, find it hard to become mentors because they tend to expound whenever they're given an audience of students.

When is it good to stop teaching? See p. 77.

This is a big problem. Since life-on-life mentoring involves fluidly employing the six relational gestures, relational inflexibility can cause students to resist our influence. Here are some statements we can imagine hearing from students when asked if they would like to be mentored by their teachers:

- "I like Mrs. 'X,' but I would never want to have her as a mentor. I had a personal meeting with her once and she just talked me to death. I wouldn't want to do that every week."
- "Coach 'Y' is a great guy, but he only sees one way of doing things. It's either his way or the highway. If he mentors you, he'll take over your life."
- "Mr. 'Z' is a nice teacher, but he doesn't really seem to have it together. I don't want to be like him when I grow up, so why would I want to have him as my mentor now?"

If we want to be life-changing mentors, we've got to become thoughtful practitioners of the six relational gestures to the point where we can model, befriend, advise, coach, teach and sponsor in a flexible and natural fashion. Everyone can do this; relationality is not an inborn trait but a skill that can be developed.

It takes work, but becoming aware of the relational gestures we frequently use and expanding our repertoire can bring a whole new level of freshness – not to mention effectiveness – to our ability to mentor life-on-life. This idea about expanding our repertoire reminds Jeff of when he began running for exercise:

> I was already in pretty good shape when I first started running, or so I thought. Imagine my surprise when I almost immediately began developing knee pain and shin splints. I thought to myself, "Maybe I'm just not genetically cut out for running." Our campus doctor is an orthopedist, so I asked him about it. He said: "We're going to do two things. First, we're going to have you do some different kinds of stretches. Second, we're going to have you exercise more muscles - you've exercised some but not others and it is creating an imbalance." Within a couple of weeks the pain diminished so significantly and has stayed away for so long that that I am able to run much farther, faster and more frequently than I could five years ago.

Relational inflexibility can cause students to resist our influence.

Exclusively running actually had a negative effect on Jeff's overall physical fitness. When he added in the new "gestures" of stretching and muscle-strengthening, however, his overall fitness improved *and* he ran better than ever.

To apply Jeff's example, when we exclusively exercise only one relational gesture, things get out-of-whack and we develop relational shin splints. Conversely, when we move toward an overall fitness approach to relationships rather than a one-dimensional manner of relating, the pain is reduced and we can relate better than ever.

Start stretching. Exercise some new relational muscles. It will almost certainly cause soreness at first, but the payoff will be immensely rewarding. Greater flexibility with the relational gestures will result in greater influence in the lives of those in the emerging generation.

Start stretching. Exercise some new relational muscles.

CHAPTER 4:
The Relational Gesture of Coaching

What To Expect

- A definition of the relational gesture of coaching.
- Six reasons the coaching gesture is an indispensable tool for the mentor.
- Three skills of effective coaching: active listening, asking good questions, and setting worthy goals.
- A suggested model for coaching conversations.

At Passing the Baton International, we're passionate about coaching. The gesture of coaching not only significantly increases mentoring success, it also significantly decreases the tension would-be mentors feel at having to know all of the answers. Training mentors in coaching is a key distinctive of our organization, and because coaching is the relational gesture that our readers are least likely to be familiar with, we wanted to invest a chapter to explain it further and offer some key coaching concepts.

What the Coaching Gesture Is

"Coaching" can mean a lot of things. Often, the word "coach" is used to refer to an athletic coach, a sage advisor, or even a New Age life coach who advocates looking inward to find answers to life's questions. There are also increasing numbers of Christians who are excellent professional life coaches, such as Joseph Umidi, Gary Collins, Tony Stoltzfus, and our friends at the Center for Coaching Excellence. Those in the growing coaching profession have developed top notch communication practices for supporting growth, and we feel that identifying and applying some of those skills in the mentoring context can significantly increase the positive impact of mentoring. That's why we include coaching as one of the gestures in our M-FACTS list.

The coaching gesture is a growth-focused, mentoree-centered, conversational approach that seeks to promote sustainable change through goal setting and positive accountability. In the context of mentoring, the coaching gesture is used as a mentor applies the skills of listening and questioning to support the mentoree's growth and forward motion. These skills create a conversational greenhouse where flourishing comes naturally. Teachers can certainly use coaching skills in classroom settings, but it should be noted that these skills are most effective when used in one-on-one situations.

In some ways, the coaching gesture could be viewed as the counterpart of the teaching and advising gestures. When coaching, mentors make a choice to *not* instruct or give advice, but instead to simply support mentorees in their processing and decision-making. Coaching is about *drawing out* potential and *calling forth* capacity, rather than *pouring* in information. This doesn't mean that teaching and advising have no role in mentoring.

Teaching and advising are absolutely necessary gestures when a mentoree doesn't have knowledge or wisdom needed on a given topic. If a person asks, "How do I get to the hospital?" it is extremely unhelpful to reply, "How would *you like* to get to the hospital?" Certainly our mentorees need wisdom, perspective, and guidance from trusted outside sources. We'd like to propose, though, that defaulting to the teaching and advising gestures shortchanges mentorees by bypassing a significant avenue for growth.

Coaching hinges on the growing realization in the helping professions that sometimes *withholding* advice does more good than *dispensing* it. Whether you should *tell* or *ask* depends on your goal. If all you care about is getting something off your chest, then by all means – tell away. Just don't be surprised if the result is a lack of understanding or follow-through. On the other hand, if you care about bringing another person to the point of meaningful change, asking may be the way to go. In support of this idea, persuasion studies show that traditional persuasion results in short term *attitude* change, but self-persuasion leads to long-term *behavior* change. Eminent psychologist Elliot Aronson explained it this way:

> Self-persuasion is almost always a more powerful form of persuasion (deeper, longer lasting) than more traditional persuasion techniques – that is, than being directly persuaded by another person, no matter how clever, convincing, expert, and trustworthy that other person might be – precisely because in direct persuasion, the audience is constantly aware of the fact that they have been persuaded by another.[55]

In mentoring, self-persuasion occurs after the mentoree thinks and reflects. Question-asking provides an environment for that kind of thinking and reflecting. *Asking* rather than *telling* is a somewhat radical notion that is founded on the belief that our mentorees' overall growth is more valuable than their short term attitude change. We believe life-on-life mentors should follow the example of coaching expert Tony Stoltzfus and be able to honestly say to their mentorees: "I'm more interested in seeing you become a great decision maker than I am in your making a great decision."[56] The practice of asking rather than telling is an investment in a mentoree's decision-making capacity. And, a side benefit of the coaching gesture is that it relieves the

Sometimes withholding advice does more good than dispensing it.

pressure of having to have all the answers. You don't need to be an expert or know the best response to every question. Answers are great, but sometimes a well-placed question brings about more significant results.

One quick note before we move on: some people use the term "coaching" to refer to a process by which clever mentors use questions to help mentorees arrive at the mentors' pre-determined conclusions. That's not coaching; it's manipulative advice disguised in coaching clothing. True coaching is not another way to bring mentorees to know or believe what you know or believe; It's a process of building mentorees into more able and confident thinkers, discoverers, and actors who take responsibility for their own lives, solutions, and decisions.

The gesture of coaching is like offering conversational hospitality to another person.

Six Reasons the Coaching Gesture Is Valuable To Mentors

The coaching gesture offers six unique benefits for the mentor and mentoree, making it well worth learning and implementing.

1. Coaching deepens growth.

The coaching gesture provides the tools mentors need to strategically create space for the mentoree to develop. The gesture of coaching is like offering conversational hospitality to another person. Hospitable conversationalists offer others a safe, inviting place in which to be themselves as they talk, as well as a natural and supportive environment in which to grow.

2. Coaching increases application.

Studies are showing that people who have been coached are able to retain and apply a significantly higher percentage of learning. In one study, coaching was found to increase performance of those who were trained at a training event by 400%.[57] In other words, if you add even just two months of follow-up coaching to a training event, participants will be four times as likely to apply what they learned. Coaching propels learning from the level of simple intellectual assent to the level of real life application.

This is especially helpful for the emerging generation, as they find it particularly difficult to commit. See p. 51.

3. Coaching encourages action.

Coaching enables mentorees to move to action in a way that makes sense to them – and without having to be persuaded. Mentors can support mentorees in taking action towards worthy goals through asking action-oriented follow-up questions and goal strengthening questions.

4. Coaching develops responsibility.

The coaching gesture helps mentorees be responsible for their own lives by encouraging them to come up with their own solutions and find ways to follow-through. Mentorees' level of engagement and commitment soars as they participate in the planning process. Their level of buy-in grows. They take ownership. They are more likely to follow-through without requiring close supervision. Instead of fostering *dependence*, the coaching gesture fosters *development*.

This is crucial for a generation struggling with perpetual adolescence. See p. 96.

5. Coaching expresses support.

The coaching gesture is a gesture of support. Now, that doesn't mean supporting mentorees' *decisions* even if they are awful ones. Rather, it means supporting the *mentoree*. It is about expressing a belief in a mentoree's capacity for success. As Tony Stoltzfus says: "In coaching, your greatest value to clients is in the fact that someone believes in them – believes that God is working in them, that they can solve the problems they face, and that their coach is pulling for their success."[58]

6. Coaching promotes selfless communication.

The coaching gesture is others-centered and is focused on seeking the mentoree's good. Because we are fallen creatures, the way we communicate is marred by our selfishness; our default mode is to communicate in ways that serve our own interests. If our interest is to look clever, we might listen half-heartedly while trying to think of a wise thing to say next. If our interest is saving time, we might impatiently dispense a remedy so we can close the conversation. Coaching turns conversations into opportunities for mentors to practice selflessness as they stay aware of their own bad communication habits and choose to focus on the interests of their mentorees.

This approach recognizes the dignity of a young person. See p. 26.

Three Keys to Effective Coaching

The coaching gesture involves three main skills: active listening, asking good questions, and helping others set and achieve worthy goals. Each

A Classroom Marked by Listening

When I was in high school I helped a 4th grade teacher, Mrs. T., with her classroom. She knew that I wanted to be a teacher, and gave me opportunities to develop those gifts. Mrs. T. always took a few minutes to share something she had noticed me doing well. She would invite me to go shopping with her or join her for lunch, and ask about how classes were going, what I was involved with at church, and my plans and dreams for the future. No one in my family had ever gone to college, but Mrs. T. insisted that I could do it.

One thing that Mrs. T. did really struck me. Every day, she spent a full 30 minutes of classroom time intentionally listening to her 4th graders. The kids would have silent reading for that half hour, and one by one she would call them to her desk. She'd turn over a one-minute hourglass, look them right in the eye, and they could tell their teacher anything they wanted to. This was the kids' favorite time of each day. They loved it. She told me that she did this because she was teaching children, not math or reading or science. Each child got their minute of completely undivided attention–she looked in their eyes, saw them, heard them, and remembered they were there. I continue this practice in my own elementary classrooms, and I am convinced it has made a world of difference for many children.

- Rebecca R.

of these skills takes practice. For most people, they involve a fairly radical change in conversational behavior. The powerful tools we've provided in the following pages are ones we've learned, used, and taught to others with great results.

Coaching Skill #1: Active Listening

Studies show that young adults crave a listening ear. See p. 33.

When you truly listen well, you give a priceless gift to others: they feel *heard*. It takes discipline to listen selflessly, and even people who are considered to be great communicators often find listening to be difficult. Distractions, judgments, and planning what you'll say next all make it tough to *really* hear what mentorees say. As communication scholars, we've heard many people claim that they can effectively listen to another person, watch television, and check messages all at the same time. However, our experience is that trying to simultaneously listen while thinking about something else is like trying to sing one song while humming another (try it sometime!). The bottom line is: if you're doing other things while listening to someone, that person will not *feel heard*. Whatever credit you gain for your efforts at efficiency you immediately gamble away in terms of credibility.

It seems like most books on listening simply highlight things good listeners have been *observed* to do. This approach is kind of like teaching someone to be a football coach by having classes on striding purposefully down the sideline, speaking authoritatively to players, and glaring at referees. Rather than focusing on what good listening *looks like*, ask yourself: "does the other person feel heard?" Ponder these questions:

- Am I engaged? If not, how do I eliminate the factors that prevent engagement?
- If I were the other person, and was looking at and listening to me, would I feel heard?

In addition to discerning whether the other person feels heard, it is also good to listen *for* certain things, such as hints about where a good question could create a breakthrough in the conversation. The Center for Coaching Excellence uses the acrostic RADAR to list five things to listen for: red flags, ardent emotions, discernment, archives, and repetition.[59] If you're actively listening, the presence of any one of these five should be a "blip" on your proverbial radar screen and tip you off that following-up might be in order.

R – Red Flags

This is when something just doesn't quite add up. If something doesn't sound right, there may be more going on underneath the surface. Perhaps an inconsistency is becoming evident. Here's an idea for following-up: "May I have your permission to share an observation with you? It seems like there are some contradictory things going on here. Here's what I see. What are your thoughts?"

A – Ardent Emotions

This is when a strong emotion comes to light. Whether positive or negative, ardent emotions are a window into the significance of a situation

*If you're doing other things while listening to someone, that person will not **feel heard**. Whatever credit you gain for your efforts at efficiency you immediately gamble away in terms of credibility.*

or topic. Go deeper through gentle inquiry: "It sounds like something here is really important for you. Tell me more about that."

D – Discernment

This is when mentorees give their perception of what needs to be done. When someone says something like "What I really think we need is..." or "I know I need to do such-and-such, but..." – it may be a good place to key-in for further conversation. Example: "I've gathered that you've identified what you think you need to do, but it seems that something might be standing in the way. What do you think about that?"

A – Archives

This is when mentorees reflect on the past and reveal events from their history that might apply to the current situation. For instance, if a mentoree mentions having done something well in the past, take the opportunity to ask, "What could your past experience in this area reveal or suggest for your current situation?"

R – Repetition

This is when a mentoree repeats certain words or ideas. Because patterns may evidence significance, a closer look may be warranted. Example: "I've noticed you've said 'I can't' a few times in our conversation today. Talk with me for a moment about that."

Here's one final word on listening: you don't have to be silent. Simple vocal cues such as "Mm-hmm" or "Yeah" or "I hear you" let the mentoree know you're tracking with the conversation. Vocally showing that you're engaged helps the mentoree feel heard, which is crucial to listening well.

Coaching Skill #2: Asking Good Questions

A good question goes far beyond gathering information. In fact, it can be a gift to others – changing everyday conversations into memorable moments of transformation. Of course, whether a question does this depends on a number of factors. To become better question askers, let's take a look at the kinds of questions we commonly use that are actually less helpful than they could be, and let's discover how to make them better.

Six Types of Unhelpful Questions:

The Center for Coaching Excellence teaches that there are six types of unhelpful questions.[60] Here's what to *not* ask:

1. Closed Questions

Example: *"Did you enjoy the chapel speaker today?"* Such questions call for either a "yes" or a "no" response. This kind of question could make mentorees feel like they're being cross-examined. In contrast to closed questions, the most helpful questions are usually open-ended, which means they require more than a prescribed one-word answer. Example: "What did you think about the chapel speaker today?" Hint: open-ended questions often use words like "what" and "how." For instance, rather than asking: "Did you do well on your assignment?" ask: "How did you do on your assignment?"

Note that there is a time for closed questions. See p. 191.

2. Leading Questions

Example: *"What would happen if you started scheduling homework into your daily planner?"* Such questions lead mentorees to follow *your* train of thought or idea as opposed to really exploring their own thoughts or options. By suggesting a course of action, leading questions remove the mentoree's responsibility for solving the problem. Ask instead, "What could you do to remember your homework?"

Leading questions remove the mentoree's responsibility for solving the problem.

3. Advice Questions

Example: *"Have you thought about cutting back on the amount of time you spend on the computer?"* Much like leading questions, advice questions contain a piece of advice disguised as a question. However, good questions tend to expand a mentoree's range of thought rather than narrowing it. Try asking a question that doesn't hint at your option: "How could you find more time in your day?"

4. Why Questions

Example: *"Why did you try out for basketball?"* "Why" questions imply a questioning of the others' motives and can create defensiveness. Try changing "why" to "what." Example: "What are some reasons you tried out for basketball?"

5. Small Questions

Example: *"You mentioned you're considering taking an extra class. Which class would it be?"* Small questions are limited in scope, forcing the mentoree to think and answer within a certain box. This could be quickly remedied by broadening the question in its scope: "You mentioned you're considering taking an extra class. Tell me more about that."

"Tell me more about that."

6. Judgmental Questions

Examples: *"What's gotten into you?"* or *"Why on earth would you do a thing like that?"* Judgmental questions can be counter-productive because they create defensiveness. Remember: using the coaching gesture in mentoring is not about showcasing your rightness; it is about your mentoree moving toward worthy goals.

A word about conversational space: good questions really make others think. So, give them time to think. Don't be intimidated by long silences, and let them ask for clarification if needed. Sometimes a long pause following your question just means you've asked a powerful, thought-provoking question. Coaching conversations can have a different pace and take some getting used to.

Five Conversation-Altering Words

For some great relationship-building questions, see p. 181.

If you're absolutely stumped for a good question, consider coaching with what may be the most powerful response-leader there is: "Tell me more about that." These five simple words can make all the difference when it comes to the depth of a conversation. The key word is: more. If you want to go deeper with your mentoree, simply ask to hear more. The following are variations of that question:

- "I'd like to hear more."
- "I'm curious to hear more on this."
- "Can you tell me more?"
- "Could you expound on that?"
- "Would you fill that in some more for me?"
- "Could you explain in a bit more detail?"

What To Say When You Aren't Asking

There's lots of room within the coaching gesture to speak up – even if your sentence doesn't end in a question mark. Here are some examples of the kinds of things to do and say when you aren't asking:

Encourage:

- "Insightful. You've really dug deep here and come to some significant conclusions."
- "That statement was said with clarity. You do an excellent job putting your thoughts into words."

For more on encouragement and celebration, see p. 128.

Celebrate:

- "I just want to stop you here for a second and encourage you. Do you realize that this is the third week in a row you've met your goal? Let's just celebrate that for a moment before we go on!"

Reiterate:

- "You want to do such-and-such, but you aren't sure what your friends will think."
- "You're thinking about all three options, and you aren't settled on any of them yet."

Bottom Line:

- "So it all boils down to _____."
- "Sounds like you're wanting to _____."
- "Perhaps it could be summed up by saying _____."

Challenge:

- "I know you can give me one more option for how you could do that project."
- "I'd like to push you just a bit further to think of one more way to _____."

Give Feedback:

- "Can I share with you something I've realized as we've been talking? _____. What do you make of that?"
- "May I tell you what I just observed? _____."

Coaching Skill #3: Setting Worthy Goals

The goal of the coaching gesture is to create a space where mentorees can move forward. This involves two steps: following-up with action-oriented questions and helping them decide on a purposeful course of action.

Follow-Up With Action-Oriented Questions:

These questions bring about immediate application and continued learning.

- "What is your biggest takeaway?"
- "Where will you go from here?"
- "What's next?"
- "What could you do *this week* with what you just told me? This month? This school year? In the future?"

Help Them Strengthen Their Goals:

These questions follow the S.M.A.R.T. goal structure for honing goals and making them more focused, powerful, and realizable.

- **S – Specific.** "How could you make your goal more clear/straight forward?"
- **M – Measurable.** "How will you know you have succeeded?"
- **A – Attainable.** "Is this goal possible/challenging enough?"
- **R – Relevant.** "How compelling/motivating is this to you?"
- **T – Time-sensitive.** "When will you start/finish?"

The G.R.O.W. Model For Coaching Conversations

G.R.O.W. is a simple way to organize a coaching conversation.[61] It's easy to remember, it really works, and it can be easily modified for a wide variety of conversations.

G – Goal. Start off by inquiring as to what the ideal situation would be. Questions could include:

- "What would you like your situation to be like?"
- "What is your hope in this area?"
- "Paint me a picture that describes what you would want to see happen."

R – Reality. Next, check into the difference between their ideal (the goal) and their present reality. Questions could include:

- "Where are you at currently?"
- "Tell me about your present situation."

O – Options. Now, help them figure out how they can get from the reality of the present to the ideal goal they desire. Questions could include:

- "How could you get from here to there?"
- "What options do you see for moving from where you are now to where you want to be?"
- "What are some ways you could begin to make that goal a reality?"

W – Walk. Finally, support them in turning ideas into action steps and really walking it out. Questions could include:

- "Which of those options sounds the most compelling?"
- "Which idea would you like to act on first?"
- "How could you act on your new insight?"
- "How can you begin putting that into practice this week?"
- "How could you make that goal S.M.A.R.T.er (more specific, measurable, attainable, relevant, and time-sensitive)?"

Coaching is an effective way for the established generation to mentor the emerging generation. Young adults are poised and ready to be listened to and asked good questions. They're desperate to have someone in their corner, believing in their ability to succeed. And they need space to develop and encouragement to stand on their own two feet. In our research, we've come to believe that there are three key growth areas for young adults: gaining life purpose, knowing and living the truth, and influencing others to create change. That's what we'll dive into in the second section of *Cultivate*.

S.M.A.R.T. goals are focused, powerful, and realizable.

After determining the goal, you'll want to give great accountability. See. p. 191.

PART TWO:
GROWING SEASONS

Focusing on Three Areas of Flourishing

What You'll Find In Part Two

- Three key questions to help the emerging generation wrestle through: "What is the purpose of my life?", "What is true?", and "What difference do I make?"
- How to help mentorees be free from self-centeredness, grow in maturity, and embrace their God-given design.
- The significance of incarnating the truth and expressing openness without being a relativist – especially when it comes to what mentorees need to know about God, about being human, and about interacting with culture as Christians.
- How to call out, walk with, and send out young adults to become leaders who will exert a positive influence on others.

CHAPTER 5:
Cultivate Design:
Helping the Emerging Generation Form Life Purpose

What To Expect
- Preparing mentorees to avoid the trap of narcissism.
- Helping mentorees to mature within a culture that worships adolescence.
- Strategies and questions to help mentorees focus on finding their life purpose based on God-given design rather than man-centered desires.
- Walking with mentorees as they make sense of their lives from the standpoint of God's providence.

William Wilberforce, widely celebrated in the movie *Amazing Grace*, tirelessly opposed the Trans-Atlantic slave trade until it was abolished in Great Britain. His epitaph in Westminster Abbey includes the following excerpt:

In an age and country fertile

In great and good men,

He was among the foremost of those

Who fixed the character of their times,

Because to high and various talents

To warm benevolence, and to universal candour,

He added the abiding eloquence of a Christian life.

Someday someone will write your epitaph and mine. What do you want them to write? And what would stop you from dedicating the rest of your life to being the kind of person your epitaph says you were?

When we ask questions like this, we're talking about the idea of life purpose. At the heart of the life purpose conversation are three questions:

- What is God's will for me?
- What goals are worth pursuing in life?
- What gifts and abilities make up my particular design?

In his book, *The Path to Purpose*, Stanford professor William Damon notes that only about one in five young people (ages 12 to 22) express a clear vision of where they want to go, what they want to accomplish in life, and why.[62] Damon demonstrates that this is tragic because young people who lack purpose:

- Report an inner life of anxiety
- Feel disappointed in themselves
- Feel discouraged by what life has offered them
- Despair at the emptiness of daily activities

On the other hand, people *with* purpose:

- Are filled with joy, despite sacrifices they must make
- Have a sense of energy
- Experience satisfaction when they accomplish their goals
- Display persistence when they run into obstacles[63]

It is important to note that life purpose is much more than being able to answer the question: "What do you want to be when you grow up?" Plenty of people who are on track in their careers lack purpose. Purpose isn't about knowing *what* to do, it's about knowing *why* what you do matters.

The emerging generation is struggling tremendously with life purpose questions and is coming up with convoluted answers that distort God's purposes. There are two things those in the emerging generation must *stop* doing and two things they must *start* doing to arrive at meaningful life purpose. They must reject self-centeredness and immaturity, and embrace their God-given design and trust in His sovereignty. We'll explore each of these in detail in this chapter.

Rejecting the Poison of Self-Centeredness

Well-intentioned mentors too often begin the discussion of life purpose by asking, "What do you want to do with your life?" Such a question contains three unwarranted assumptions:

- That we can do what we want.
- That we know who we are.
- That our lives belong to us.

All three of these statements ignore the truth of a biblical worldview. What if we cannot – or should not – do what we want? What if the way we think about ourselves actually obscures who we were designed to be? What if our life consists of something that is higher than our actual physical existence? It's impossible to arrive at the correct answers when we're asking the wrong questions.

The focus on the "self" and what it "wants" not only creates confusion, it generates narcissism. Derived from the Greek myth about a boy who fell in love with his own reflection, narcissism refers to people who have an

*Purpose isn't about knowing **what** to do, it's about knowing **why** what you do matters.*

What is the purpose of our lives? See p. 225.

93

overinflated view of their own abilities. One way that narcissism manifests itself is when someone views life as a chance to accumulate stuff and receive glory. And yet, according to Kinnaman and Lyons, this is precisely what the emerging generation wants from life:

> By a wide margin, the top life priorities of eighteen- to twenty-five-year-olds are wealth and personal fame. Objectives like helping people who are in need, being a leader in the community, or becoming more spiritual have much less traction among young Americans than they do among older adults.[64]

These findings are corroborated by Luton First, sponsor of Britain's National Kids' Day, which asked British school children under age 10 "What is the very best thing in the world?" The number one reply was, "being a celebrity," followed by, "being rich." "God" was the 10th – and last – item on the list.[65]

It's not just an obsession with material possessions – it's an obsession with self-obsession, according to Jean Twenge and Keith Campbell, psychologists from Case Western Reserve University.[66] In their book, *The Narcissism Epidemic*, Twenge and Campbell lay the blame at the feet of endlessly repeated mantras, such as, "You are special," and suggest that this blatant promotion of self-love is turning into a pandemic among young adults.

This ties back to moral relativism. See p. 49.

Among other things, narcissism promotes a desire to get ahead at all costs, and the social consequences are devastating. Take cheating for example. The percentage of students who admit to having cheated has doubled since 1969, and yet 93% of students say they are satisfied with their personal ethics.[67] This bizarre disconnection leads us to believe that the chickens of moral relativism have truly come home to roost.

So is narcissism a cultural problem? Twenge and Campbell point out a number of symptoms that they say indicate the presence of narcissism in a culture. See if you recognize any:

- Vanity: an obsession with appearance.
- Materialism: an insatiable desire to acquire possessions.
- Uniqueness: a strong desire to stand out, to be unique and different.

- Antisocial behavior: a belief that a person's needs take precedence, and a willingness to act aggressively to ensure that those needs are met.
- Relationship troubles: using relationships to look and feel powerful, special, admired, attractive, and important.
- Entitlement: a person's belief that he or she deserves special treatment.
- Religion and volunteering: using church and community service as ways of boosting self-admiration.

It's sobering to realize that narcissism affects every aspect of our culture, even, as the seventh bullet point reveals, some aspects that are seemingly positive.

Narcissism is a sticky problem. You may ask, "Doesn't telling someone 'You have a special life purpose' feed the tendency toward narcissism?" That's a great question, and we certainly don't want to puff up our mentorees to even greater heights of self-centeredness. Our view, however, is that a proper approach to life purpose is actually the *antidote* to self-centeredness because it helps us see ourselves as God sees us: awesome creatures who are thoroughly corrupted by sin and desperately in need of redemption. This spiritual reality check raises our esteem of God, replacing the self-esteem that obscures what is truly worth living – and dying – for.

David Livingstone's life serves as a powerful illustration of knowing what is truly important. Livingstone dedicated his life to missions in Africa and was credited with helping abolitionists by bringing to light the horrors of the African slave trade. Livingstone's motto was "I will place no value on anything I have or possess, except in its relationship to the kingdom of God." This zeal inspired millions around the world, as Harold J. Sala reports in his book, *Heroes*:

> Upon his death, natives gently removed his heart and buried it in the Africa he so loved. Then his body was carried to the coast, where it was shipped back to England for burial…. As the body of Livingstone was carried through the streets of London on its way to its final rest-

*A proper approach to life purpose is actually the **antidote** to self-centeredness because it helps us see ourselves as God sees us.*

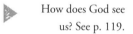

How does God see us? See p. 119.

ing place in Westminster Abbey, one man wept openly. A friend gently consoled him, asking if he had known Livingstone personally. "I weep not for Livingstone but for myself," the first man said, adding, "he lived and died for something, but I have lived for nothing."[68]

He lived and died for something, but I have lived for nothing. That statement should give us pause. The fact of the matter is – everyone who lives eventually dies; will our purpose for living transcend death?

What are we asking students to live for? See p. 225.

The opposite of narcissism is self-sacrifice – giving your life to a cause that's greater than yourself. When we speak of life purpose to students, we aren't telling them that they are incredible and worthwhile; rather we're telling them that there is a God who is incredible and worth living for.

Rejecting the Emptiness of Immaturity

In her book, *The Death of the Grown-Up*, Diana West pinpoints one of the biggest issues stunting the growth of Western culture: people just don't want to grow up. Some of the cultural indicators she highlights are both bizarre and amusing:

Adults are not growing up. How do you deal with this issue in your own life? See Chapter 13.

The opposite of narcissism is self-sacrifice – giving your life to a cause that's greater than yourself.

- More adults, ages eighteen to forty-nine, watch the Cartoon Network than watch CNN.
- The average video gamester was eighteen in 1990; now he's going on thirty.
- The National Academy of Sciences has redefined adolescence as the period extending from the onset of puberty, around twelve, to age thirty.
- In Italy, nearly one in three thirty-somethings have still not left home.[69]

It's no wonder that young adults struggle with what it really means to really grow up. They see 28-year-olds living like teenagers, and a society that officially recognizes this as expected and acceptable.

Fortunately there is growing pushback against perpetual adolescence. Two of those encouraging the resistance are Alex and Brett Harris, twin brothers who just turned twenty years-old as of this writing. In their best-selling book, *Do Hard Things*, they ask:

Called to Responsibility

Mrs. W. was my sixth grade teacher at the elementary school in our small Virginia town. My older siblings had raved about the fun they had when she had taught them, so I was excited to enter her classroom.

Sure enough, she lived up to all of my expectations. Her teaching style was uniquely exciting, flowing from her joy in her work and love for us. The students in our class had so much fun doing science experiments, helping in younger classrooms, and studying other cultures and their foods. I specifically remember her serving us chocolate-covered ants, octopus, and escargot – and laughing with all of us sixth graders as we sampled the strange foods.

Perhaps most importantly, Mrs. W. demonstrated trust in us. She gave us confidence. We were entering an awkward stage in life, and Mrs. W. helped us begin the transition out of childhood into adulthood. She treated us like we were responsible and could be trusted. When she assigned tasks, she would not hover over us, micromanaging our every move, but instead would give us a few instructions and then leave us to it. She encouraged us, built us up, and expected the best from us – and we responded heartily. We even did the small tasks (like lowering the flag at the end of the school day) with a sense of great responsibility and personal satisfaction. My life was deeply impacted by this teacher who not only had fun with us, but called us to responsibility and, in that sense, welcomed us to burgeoning adulthood.

– Danny M.

Isn't it ironic that many teenagers, though fluent in multiple computer languages (we're considered trendsetters and early adopters), are not expected to understand or care about things like personal finances, politics, or our faith? We're not even expected to be capable of carrying on an intelligent conversation with an adult.[70]

Alex and Brett hope to stir up what they call a "Rebelution," throwing off

the shackles of lies and low expectations and returning our generation to a true and very exciting understanding of the teen years – not as a vacation from responsibility but as a launching pad for the rest of our lives.[71]

What a counter-cultural challenge!

When Alex and Brett encourage their readers to do hard things, they actually specify "five kinds of hard":

1. Things that are outside your comfort zone.
2. Things that go beyond what is expected or required.
3. Things that are too big to accomplish alone.
4. Things that don't earn an immediate payoff.
5. Things that challenge the cultural norm.[72]

These five kinds of hard are a great place to challenge students in mentoring relationships. Here are some corresponding conversation ideas:

- "What was it like the last time you did something that took you out of your comfort zone? What other kinds of out-of-the-box things could you do, and how could I support you?"
- "Before we finish our time together, let's think of one clear way in which each of us will go beyond what is expected or required of us this week, and then we'll report back in our next meeting."
- "A lot of important things in life can't be accomplished alone. Who are the people who could walk with you, and how will you call them out?"
- "What is an area in which you're looking for a fast payoff? How would it be different if you instead patiently waited for long-term results?"
- "You can't make a difference unless you are different. What are some good ways you see God making you different than the norm? In what ways (that you might wish to push back against) do you look just like the cultural mold?"

Becoming an adult involves more than just doing hard things, though. Diane Dumas and Robert Epstein reviewed academic literature, interviewed adults, and consulted with professionals before concluding that there are 14 different "competencies" that distinguish adults from non-adults [73]:

1. **Love.** Adults know the difference between sex and love and know what it means to experience love.
2. **Sex.** Adults know about making babies, about self-control, about being pure.

3. **Leadership.** Adults know how to act as leaders of other adults, of children, and of pets.
4. **Problem solving.** Adults know the difference between right and wrong and are able to solve a wide variety of problems.
5. **Physical abilities.** Adults are supposed to be physically self-sufficient.
6. **Verbal and math skills.** Adults know "reading, 'riting and 'rithmatic" and can apply what they know to their stewardship of time and money.
7. **Interpersonal skills.** Adults know how to converse with, show respect for, forgive, apologize to, get along with, and assist other people.
8. **Handling responsibility.** Adults know to accept blame for their wrongdoing and how to honor the commitments they've made.
9. **Managing high-risk behaviors.** Adults know how to handle risky items and activities responsibly.
10. **Managing work and money.** Adults know how to get and keep jobs.
11. **Education.** Adults have obtained a basic education and know its value.
12. **Personal care.** Adults practice basic hygiene and good nutrition.
13. **Self management.** Adults can manage their own behavior: keeping appointments, accomplishing tasks, and preventing their anger from getting out of control.
14. **Citizenship.** Adults know about government and how to be good citizens.

These 14 clues to adulthood are a great starting place for discussions. As you discuss adulthood, consider challenging your mentoree with these thought-provoking questions:

- "A lot of people think that the emerging generation has a hard time figuring out how to grow up. What do you think?"
- "Have you ever thought about what it means to be an adult? What are your thoughts?"

- "What are some of the indications that someone has grown up? What makes a boy become a man and a girl become a woman?"
- "Much of our life purpose can only be understood as we commit to becoming more mature...Would you like to discuss how to grow in maturity?"

A call to adulthood is literally a call to a life of purpose. Be careful to have these conversations about maturity in a tone that doesn't come across as scolding or lecturing. Rather, paint a picture of adult life as it is: epic, adventurous, and real. Help them understand that the story that God is telling is so compelling that we ought not sit at home like helpless little children. Capture their imagination with the story, call them to rise to the occasion, and invite them – like Peter in C.S. Lewis's *The Chronicles of Narnia* – to become young rulers who look like children but fight like men.

Grasping the big picture is crucial for young adults. See p. 114.

Overcoming adolescence is part of a bigger question: "How do we live based on the way God made us?" Let's take a look at what that can mean for you and your mentoree.

A call to adulthood is literally a call to a life of purpose.

Embracing Our God-given Design

It's tempting to encourage mentorees to succeed by offering the timeless advice, "You can be anything you want to be." Don't do it! In his video series on life purpose, *Secrets of World Changers*, Jeff explains why the be-anything-you-want-to-be advice is wrong:

- **It is selfish.** It emphasizes what we *want to seek* rather than what we *ought* to seek. It is not you but is Christ in you that is the hope of glory (Colossians 1:27).
- **It is covetous.** When I seek satisfaction apart from God's purposes, I end up imitating others and coveting their abilities (Exodus 20:17).
- **It is self-defeating.** How many people have been deceived into trying to succeed at something they're not gifted to do, and have caused a proverbial train wreck for themselves and others? We should remember that each Christian is part of the body – no one is designed to do everything (I Corinthians 12:11-12).

The Life-Altering Effect of Discovering Your Design

My seventh grade English teacher, Mrs. W., helped me to find confidence in who God made me. I was a very insecure girl whose most-used phrase was "I can't." I deeply feared rejection and humiliation. My nemesis was oral reports – they petrified me. Mrs. W. noticed my fear and decided to work one-on-one with me throughout the process of crafting a speech. After my report, she encouraged me to take a communications class. I was still terrified, but agreed.

The next semester Mrs. W. would come by the class to hear me make presentations, and continued to give me feedback and encouragement. By the end of the semester I had fallen in love with speaking and drama. By my senior year in high school I was class president. I would go on to be involved in college drama and pursue a career that involved speaking and presentations. Communication is now what I love rather than what I fear.

I trace that all back to Mrs. W., who saw something in my design that I didn't see and drew it out. Because she took the time and effort to invest in my gifts, my life has been forever changed.

– Sarah H.

- **It is schizophrenic.** How do you really *know* what you want, anyway? Maybe what we think we want isn't what we truly want, meaning that it isn't what is best for us. What seems right to us may actually be wrong and dangerous (Proverbs 14:12).[74]

We think a better approach is to help mentorees understand that they have been uniquely designed by God to do certain things, in certain ways, for certain outcomes. For nearly 40 years, Arthur F. Miller has been offering a perspective on understanding design that has recently been highlighted by Max Lucado in *Cure for the Common Life*. God has designed us to be motivated to achieve certain outcomes, Miller teaches, and we each feel drawn to fulfilling those specific purposes as if a magnet were pulling us in.[75]

As people use their God-given design to achieve desired outcomes, patterns emerge. Miller calls these patterns "motivated abilities." Secular psychologists have struggled in vain to come up with naturalistic explanations for motivated abilities. In *Designed for Life*, Miller gives extensive proof that motivated abilities are of supernatural design, that they cannot be explained by cultural circumstances, that they cannot be added to or taken away from, and that they exist even in the midst of hardship and tragedy. According to Miller, every invention, discovery, or creative act in all of human history goes back to the motivated abilities God has placed inside those inventors, discoverers, and creators.[76]

If Miller is correct, and we think he is, then our job as mentors is to ask questions that help our mentorees become more aware of the particular ways in which God has designed them. Here are some questions that can move the discussion in that direction:

- "What are some things you understand about your gifts and design?"
- "Have you had experiences that thoroughly captured your imagination? What do you think was happening in those experiences?"
- "What are some experiences where you've accomplished something that gave you a tremendous sense of satisfaction?"
- "When you recall experiences that gave you a tremendous sense of satisfaction, what do those experiences have in common?"
- "Tell me some stories, as detailed as you can remember, about things you've done that returned energy to you and made you feel more alive."
- "What kinds of things do you like to work with (ideas, tools, etc.) and in what situations?"
- "What are some things that trigger you into action?"
- "What interesting things have you always wanted to try? What is stopping you from trying them?"

Looking for patterns of motivated abilities can be eye-opening and enjoyable, so have fun with these questions. Convey to mentorees your enthusiasm for seeking patterns and looking with them at their unique design. Note, though, that this process doesn't stand alone for discovering God's will because it doesn't deal with character issues or moral choices. The goal here is not to use these questions as some sort of magic formula that will

Motivated abilities are of supernatural design, they cannot be explained by cultural circumstances, they cannot be added to or taken away from, and they exist even in the midst of hardship and tragedy.

reveal a mystical truth, but for the mentors and mentorees to slowly gain a better understanding and awareness of who they are.

This exercise is hard for many people – perhaps because they are overly focused on society's values, or perhaps because they don't believe their gifts have value in light of gifts others possess. Young adults who struggle with analyzing their gifts might do well to reflect on what it means to understand and act on God's will. Garry Friesen's thorough book, *Decision Making and the Will of God*, is helpful here. Friesen basically makes four arguments:

1. Where God commands, we must obey.
2. Where there is no command, God gives us freedom (and responsibility) to choose.
3. Where there is no command, God gives us wisdom to choose.
4. When we have chosen what is moral and wise, we must trust the sovereign God to work all the details together for good.[77]

If you want, you can talk about these four axioms with your mentoree and ask him or her to imagine applying them to various decisions. Encourage your mentoree to identify and set goals, trusting God for the outcome.

Trusting God's Providence

God knew what He was doing when he made you and arranged the circumstances of your life. Learning to trust this fact is essential to understanding life purpose, but many people can't do that because they make one of three faulty affirmations:

- "Whatever will be is up to me." This belief says that God either doesn't exist or isn't involved; we are the masters of our own destiny.
- "Whatever will be, will be." This is fatalism – the notion that unseen forces of nature have determined what will happen to us, both for good and for bad.
- "Whatever." Some people just give up and surrender to chance; life is random and unexplainable, so why try to do anything at all?

The biblical perspective rejects these faulty affirmations and focuses on God's providence. Providence comes from two words "pro" = before, and "noseo" = to think. To think before. Forethought. The doctrine of providence says that God has already thought of what resources you will need to glorify Him, and he has provided for this by designing you and arranging the circumstances of your life. God supplies all of your needs (Philippians 4:19), instructing and teaching you in the way you should go (Psalm 32:8).

One reason it is difficult for young adults to accept God's providence is that they are dissatisfied with the unchangeable traits they possess, or the life circumstances over which they have no control, such as:

- Birth parents
- Siblings
- Birth order
- Gender
- Nationality
- Innate physical features[78]

When faced with traits or circumstances beyond our control, we have a choice to be bitter and angry, or to decide to trust that God will ultimately use these things to His glory and our blessing even though we can't see how it might happen.

Remember, the quality of your questions and willingness to listen will account for much of what your mentoree takes away from your discussion of life purpose.

Remember, the quality of your questions and willingness to listen will account for much of what your mentoree takes away from your discussion of life purpose. Here are some questions that focus on making sense of life circumstances. Prayerfully ask a question or two, listen to the answer, and help your mentoree draw conclusions:

- "Why do you think God chose to have you born when He did?"
- "Have you ever thought about why God placed you in the family, school, town and nation that He did?"
- "What opportunities or challenges have you been given by God?"
- "What life experiences have been very difficult to understand? How have they shaped you? How have they formed your view of God?"
- "What life blessings have been given undeservedly to you? How have they shaped you? How have they formed your view of God?"

Processing through these questions honestly can be difficult. Persist! Though answers may be hard to come by, what these questions do is begin forging the link between God's providence and your mentoree's character. Often the best answer students can come up with is: "I don't know." When Jeff gets this reply, he often asks, tongue-in-cheek: "I know you don't know, but if you *did* know, what would the answer be?" It's a silly question, but it often leads to breakthroughs.

Life purpose questions are not designed to be answered in isolation. We all need wise counselors. Encourage mentorees to go beyond your mentoring relationship and surround themselves with people who can have a strong shaping influence on their character. Here are some questions to lead in that direction:

This is a form of sponsoring. See p. 201.

- "Who knows what you need to know?"
- "Who is doing what you would like to do?"
- "Who knows you better than you know yourself?"
- "Who will give you honest, constructive feedback?"
- "Who can encourage you and guide you?"

Our friend Kathy Koch from the organization Celebrate Kids calls this identification process "developing your own personal board of directors." Encourage mentorees to boldly ask for character-based feedback by using questions like:

- "When you observe my life, what do you see are my strengths and weaknesses?"
- "Based on what you know about me, what do you think I would be good at?"
- "I want to take my work to the next level. What are some areas of strength or weakness that you think I could focus on to strengthen/ improve?"
- "What kind of character qualities do you see in me?"

Clearly, mentoring in the area of life purpose is one of the most involved aspects of mentoring. It's also deeply rewarding. These sorts of discussions, conducted with a listening ear and an encouraging (courage-giving) attitude will become a significant part of your life's legacy, flowing from your own life purpose.

CHAPTER 6:
Cultivate Wisdom:
Guiding the Emerging Generation to Know and Live the Truth

What To Expect

- How to move from getting the word *out* to getting the word *in*; bringing mentorees into an unforgettable encounter with truth.
- Four ways to communicate the truth openly and humbly to the emerging generation.
- How to communicate God's truth to a generation that isn't even sure that truth exists.
- How to help mentorees answer the toughest questions about God, humanity, and culture.

This is God's normative pattern. See p. 29.

The Apostle Paul says in 1 Corinthians 15:3: "For I delivered to you as of first importance what I also received: that Christ died for our sins in accordance with the scriptures." Notice the word "deliver," the Greek for which is "paradidomi," which means "to hand over." Quite literally, delivering God's truth to the next generation is the most important thing you can do as a mentor. To discuss matters of truth with mentorees is to engage them in thinking about reality, who God is, and how we should live.

Oftentimes the call to share truth sounds more like a call to impart information. Some traditions have elevated knowledge and reason to such a high level that they risk idolatry: worshiping what they know rather than the One who knows all things. But, as Matt Benson, Vice President of Spiritual Formation at Bryan College, phrases it, "We forget that truth is a person, not merely a position (John 14:6). We aren't called to know truth per se; we're called to know God. A mentor connects a person to God, not to information."[79] As Proverbs 9:10 states, "The fear of the Lord is the beginning of wisdom." When we know who God is we can begin to be wise – knowing what truth is and how to live based on that truth.

*Mass communication has made it simple to get the word **out**, but it utterly fails at getting the Word **in**.*

The over-emphasis on passing on knowledge for its own sake is partially responsible for the marginalizing of life-on-life relationships. Think about it this way: if the important thing is what people know, mentoring is an *inefficient* act. Why mentor life-on-life when you can teach a large class, create a website, host a radio show or do some public speaking in order to transmit knowledge to many more people at once?

The fact is, mass communication has made it simple to get the word *out*, but it utterly fails at getting the Word *in*. Here's how Norman Willis put it:

> The ways of modernity have replaced the ancient paths of generational transfer. The one on one relationship of mentor and disciple has been replaced with one impersonal instructor and a classroom of a hundred students. A lifetime of *formation* has been replaced with a few short years of *information*.[80]

The mentoring relationship is inherently incarnational. As we do life together, and are present with one another, *Who* we know is the only reliable foundation for *what* we know.

In this chapter we'll talk about the relational gestures that work best in helping your mentoree grapple with deep spiritual issues. We'll begin by discussing how to express openness without falling into relativism. Then we'll delve into the specific topics about God and truth that the emerging generation seems to be most concerned about. Along the way, we'll focus on the practical strategies – and even specific questions – you can use to begin engaging students in vibrant, significant conversations.

Incarnating the Truth

As mentors apply the relational gesture of modeling, it is essential that they live out truth in front of their mentorees. A recent study of Christian college students by Jennifer Ripley and her colleagues demonstrates that modeling is really at the heart of what the emerging generation is concerned with. The study identified 23 different things that professors do to make the Christian faith real to students, six of which rose to the top as more significant than the others. Here they are, along with the underlying questions we have concluded that students seem to be asking:

How do you cultivate a life worth modeling? See Chapter 13.

1. **A firm commitment to Christian beliefs.** The emerging generation is asking: "Do you really believe this?"
2. **Evidence of ongoing process in personal relationship with God.** The emerging generation is asking: "Do you know God personally and are *you* growing in your relationship with Him?"
3. **A well developed Christian worldview.** The emerging generation is asking: "Does a biblical view of the world really fit with reality, and is it livable?"
4. **Openness to differing points of view.** The emerging generation is asking: "Have you carefully listened to others before forming your views?" and "Are you defensive or resentful when asked questions about your viewpoints?"

5. **Richness of Christian insights and wisdom.** The emerging generation is asking: "How does understanding what God says enable us to live more rightly?"

6. **Strength in the unchanging wisdom of our faith.** The emerging generation is asking: "Is your faith wise and deep, and does it give you strength in every area of your life?"[81]

When these six attributes were present in the life of a professor, students saw truth incarnated. As a result, the Christian faith was more compelling and inviting to those students.

Before we move on too quickly, though, did point #4 catch your attention? On the one hand, students wanted their professors to have strong, well-established views. On the other hand, they wanted their professors to be open to differing views. Isn't this a contradiction? Is this just the relativism of the emerging generation rising to the surface? And if it isn't, what on earth does it mean for us as we seek to connect students with the one true God?

Let's take a close look at this seeming contradiction, because how we interact with mentorees about the truth is critical to how they come to know and live it.

How to Be Open-Minded without Being a Relativist

Some time ago, we sent the above six points to our weekly e-mail newsletter list. We suspected that point #4 would open a can of worms, and we weren't disappointed. Our subscribers felt very strongly about this point and, as they are an unusually articulate bunch, the comments we received were fascinating. The crux of the issue was well stated by a subscriber named Mary:

> My only concern with the response on the "differing views" is that the culture doesn't understand Truth and absolutes...the emerging generation needs to understand that God's Word is not just another viewpoint. Rather than treating it as my opinion vs. your opinion, we should ask, "What does God's Word say?"

Christians believe strongly that even though we are fallen creatures, we can still know the truth. Further, we believe that we must engage people who believe differently than we do. But here's the rub: engagement without openness equals insincerity. If we are not sincere, we ought to disclose that fact upfront to non-believers: "I know the truth and you don't, so I'm going to be polite and let you talk. In return for this politeness, I expect you to pay better attention when I reveal the truth to you." As John Stonestreet, Executive Director of Summit Ministries, points out, young people are reacting against this: "They have reacted to seeing *certainty* with no *humility* by choosing *humility* with no *certainty*. We need to offer them certainty *with* humility."[82] Here are four ways to create open space to discuss and share truth:

Engagement without openness equals insincerity.

1. Embrace humble transparency.

The term, "humble transparency," was used by one of our subscribers, Candace. We've also become familiar with the term "epistemological humility," which roughly means that our understanding of truth is valid but incomplete. We see now dimly, as in a mirror. This leaves room to be honest about our own struggles without being dangerously wishy-washy in our faith. Here are some suggested ways to articulate humble transparency:

- "We certainly cannot know everything. But there are some things we can be sure of. Let's talk about what some of those things might be."
- "I am a fallen creature so my ability to reason is far from perfect, but here is what I understand to be true..."

Don't forget to acknowledge complexity where it exists. See p. 43.

2. Trust God's sovereignty.

Most Christians will say that their spiritual growth has involved honest wrestling with significant issues. When we fail to give the emerging generation space to wrestle in a similar fashion, we're basically saying to them: "We've already done your thinking for you – here's the correct pre-packaged conclusion." Many on the receiving end of such a statement would see it as insulting, as you can well imagine. The established generation must ask itself, "Do we trust God enough to surrender the outcome to Him, walk faithfully with others, and avoid trying to manipulate the situation?" Here are some suggested ways to show faith in God's sovereignty:

- "This is a big issue and I'm glad you're not taking it lightly. I'll pray and ask God to give you insight..."
- "I'm so glad you're interested in asking the tough questions, and I hope we have the chance to talk more about this..."
- "I've wrestled a lot with that issue myself. Here are some resources that I found helpful..."

3. Avoid indoctrination.

It's a good thing to want the emerging generation to embrace God's truth, but *how* we go about reaching them really matters. Ken Van Meter, one of our newsletter subscribers, alerted us to some dissertation research he had recently conducted with top students in Christian schools. He found that "If students believed that Christianity was being forced upon them instead of giving them time and intellectual space to reach their own conclusions, they became resistant to the Biblical worldview message." Here are some suggested ways to avoid this brand of indoctrination:

- "If you're like me, I would guess you have genuine questions and doubts. I want to hear your honest questions."

We've recommended excellent books on a variety of topics. Do some research and share what you learn with your mentoree. See p. 257.

- "May I share with you how Christians throughout history have come to grips with this issue?"

4. Listen in an engaged fashion.

One Christian school leader, Nancy, e-mailed us with the following view:

> Listening to another's beliefs before speaking makes the listener credible and compassionate. However misguided the other's beliefs may be, why should they listen to me if I cannot listen to them?...Is my faith so small that I have to cover my ears?

Our friend and Passing the Baton board member, JR Kerr, says: "The established generation asked, 'Can you prove it to me?' The emerging generation asks, 'Can you hear me?'"[83] Here are some suggested ways to listen in an engaged fashion:

For more on active listening, see p. 80.

Refusing to Spoon-Feed

Dr. R., who taught Biblical Studies, was my favorite professor in college. When he taught, he didn't just pass along information – he passed along his heart. He was excited about what he taught. It made us, his students, excited. Don't get me wrong – he was very knowledgeable, but what stood out to me was his conviction. I remember many days when tears would pour out because of the deep love he had for his Lord. Other times I would find myself forgetting to take notes because I was overwhelmed by his passion for God.

But what made Dr. R. so unique was that although he had deep convictions, he refused to spoon-feed them to us. He structured his lectures in a way that invited tough questions– and he rarely gave us answers. He was not afraid to let us wrestle. Why? Because He trusted that God would reveal Himself and guide us. He fully believed that the Holy Spirit in us was more powerful and able to guide us better than himself. And the result of all this was a change to my spiritual core: he made me develop and own my convictions. Because of this, Dr. R. influenced me more than any other teacher I've had.

– Name Withheld

- "Tell me more about that." (Nothing says "I'm listening!" as clearly as a question which honestly solicits further communication.)
- "I want to hear what is important to you."
- "Can we take some time to share our points of view with one another?"
- "Thank you for honoring me by trusting me with your thoughts on these real-life matters."

As much as we value openness and encourage conversation, we *never* want to give the impression that God's truth is up for debate, because it is not. God's nature and character are revealed in scripture, and He means for us to know what is true. John Stonestreet suggests, "Be straightforward with students. Look them in the eye and say that you're willing to stand on these ideas. When you don't know something you have to be humble enough to say 'good question.'"[84] The proper attitude is memorably phrased by Dan Egeler, author of *Mentoring Millennials:* "Our challenge is to uncompromisingly teach absolute truth while coming across not as the bug spray of condemnation but as the perfume of Christ's grace."[85]

Truth and Worldview: The Big Picture

This ties directly back to the emerging generation's love of complexity. See p. 43.

Kinnaman and Lyons have affirmed our thinking on connecting mentorees to God's truth. They point out that most young people don't have an objection to the truth; what they're objecting to is the way in which Christians fail to relate God's truth to the complexities of modern life. Here's how they put it:

> Young outsiders and Christians alike do not want a cheap, ordinary or insignificant life, but their vision of present-day Christianity is just that – superficial, antagonistic, depressing. The Christian life looks so simplified and constricted that a new generation no longer recognizes it as a sophisticated, livable response to a complex world.[86]

They need to be swept up into the epic story.

To know and live the truth, our students need more than just facts or a list of right and wrong rules. They need a compelling vision of the bigger picture. They need to be swept up into the epic story. They need to be awed by a view of reality that is much greater than themselves. In essence, it must be presented as a way of seeing that affects the way they make decisions about everything in life. It's a *worldview*, which David Noebel, president of Summit Ministries, defines as "an overarching approach to understanding God, the world, and man's relationship to God and the world."[87] A worldview is what you get when you respond to ultimate questions, including:

- "How did I get here?"
- "What is the purpose of life?"
- "How should I live?"
- "What happens when I die?"

Everyone, even people who have never consciously thought about it, form answers to these questions and live accordingly. Everyone has a worldview, and this worldview is, by its very nature, spiritual. Nancy Pearcey, author of *Total Truth*, points this out with eloquence:

> We have to reject the division of life into a sacred realm, limited to things like worship and personal morality, over against a secular realm

that includes science, politics, economics, and the rest of the public arena. This dichotomy in our own minds is the greatest barrier to liberating the power of the gospel across the whole of culture today.[88]

Most young adults we've met are oblivious to the relationship between spiritual things and the rest of their lives. Helping them understand the Christian worldview could be one of the most eye-opening, life-shaping things you do as a mentor. It will move them from viewing truth as a discussion of occasional dilemmas to an understanding of all of life. Unfortunately, as you're about to read, this is very far from how most young Christians understand their faith.

As a mentor, where should you turn for worldview training? See p. 264.

Knowing that Spiritual Truth is Knowable

Many of today's Christian young adults are oblivious to the actual content of their beliefs. In his book entitled *Soul Searching: The Religious and Spiritual Lives of American Teenagers*, Christian Smith concluded that most young adults who claim to be Christians don't actually express Christian convictions. Instead, they are moralistic therapeutic deists whose deepest spiritual thought is "God loves me and wants me to be happy."[89] This illusion must be confronted – but how do we do it?

Sean McDowell is one guy whose finger is on the pulse of young Christians in America. Growing up with a father (Josh McDowell) who has spoken to millions and written dozens of books explaining the truth of Christianity, he's been around worldview studies all of his life. Today, as a Christian school teacher and Bible department chairman, Sean has successfully focused on helping his students know and live the truth through life-on-life influence. In our interview with Sean, he said:

> It's not enough to just give people the truth. It's not even enough to *know* the truth. Young people need to *know* that they *know* the truth. [In other words, they need to realize that truth is knowable – that it can be known – and that the truth they know is true.] That's what brings confidence. Imagine two kids taking a test. One thinks he knows the right answer but isn't sure. The other actually knows the answer. The first student might get it right, but the second student is the one who

"It's not enough to just give people the truth. It's not even enough to know the truth. Young people need to know that they know the truth."

115

will be able to make a coherent argument if he is challenged. That's what we need today.[90]

Based on Sean's work in a Christian school, he points out:

> There really is such a thing as knowledge and objective truth and we seem to be willing to deliver it in every topic except "spiritual" ones. We do it in math class. We do it in biology class. But in religion class, we talk about feelings and experiences as if spiritual knowledge is uncertain. If we help students know that it *is* actually true, then they can defend the truth with confidence.[91]

We couldn't agree more. If the students we are in relationship with are going to have a vibrant faith that speaks to all of their lives, they'll need to develop a biblical worldview that applies to every area of life. Though the purpose of this book is not to deal exhaustively with worldview issues, let's take a brief look at what truth looks like in relation to God, humanity, and culture.

Truth About God

Many young adults today are unaware of basic truths about who God is. It may be that you, as their mentor, will have the privilege of introducing them to the great and vital doctrines about God's attributes. In his book, *TruthQuest Survival Guide*, Steve Keels points out that there are seven clear attributes of God given in scripture. Along with these seven we're including a handful of scripture passages you can study with your mentoree:

- **God is omnipresent.** "He is always available, always ready for you to call on Him, worship Him, pray to Him, and enjoy His presence."[92] (Jeremiah 23:23-24, Psalm 139:7-10, Acts 17:24-27)
- **God is omniscient.** "God is truly amazing in His knowledge! There is nothing that is possible to know that God does not know…He is infinite in His knowledge and understanding."[93] (1 John 3:20, Psalm 139:4, Psalm 94:11)
- **God is omnipotent.** "God can do what to us seems impossible."[94] (Genesis 18:14, Job 42:2, Matthew 19:26)

If students are to have a vibrant faith they need a biblical worldview that applies to every area of life.

- **God is love.** "He doesn't love us because of our performance or because we are worthy of His love. He loves us because it is His nature to love us."[95] (Psalm 103:17, 1 John 4:8, Titus 3:4)
- **God is jealous.** "God is jealous for your affections. He wants you to desire Him more than any other thing in this world."[96] (Exodus 20:5, Exodus 34:14, Deuteronomy 5:9)
- **God is all wise.** "God knows how life works."[97] (Job 12:13, Psalm 147:5, Romans 16:27)
- **God is trinity.** "God is the Trinity…He exists in a perfect, eternal relationship with Himself."[98] (John 8:41, Hebrews 1:8, 1 Corinthians 3:16)

The conversations you have with your mentoree about who God is may bring up tough questions about His character. As we were talking with Sean McDowell about the attributes of God, he made the following thought-provoking comment:

> Most attacks on Christianity have to do with the goodness of God. It ultimately comes down to whether you believe God is good or not. This is the first area that Satan attacked – is God really good? The new atheists are attacking this; it's particularly relevant today.[99]

When we asked Sean "If that is the case, what should mentors do?" he replied:

> Mentors should share stories/experiences from their own lives where pain and suffering turned out ultimately for the good. They should also reflect back on their life and periods where they didn't understand truths (such as sexual purity) and – now that they're further in life – they realize that God's rule is good. His commands are good. God wants to bless you and you have to trust Him.[100]

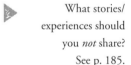

What stories/experiences should you *not* share? See p. 185.

Many young adults have serious questions about God's goodness. Your mentoree may be wondering:

- What about the God we read of in the Old Testament, who ordered the slaughter of children and babies?

- What about the suffering we see around the world – not to mention the pain we have in our own lives?
- What about God's seemingly arbitrary rules and commands which, if violated, invoke harsh judgment?

We'll take a look at each of these three in turn.

1 Corinthians 13:12 says, "For now we see in a mirror dimly, but then face to face. Now I know in part; then I shall know fully, even as I have been fully known." In other words, we can't understand everything about God because our relationship with him is fractured. The only way to grapple with our questions and doubts is to recognize that they exist because of this broken relationship. We can understand each of the above questions best in the context of relationship. We don't know why God did what the Old Testament says He did, but we believe that His wrath is part of the greater story of Him redeeming a people for Himself. Ultimately it is about His restoring relationship with us.

The same goes for pain and suffering, which are the direct result of our broken relationship with the God who made goodness, truth, and beauty. And the good news is that our God is not unfamiliar with pain and suffering. Every worldview must explain pain and suffering, but only the Christian story paints a picture of a God who is not distant or uninvolved. Quite the opposite in fact: He entered into our suffering to bring us back into relationship with Him.

Again, the question regarding the rules and commands given in scripture are part of the bigger story. God gave those rules to His people with the promise of incomprehensible blessing. If we step back from our self-oriented perspective, we can see that these rules and boundaries tell of a God who desires His people to live whole, rich, blessed lives. Sexuality, for example, is so valuable that God went to great lengths to protect it inside the marriage relationship. There, it can be experienced joyfully in a way that connects the man and woman at the deepest levels. We've heard it said that sex is like fire: inside the fireplace of marriage it is warm, delightful and life-giving – but once it skips over the boundaries of the fireplace it is a ravaging, devastating

Every worldview must explain pain and suffering, but only the Christian story paints a picture of a God who is not distant or uninvolved.

force that brings destruction. In His love and wisdom, God set up "fireplaces" for our health and joy.

These difficult questions regarding God's goodness can only be discussed in light of the greater story of Creation, Fall, and Redemption – and how God's purpose is to restore all to relationship with Himself. This is quite possibly the most pressing truth that young people need to know about God.

Truth About Being Human

Acts 17:28 says, "In Him we live and move and have our being." Who God is determines who I am, and who I believe Him to be has implications for all of my life. But the reverse is also true: who I believe I am affects what I believe about God as well. John Calvin began his extensive work, *Institutes of the Christian Religion*, with the heading: "Without knowledge of self there is no knowledge of God."[101] This quote is alarming when read in the context of a society in which what it means to be "human" is being called into question more and more by evolutionary theory, bio-ethical research, political battles over abortion and even technological advances in robotics. In the midst of this cultural confusion, mentorees are desperate to know who they are and why it matters. They are asking: "What does it mean to be human?"

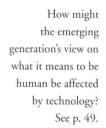

How might the emerging generation's view on what it means to be human be affected by technology? See p. 49.

In ancient times, kings erected statues of themselves throughout their kingdoms. These statues bore the image of the king, and in a sense, they ruled in his place. Genesis 1:26-27 says that God made man and woman in his image. Throughout history, the church has interpreted "image of God," or *imago Dei*, in a number of ways. Some suggest that *imago Dei* means that humans are uniquely equipped with the attributes of reason, morality and will. Others suggest that it means relationship; just as God is relational within Himself, humans are uniquely relational and are designed to know God and each other. Still others suggest *imago Dei* is all about God's purpose for us to have dominion. When taken together, all of these perspectives on *imago Dei* give us a beautiful picture of how we were made: equipped with reason and morality, designed for intimate relationship with God and each other, and given the awesome task of ruling creation.

The Value of People

Toward the end of my college years I was able to establish a close friendship with my college advisor, Dr. H. Like a true Barnabas, he poured words of wisdom, encouragement, correction and affirmation into my life. He saw potential in me that no one else saw, telling me that I was a leader and could work in administration one day – something I could not imagine at the time.

But Dr. H. was right. When I was offered a position to be an Assistant Principal, he was one of the first people I called. His advice was priceless. He told me to value people, whether they were students, co-workers, support staff, or custodians. "There's a lot to be done in administration," Dr. H. told me, "but don't lose perspective on why you are doing the job God has called you to do. Invest in people! Invest time in them!"

These weren't just wise words – they were the very words by which Dr. H. lived his life. Every time I had gone to meet with him in his office, regardless of what the issue was, he would always unplug the phone and close in prayer. Even in the midst of a busy professor's schedule, he showed me that I had great value as a person, as an image-bearer of God. This is a lesson I will keep with me for the rest of my life.

– Andy C.

Unfortunately, Adam and Eve's desire to *be* God, resulting in our subsequent, ongoing desire to be God, has broken our relationship with the one true God. The question, "What does it mean to be human?", is answered in part by the Fall: we are deeply broken, twisted, and scarred by sin. Our reason and morality are marred. Our relationships with God and each other are broken. Our dominion is in shambles. Beyond that, because we are in imperfect relationship with the God whose image we bear we don't know how to answer the question of what it means to be human. We're left to our own devices – and those devices aren't working. We're confused. We can't fix what's broken. We don't understand ourselves or others. One area in which this can be seen today is in how obsessed Americans are with altering their bodies to be more attractive and, hence, more valuable. We're trying to mend ourselves.

The power and beauty of God's story is that redemption includes humanity – the image of God is being restored. We will be what we were meant to be. What hope we can find in that truth! Here are some ways you can discuss these ideas with your mentoree:

- "Why is it that human beings seem wired to be in relationship?"
- "When you look around, it is stories, not mere lists of information, that capture our imagination (TV shows, books, movies, songs, photo albums, blogs). Why is it that we gravitate toward stories and look for everyday life to have a deeper meaning? What does that tell us about ourselves?"
- "What are some of the things in culture that are broken because of human sin? What are some of the things in humans that are broken?"
- "What do you see around you that wouldn't be this way if all humans perfectly followed the 10 Commandments?" (Examples: security cameras, jails, some commercials, shrines, many products, etc.)

We expect you'll think of even better questions on your own as you work together with your mentoree to focus on God's story and what it means for our identity as human beings.

Truth About Culture

Culture, simply defined, is *what human beings do*. It does not have some sort of nebulous existence on its own, but is the result of human acts of creation. It's actually what God designed humans to do – form and fill, subdue and have dominion over, create and cultivate. God gave Adam the garden and asked him to make culture; He created and asked humans to form and create in response.

Unfortunately, like our other relationships, our relationship with creation is broken. As Bonnie-Marie Yager, Assistant Director of Worldview Formation at Bryan College, puts it:

> Everything is about relationships, our relationship to God, to others, to ourselves, and to creation. All of these relationships are affected by the

A great way to frame the discussion of culture would be to create something together. See p. 241 for ideas.

Fall, and redemption means restoring these relationships – calling them back to what they were intended to be.[102]

This way of understanding redemption hints of God's plan to redeem our relationship with creation. Nature and culture, both created things, will be restored. Our calling, the "cultural mandate" to fill, form, and create, is renewed through the redemptive work of Christ. Christ himself articulates this perfectly in Matthew 28:18-20 by commanding his disciples to teach everyone in the world to obey God in every area of life. Because "all authority in heaven and on earth" belongs to Christ, every area of life and culture is brought under his rule. The cultural mandate is renewed.

What does this mean for us? In his book *Culture Making*, Andy Crouch suggests that as humans we engage culture in two distinct ways.[103] First, we are cultivators – God gave us His good creation to care for, tend, and form. We are to cultivate not only what is good in God's creation (nature), but what is good in human creation (culture). Celebrate good culture. Enjoy it. Increase its influence. Second, we are creators – God gave us the tools and calling to make culture. We are to take initiative, to be productive, to make wise decisions and to create new cultural artifacts that reflect who God is and the story He is telling. It's critical to have this discussion with mentorees because most assume that the culture just is what it is, and isn't shaped at all by their actions. Here are some ways to spark the discussion:

- "Let's spend some time talking about culture. What is culture, really? How do we know it when we see it?"
- "You're familiar with the term 'popular culture.' What does that mean? What are some examples of it?"
- "If the influential people who form culture genuinely believed in God's goodness and sought to bring redemption to bear on what they formed, how would the culture be different?"
- "What should our stance toward culture be as Christians?"
- "What are some ways we can make a difference in the culture even if we can't affect everything about it?"

To paraphrase Sean McDowell, it's critical to get students to talk about these issues as a way of coming to know that what they know is true. The

Our calling to fill, form, and create is renewed through the redemptive work of Christ.

goal isn't to come up with a specific set of answers, but to challenge your mentoree to ask the right questions. Here are some powerful follow-up questions you can gently use to help mentorees go deeper:

- "What do you mean by that?"
- "How did you come to understand that?"
- "How do you know that is true?"
- "Where do you get your information?"
- "What happens if you're wrong?"

Keep asking questions, keep probing, and keep looking for opportunities to share your story along the way.

In Appendices G and H, you'll find a list of resources we've found most helpful in provoking discussion and building knowledge based on a biblical worldview. But – please – don't ever forget that the way you live out God's truth is the greatest witness to its trueness. Mentorees may not see that right away, but years from now it will be the main thing they remember about your relationship.

CHAPTER 7:
Cultivate Leadership:
Preparing the Emerging Generation to Influence Others

What To Expect
- Natural ways to invite mentorees to accompany you on your life journey.
- Three steps to prepare mentorees for greater lifelong influence.
- The key elements of great calling-out conversations: complimenting, acknowledging, and championing.
- Twelve skills mentorees need in order to become culture-shaping leaders.

John Cook, one of our Passing the Baton board members, tells of how he got his start in leadership…way back in middle school:

> I didn't think that I had done much to distinguish myself with Ms. Elinor Black or any of my other eighth grade teachers. Late in that school year, however, as Student Council elections approached, Ms. Black called me out – literally. One day before class she asked to speak to me privately in the hall. "Have you considered running for Student Council office?" I really don't recall what I said except that it amounted to "No!"
>
> Ms. Black then proceeded to point out four or five reasons why I should run and asked me to think about doing so. I accepted the challenge and won. For each of the next four years I was either appointed to or won election to an office of the executive committee of the Student Council. This eventually led to running – unopposed – for President in my senior year of high school. In that senior year I also represented my high school to serve as the president of the Southern Association of Student Councils. Student council taught me much about leadership, lessons I would have never learned if Ms. Black hadn't called me out.

Just about every leader was called out at one point or another – most often by an everyday person who saw their potential, voiced it, and encouraged it to bloom. In theological terms, this is called "the blessing." Ms. Black gave a blessing to John by identifying his leadership ability and encouraging him to use it. As John honed his leadership skills, many other people were blessed. Since that time John has served as a devoted husband and father, a corporate executive, a school board president, and an executive coach. Imagine the thousands of people who have been blessed because Ms. Black took a few minutes to stiffen the spine of an insecure middle schooler!

Blessing: The Power of Good Words to Create a Leader

It used to be a common thing for a young person to receive a blessing upon leaving home. No longer. The word for blessing in the New Testament comes from two Greek words: "eu" which means "well," and "logos" which means "word." Put them together and you get "eulogos". Say that aloud a couple of times. Does the word sound familiar? It's the root word for *eulogy*. American culture dictates that eulogies are delivered at funerals. We say nice things about people when they're dead. In his book, *Handoff*, Jeff suggests that we reverse the trend and start having "funerals" for people while they're still alive – literally giving eulogies to people as they are preparing to go out into *this* world, rather than the next.[104]

In high school, Paul and a few dozen of his friends decided to do just that. Instead of calling it a funeral, they deemed it a "*fun*-eral," and they each gave a serious eulogy for another person in their friend group – with everyone listening. It was silly, to be sure, but it was also meaningful to hear words of blessing spoken. It even brought tears to some of the teenage guys' eyes.

One of the most important eulogies, or blessings, we can give to young adults is to help them understand their responsibility to lead others. This kind of blessing can have a transformational effect on a young person. Consider the example of John Wooden, the phenomenally successful basketball coach from UCLA who is widely considered to be the most successful college coach of all time. Upon graduating from the county school in Centerton, Indiana, John's father, a rural mail carrier and farmer, gave John the following written creed:

> Be true to yourself; make each day your masterpiece; help others; drink deeply from good books, especially the Bible; make friendship a fine art; build a shelter against a rainy day; pray for guidance; count, and give thanks for your blessings every day.[105]

Can you imagine the impression this advice made on young John – clear, simple, specific advice from a father who was counting on his son to make him proud? These words went beyond mere advice and actually created an expectation for young John that he could live the good life – a blessing from his father that raised John's expectations for himself. Successful mentors do this same thing in terms of preparing future leaders.

*We should start having eulogies for people while they're still alive, as they are preparing to go out into **this** world, rather than the next.*

How Jesus Formed World Changing Leaders

If we could form the idea of leadership as a mathematical equation, it would simply be L = I + C (*leadership* equals *influence* plus *change*). To influence others and change things glorifies God and allows us to be a blessing to the nations. Scripture tells us that Jesus employed a three-part strategy for unleashing his followers. He used this strategy to identify and equip 12 ordinary men who went on to change the world. What better example could we have of long-lasting impact?

Small, personal influence seems to be a pattern in scripture. See p. 33.

As we mentioned briefly in Chapter Three, the gospel of Mark gives us some insight into Jesus' overall strategy:

> And he went up on the mountain and called to him those whom he desired, and they came to him. And he appointed twelve (whom he also named apostles) so that they might be with him and he might send them out to preach and have authority to cast out demons. (Mark 3:13-15)

Recall that Jesus did three things:
- He called to him those whom he desired.
- He appointed 12 to be with him.
- He sent them out to preach and have authority over the spiritual realm.

Let's take each of these three points in turn.

First, Call Them Out

To call a person out is to identify the shape of his or her soul and give voice to what you see.

To call a person out is to identify the shape of his or her soul and give voice to what you see. There are lots of ways to do this:
- "I've heard that you're a really sharp student. I'd like to get together and talk about your potential to influence our school."
- "I see potential in you that goes far beyond what you are exercising at the present time. If you are interested, I would like to help you utilize that potential."

Just a Few Minutes, Just a Few Words

Mr. C. was a science teacher at my public high school. I didn't like to ride the bus so I usually just walked home. One day he saw me walking and offered me a ride. Since my house was on his way home, from time to time he gave me rides.

Mr. C. had a knack for asking good questions. In the few minutes we shared on the way home, he asked me about my likes and dislikes, my goals (or lack thereof), and my attitude toward life and people. After listening carefully, he planted seeds of encouragement by saying things like, "I can see you as a successful business man. Work hard when you go to college, but I have no doubt you will be successful." I'd never heard words of blessing like that – even from my own father, who was a good man.

I knew that Mr. C. wanted to get to know me. That's why his encouraging words sank deep and inspired me long after the car rides ended. Interestingly, I went on to college, graduated, and went into business. I now own a successful company, and I often reflect back on his words of encouragement and the impact they have had on me – all from just a few minutes on his way home every day.

– Ken J.

- "I think you're selling yourself short by not trying as hard as you could. What do you think about working through a process to figure out the true extent of your giftedness?"
- "Can I share something in a spirit of love? I've noticed that you follow the crowd when I think you could be leading them in a more positive direction. If you're interested I'd like to show you how it's done."
- "Has anyone ever told you that you have the gift of _____? What do you think about grabbing some coffee and talking about what I've observed?"
- "Most people are interested in shallow things: wealth, fame, etc. I've observed you and I think you're a deeper thinker than people give you credit for; I think you could pursue higher goals that could

really make a difference in the world. How does that idea strike you?"

To a cynical person, these kinds of "calling out" statements may appear to be little more than shameless flattery. Far from it. Flattery is hollow praise given for the purpose of gaining power over another person. These calling out conversations are a critical combination of *complimenting, acknowledging* and *championing*.

Be careful to avoid flattery with the emerging generation. See p. 38."

- Complimenting, according to the Center for Coaching Excellence, is saying *what* someone did well. Complimenting takes practice. Many of us are used to giving (and receiving) vague, minimally helpful compliments such as "You're awesome!" and "Great job!" Kind words like these certainly have their place, but the compliments that really make a difference are typically much more specific. Example: "You did that report very well. I loved how you organized it so thoroughly and provided such detailed handouts for the class." Now you try it. Start with the framework and fill it in: "You did ____ well."

- Acknowledging is saying who someone is and how you saw it. Be honest and specific. Acknowledging is a simple way to express the value you see in another person. The power of these words in building another person up cannot be overestimated. Example: "You are compassionate, and I observed it when you sat with the new kid at the lunch table last week." Now you try it: "You are ____, and I saw it when you ____."

- Championing is expressing your belief in another person by saying what you see in them (that they likely do not even see in themselves). Championing instills confidence. Again, the key is being honest and specific. Example: "I am confident that you can accomplish your goal and stay on task this week. I've seen you keep your commitments time and again, and I know you're capable of doing what you've set your mind to do." Now you try it: "I am confident that you can ____."[106]

Complimenting, acknowledging and championing make others feel respected and increase their confidence.

Together, the skills of complimenting, acknowledging and championing make others feel respected and increase their confidence as they begin to see a more accurate view of themselves.

A quick note on giving praise: research conducted over the last couple of decades by Carol Dweck and her colleagues demonstrates that praising students for their *intelligence* causes students to care more about performance, and even to take fewer risks because their failure might disappoint their teachers and parents. Students praised for their *effort*, on the other hand, displayed greater task persistence, enjoyment, fewer low-ability attributions ("I'm not capable of doing this"), and greater task performance.[107]

Jeff recalls how one of his high school teachers called him out by focusing on effort, rather than intelligence:

> H. Gene Specht was my first debate coach. I found him to be thoroughly intimidating but was glad to have him – he was one of the most respected debate coaches in our state. On our first overnight debate trip, Mr. Specht took us to the nicest restaurant he could afford on the debate budget – complete with linen tablecloths and napkins. Quite an experience for a bunch of kids from a farming community! He took great pains that evening to help us learn how to behave in such a setting, occasionally barking out impromptu manners lessons.
>
> Later, he drove us through a very nice part of town that showcased mansions on tree-lined streets. As we gawked out the windows, he said, "If you work hard you have the potential to live in a place like this someday." Although his words seemed materialistic, I realize now that this was Mr. Specht's way of saying: "Don't settle in life. There is so much more for you than what you've experienced so far."

Encouragement of the sort that Mr. Specht offered to Jeff can be just the thing students need in order to gain confidence in their ability to lead.

Jeff teaches a leadership class at Bryan College, and for the last six years he has surveyed his students on a battery of questions. One of those questions is this: "What beliefs about yourself block your ability to be an effective leader?" The number one answer is: "A lack of confidence," and the number two answer is: "I feel inadequate." Shockingly, these responses are from a generation that was raised on the TV show *Blues Clues* which

Christ did not merely hand them the task of continuing his work; he made them part of it from the very beginning.

taught them: "...when we use our minds and take a step at a time, we can do anything that we wanna do!"

Perhaps Jeff's students are exceptionally humble, but it is more likely that they, like so many young adults, know in their heads what the right answer is ("I am a leader and I can do anything I set my mind to.") but are saying in their hearts, "This is a bunch of propaganda. The truth is, I don't know what to do and I'm scared."

Yes, there are some leaders whose self-confidence helps them naturally rise to leadership positions. But the majority of people are not this way. Thankfully, the message of scripture is that, time and time again, God uses ordinary, scared people to accomplish the extraordinary. Wise mentors emphasize this message repeatedly, calling mentorees out through acknowledging, championing, and complimenting so they see how God can use them as leaders.

Second, Take Them With You

This is a great example of the modeling gesture. See p. 59.

Roger Erdvig says, "Teaching others to be influencers requires almost purely a 'let's do it together' approach. There needs to be no agenda except to be together as I do what God has called me to do. Mentorees are just doing it with me and seeing it happen."[108] In his book, *Mentoring for Mission*, Gunter Krallmann calls this let's-do-it-together approach "transparent with-ness."[109] What a descriptive term. This is the idea behind the English word "witness," as in a person who testifies during a trial: "I know what happened because I was with them." Here's what "with-ness" might look like:

- "There's a new student in our school and I'm going over to her house tonight to meet her family. Would you be interested in grabbing a friend and accompanying me? I think she would be grateful to meet a couple of her fellow students."
- "I'm going to be heading downtown to preach at the homeless shelter. I'd like for you to come with me if you're free. Afterward we can grab a soft drink and talk about the experience."
- "Congratulations on becoming student government president! As someone who has also been called to be a leader, I think there are

some things I could teach you. Would you like to walk with me, so to speak, and learn some of the things I've learned?"

- "I'm part of a group that is seeking to make a difference in the area of _____. I think you have the kind of gifting that could really make a difference in the group, and I believe you'd find it to be a satisfying use of time. Would you join us for a meeting to see what you think?"

One of the subscribers of our weekly e-mail newsletter, Gary Carper, tells how his high school principal practiced with-ness to great effect:

> One day our principal, Mr. Moore, asked me and another senior to go with him somewhere. He took us to the juvenile detention center where we visited with a 12- or 13-year-old boy. We saw the boy's circumstances in the center: a sparse, jail-cell-like room, a uniform, and no shoes. It was not a very inviting place to say the least.
>
> Mr. Moore talked to the boy a little and then to an official. On the way back to school, he told us that the boy was there because he had been abandoned by his family and had nowhere else to go, and that he was being kept at the center until a better arrangement could be found. Mr. Moore had gone to check on him and see what was being done to help him.
>
> I never heard anything more about that boy's situation, but Mr. Moore's response made an indelible impression on me. Never again would I be able to look at people who were down-and-out and think that they deserved everything that happened to them. Mr. Moore also taught me by example that leaders do a lot of things for which they never get credit, including reaching out to those who are the least among us.

Mr. Moore influenced those boys forever without saying a word – he just took them with him. This reminds us of what Christ did with his disciples. He literally lived with them, influencing them in the ordinary, everyday moments of walking, eating, resting, and playing. He did not merely hand them the task of continuing his work; he made them part of it from the very beginning.

This reflects the theological notion of incarnation. See p. 149.

What are some ways you can do this creatively with your mentoree? See p. 241.

133

Mentorees will learn and grow far more by walking alongside you than they ever could from merely hearing your advice. Take them with you.

Third, Send Them Out to Lead

Christ was neither a "buddy" nor a "boss." See p. 26.

Jesus didn't just call out followers to be his pals and hang out with him. He called them out *in order to send them out* to influence the world. Here are some of the ways Jesus sent his followers out:

- John 14:12 – "Truly, truly, I say to you, whoever believes in me will also do the works that I do; and greater works than these will he do, because I am going to the Father."
- Matthew 10:16 – "Behold, I am sending you out as sheep in the midst of wolves, so be wise as serpents and innocent as doves."
- Matthew 28:18-20 – "And Jesus came and said to them, 'All authority in heaven and on earth has been given to me. Go therefore and make disciples of all nations, baptizing them in the name of the Father and of the Son and of the Holy Spirit, teaching them to observe all that I have commanded you. And behold, I am with you always, to the end of the age."

Here are some statements you can use to "send out" the emerging generation in your own context:

- "You are preparing to move into a season of opportunity. Most people squander it, but I'd like to help launch you successfully."
- "Here's how I see it: I've made it a ways up the ladder of life. My goal is to reach out a hand, pull you up, and then push you on ahead of where I myself could go."
- "You are on your way to becoming an incredible influencer based on your God-given design. What do you want to do with the influence you have? How can you expand your influence?"

As we've worked with young adults over the years, we've been astounded at how few of them have ever been challenged with a clear sense of mission. This is especially true for adolescent boys, who seem to be struggling today in cultures around the world. At Passing the Baton, we've concluded that it is not possible for a young man to grow into his potential without the

For a great illustration of this, see p. 172.

strong guiding influence of an older man. Several years ago, Jeff developed a teaching on this called "Where are the Men?" and has offered it both in live workshops and as an audio recording. In the workshop, he shows how youth-serving organizations can be transformed if a respected man will take a small group of five young men under his wing and disciple them in a mentoring group.[110]

Last year we received the following story from Blair, a principal at a Christian school near Seattle. Listen to how he describes the process of unleashing the boys in his school:

> For the last year, I have been meeting with a group of five young men. They were given the opportunity to participate or walk away, but they had to be all in or all out. We have met each week for about one hour. I told them that we would be changing the school and that they would become the spiritual leaders.

135

Sending-out conversations may launch mentorees into opportunities to influence that they might not have dared to consider before.

For more on cultivating purpose in a mentoree, see p. 93.

We just came back from a spiritual retreat for our high school. These five boys took seats in the front row, without being asked, and stood and worshiped in front of the entire student body. At the end of the first day, I did a male-only session asking: "Where are the godly young men?" These young men stood and gave testimonies from the year about what God was doing in their lives and expressed their vision for the school. After they shared, other young men started to come to the microphone and share, dream, confess sins, ask for help, and offer to help. It was amazing; young men that had never shared publicly stood and participated.

As we went through the second day of our retreat, students were not only caught up in worship, but they remained at the altar in tears and prayer even after being released for lunch. By the last session, the students surrounded the teaching staff, laid hands on them and prayed in the power of the Holy Spirit. The teachers were overwhelmed and stood in shock with tears running down their faces. Our speaker and worship band left on Tuesday afternoon, but the Spirit of God remains and has changed our school.

Notice how Blair called the young men to a significant, worthwhile purpose. He walked with a small group of them in an intentional way, and then he sent them out to change the culture of the school. Would you like to see that happen in your school? It's incredible to see what God does when we express confidence in the emerging generation's ability to lead in a way that genuinely makes a difference.

As mentorees gain greater understanding of their design, build on that foundation with conversations about influence and mission:

- What could you do?
- Who could you influence?
- What good thing could you create?

These sending-out conversations may launch mentorees into opportunities to influence that they might not have dared to consider before.

Next Level Leadership: Developing Twelve Pivotal Skills

Opening the world of leadership to a young person is one of the most valuable things you can do as a mentor. In Appendix G, we recommend a number of excellent leadership resources that work really well in the context of mentoring relationships. One of our favorites is Tim Elmore's *Habitudes* book series. Each chapter in these four books contains a memorable image that teaches a basic leadership principle you can help your mentoree develop.

Another helpful resource is Jeff's video course, *Secrets of Everyday Leaders*, which consists of 12 20-minute video segments, a textbook, and a discussion guide. It's set up so you can watch and discuss each lesson with one person or a group and work through the abilities all leaders must develop in order to succeed.[111] This course goes into a detailed survey of 12 leadership skills that can help your mentoree grow in the area of leadership. Here's a brief overview:

1. Identify your mentoree's leadership gifts.

Everyone is a potential leader because everyone influences others and has opportunities to create change. Help your mentoree discern areas where he or she would like to make a difference, and take a look together at his or her specific gifting. This will involve asking questions like:

- "What kinds of experiences with leadership have you had in the past?"
- "What principles can we learn from the Bible about leadership?"
- "What are the barriers that prevent you from making a difference?"
- "If you could see your potential from God's perspective, how would you see yourself differently?

2. Help your mentoree gain credibility so he or she will be taken seriously.

People decide who to follow by asking three questions: (1) Are you a good person?, (2) Do you have the passion to succeed?, and (3) Do you know what you're doing? Time and time again, we've seen young adults who were not viewed as leaders rise to positions of influence because they concentrated their personal development on answering these three questions. Have a discussion with your mentoree about those credibility questions:

- "What are some things you can do to answer those credibility questions in a way that builds trust with others?"

3. Engage your mentoree in a discussion about what it means to live above reproach.

Set the standard high and be a servant leader. The idea of being "above reproach" comes from 1 Timothy 3:2. Read the passage with your mentoree and discuss questions like these:

- "What is your reputation among your peers?"
- "Does your reputation help or hurt you when it comes to influencing others?"
- "Are there things that you have done which have damaged your reputation that need to be set right?"

4. Nurture a desire in the heart of your mentoree for wise counsel.

The best leaders are those who seek out wise counsel. Wise counselors don't usually just appear out of nowhere – they must be sought out and asked for help. Walk through this process with your mentoree:

For more on sponsoring a mentoree to another advisor or mentor, see p. 201.

- "Who are some people you trust and look up to? How could you ask for their help?"
- "What questions do you most want to have answered?"
- "How can you ask these folks in a way that will gain favor with them?"

5. Prepare your mentoree for good followership.

Even Jesus consistently pointed to His Heavenly Father when asked about the source of His authority. We can derive from this an essential principle of leadership: If you want to have authority, you must be under authority; if you want to be a leader, you must first be a follower. In essence, effective leadership means learning to lead when you're not in charge. This involves understanding the importance of authority and how to demonstrate integrity and a willingness to serve. Key questions include:

- "What are the goals of those in authority?"

- "How can you help them succeed in those goals?"
- "What can you learn from the biblical examples of Nehemiah, Daniel, Ruth, and Esther about appealing to those in authority?"

6. Help your mentoree articulate a vision and mission.

People follow those who seem to know where they are going and can articulate why they are going there. A vision is a statement answering the question: "Where are we going?" A mission is a statement answering the questions: "Why are we going there?" and "How will we get there?" Walk with your mentoree through possible answers to these questions:

For more on goal setting, see p. 86.

- "Where do you want to be that you are not now?"
- "What does the ideal future look like in this situation?"
- "What are the resources you have now to help you get there?"
- "What are the resources you will need to acquire?"
- "How will you explain to others what you're doing in a way that enlists their assistance?"

7. Prepare your mentoree to embrace a mindset of dedication.

Leaders need to know how to inspire rock-solid dedication in their followers so that folks won't give up when things get hard. The leaders with the most dedicated followers are those who walk with their followers through difficult situations and help them learn, help them become more confident, and help them thrive in the midst of opposition. Work together to come up with answers to the following questions:

- "How do we explain the importance of what you'd like to do?"
- "Why is it important and timely for people to get involved?"
- "How can we help people see that they can succeed?"

8. Unleash your mentoree's vision through smart strategy.

Lots of strategic planning tools exist. Perhaps the most common one is called a S.W.O.T. analysis. Using your mentoree's leadership opportunity as a case study, help him or her identify Strengths, Weaknesses, Opportunities, and Threats. The idea is to play to strengths, compensate for weaknesses, set goals based on the opportunities, and counteract the threats. Once you've

Vision answers: "Where are we going?" Mission answers: "Why are we going there?" and "How we will get there?"

identified each element of the S.W.O.T. analysis, identify one or two key results that are worth achieving, and brainstorm how to get there:

- "What is the specific thing you would like to accomplish? By when?"
- "Whose assistance do you need to enlist? What do you need them to do?"

9. Assist your mentoree in conquering the apathy of those he or she influences.

Leaders don't conquer apathy directly – they starve it with an inspired vision.

When vision decreases, apathy increases. But the opposite is also true: when vision increases, apathy decreases. Leaders don't conquer apathy directly – they starve it with an inspired vision. Just as Nehemiah did by rebuilding the wall of the city of Jerusalem, emerging leaders need to identify those who are highly committed (and train them to articulate and work toward the vision), to identify those who are unmoved (and deploy the highly committed to help them inch toward commitment), and to identify those who are opposed to their efforts (and invite them to carry the vision or at least to be neutral). Talk this through with your mentoree:

- "Who are the dedicated people who can help you?"
- "Who are the people who would try to stop you, and how can you get them on your side?"
- "Who are the people who seem to be stuck in the mud, and what are some small steps they can take to move closer to your vision?"

10. Prepare your mentoree to edify his or her followers through delegation.

Delegation honors team members with the opportunity to play a significant role in achieving a worthy vision. To delegate in this way involves breaking down the vision into manageable chunks so that others can understand what needs to be done and become enthusiastic about it. Questions for your mentoree include:

- "What responsibilities can you pass off to others?"
- "What are the steps to accomplishing the vision quickly and efficiently?"

- "Who are the people who can help you get there? What are their gifts? How can their gifts make this a much better project?"

11. Prepare your mentoree for opposition.

All good leaders experience opposition. In fact, it's hard to grow into an effective leader without the strength that comes from encountering resistance. Your goal is to help your mentoree tackle difficult challenges and respond to criticism with a spirit of grace. Discussion questions include:

- "How can you 'count it all joy' in this situation?"
- "How can you show grace to your 'enemies' and bless them?"
- "Which parts of this criticism are on target and which parts are off base?"

12. Assist your mentoree in learning how to grow through conflict.

Properly conceived, conflict is a tool to sharpen a team for greater leadership effectiveness. Conflict itself isn't the problem – the inability to handle it in a godly fashion is. Don't encourage your mentoree to avoid conflict or to attack those who create it. Rather, focus his or her attention on the set of skills oriented around conciliation: peacemaking, negotiation, mediation, forgiveness and so forth. Questions to discuss include:

- "What is the most important outcome in this situation?"
- "How can you discuss your brother's fault with him in a spirit of love?"
- "How are you at fault in this situation? What should you do to make it right?"
- "Jesus said that peacemakers are blessed. What blessing does God have for you in this situation?"

Your influence as a leader-developer begins with asking God: "Who do you want me to help shape as an influencer for your kingdom?" Keep in mind that your goal isn't to launch one person to tremendous success but rather to plant seeds of leadership in as many people as you can influence life-on-life. Remember: God uses ordinary people to accomplish the extraordinary, and He uses each of us to identify and unleash those ordinary people.

Now that we've explored three key growth areas for young adults, let's turn our attention toward the process of mentoring by addressing how to get started as a mentor.

PART THREE:
GREENHOUSE CONDITIONS

Creating an Ideal Environment for Growth

What You'll Find In Part Three
- Practical mentoring how-to's, including need-to-know training on getting started as a mentor and finding a mentoree.
- Wise, actionable counsel from mentoring experts on deepening, evaluating and closing a mentoring relationship.
- How to protect yourself and your mentoree by maintaining biblical standards of safety.
- Key questions you can ask yourself to evaluate your own spiritual growth and cultivation.

CHAPTER 8:
Getting Started as a Mentor

What To Expect

- Ways to move from casual to life-transforming conversations.
- Five steps to deeply formative mentoring relationships.
- Balancing mentoring opportunities with other life responsibilities.
- Eleven simple mentoring moves you can make right now that could change your mentorees' lives.

On Jeff's trips to Africa, he's presented training in how to mentor, disciple and coach the next generation. For many African educators, life-on-life influence is a radically different way of interacting than the authoritarian-teacher/compliant-student relationship they're accustomed to. It can be overwhelming in its newness, and just when our workshop participants start to seem overwhelmed, we give them a mischievous look and ask: "How do you eat an elephant?" They instantly brighten and reply with the answer known the world over: "One bite at a time!"

People who are just getting started in mentoring relationships often look at others who have spent years cultivating these kinds of relationships and think, "I could never be that effective!" And yet, the odds are good that those same effective individuals thought that very thing when they first began investing personally in others. Just as you would start eating an elephant by beginning with one bite, cultivating life-on-life mentoring is a process of trying things, learning, growing, making mistakes, and adjusting.

In this chapter we'll share what we think are the five steps to starting a mentoring relationship and answer the most pressing question we've heard from the thousands of people who've participated in our training: "How do I find the time?"

Step One: Prepare Yourself

Mentoring relationships are vital to success in life, but that doesn't mean that people automatically know how to successfully conduct them.

Here are three questions to ask as you prepare to be a mentor:

Is my heart in it? Life-on-life mentoring is a matter of the heart. Norman Willis states,

> The only way the discipleship process can work is if the hearts of the disciple and the discipler are given to each other. Without hearts given to each other, discipleship can very easily become a means of control or manipulation. But when hearts are given to each other, the process is perceived as training.[112]

Cultivating life-on-life mentoring is a process of trying things, learning, growing, making mistakes, and adjusting.

One way to give your heart to a mentoree is to share your story. See p. 184.

If your heart isn't in it, you'll find it difficult to maintain relationships for more than just brief periods. Not all mentoring relationships last a long time or maintain a sustained level of intensity, but a study done by Public/Private Ventures shows that mentoring relationships of six months or more work best.[113] This minimum length is especially important with at-risk adolescents, who need to be assured that you aren't going to abandon them as so many other adults have done. And the only way they can be assured of that is if your heart is obviously in it.

Here are some tough questions to ask yourself:

- Do I really want to mentor students, or am I just doing it because I feel that I must?
- Will I be able to develop relationships that are focused on affirmation and encouragement rather than improved performance?
- Am I willing to commit to life-on-life mentoring relationships for the long term?

Do I have the maturity? Juergen Kneifel, president of Mission2Mentor, says:

> To begin mentoring you must have a self-awareness of your own maturity. Nobody has ever actually arrived as a perfect mentor, but you must know yourself, and your capacity to form and maintain life-on-life relationships.[114]

Kneifel, who formerly served as the Director of Marketing and Recruitment with Big Brothers Big Sisters of Puget Sound, noted from his experience that approximately 8% of volunteer applicants were not selected to be matched due to immaturity. "In the mentoring field," Kneifel said, "there is a strong belief that immature mentors will do more harm than good."[115] Immature mentors can do harm in several ways by: (1) not taking the relationship seriously, (2) not committing the time or emotional space needed to maintain a strong relationship, or (3) coming to the relationship with a self-serving agenda. The mature mentor approaches a relationship with commitment, humility, a willingness to listen, and a desire for influence rather than control.

One way to become a more mature mentor is to practice the gesture of coaching. See p. 76.

Ask yourself these questions as you assess your own maturity:

- Am I willing to accept the fact that I don't have all of the answers?
- Am I interested in life-on-life mentoring because I want a better way to control students, or because I genuinely want to see God's work be done in their lives?
- Am I willing to be quick to listen and slow to speak? (James 1:19)

At this point, some readers may be thinking, "I'm not sure if I have the maturity – I have real struggles in some areas. Is there ever a point at which my own struggles disqualify me from being a mentor?" The answer is both yes and no. Yes, if your struggle isn't fully in the past but is on-going and may stand in the way of you being a healthy influence. Such struggles might include:

- On-going struggles with sexual issues such as pornography or lack of sexual purity.
- Difficulty healing from having been sexually abused.
- Substance abuse or other undisciplined behavior that would serve as a poor example.
- Inability to work through relationship difficulties.
- Uncontrolled anger.
- A rebellious attitude toward authority.

If any of these are present concerns for you (or if another specific concern has just popped into your mind), we strongly recommend that you work with a wise mentor or counselor before taking on the responsibility of mentoring students. The bottom line is that everyone is influencing all the time – the issue is whether you should seek a greater personal influence, and we believe there are certain situations in which a person should not.

But just as we must answer the question about disqualification with a "yes" in some circumstances, we can also answer it with a "no" in others because, in Jesus Christ, there is forgiveness of sins. Scripture teaches that the plague of sin affecting all human beings annihilates our ability to stand righteously before a just and holy God. The Apostle Paul makes this point clear, but also declares the hope we have of being declared righteous through Jesus Christ:

Do you not know that the unrighteous will not inherit the kingdom of God? Do not be deceived: neither the sexually immoral, nor idolaters, nor adulterers, nor men who practice homosexuality, nor thieves, nor the greedy, nor drunkards, nor revilers, nor swindlers will inherit the kingdom of God. And such were some of you. But you were washed, you were sanctified, you were justified in the name of the Lord Jesus Christ and by the Spirit of our God. (1 Corinthians 6:9-11)

This is fantastically good news! It gives genuine hope that we can, as one of Jeff's mentors puts it, "Make our mess our message."

Step Two: Walk Alongside

It's freeing to know that life-on-life influence begins with the simple step of just being *present* with someone. It seems trivial, but being present is actually counter-cultural in a society where Twitter, Facebook and text messaging make it easy to keep relationships at a shallow level.

Shane Hipps points out that authentic community is made up of three ingredients: intimacy, permanence, and proximity.[116] Choosing to be physically present in a particular time and space is called "incarnation". It's what Christ did in choosing to be physically present with us. When you choose the path of incarnation, you offer your mentoree authentic community and emulate the ministry of Christ.

Choosing to be physically present in a particular time and space is called "incarnation".

One of our friends, Renny Scott, tells of a professor named Dr. Ewing who hired him as a summer intern for the church he pastored. Listen to how Renny describes the incarnational nature of this relationship:

Dr. E., as we called him, told me on multiple occasions not to worry about receiving a recommendation from him after the summer. He said I should feel free to make mistakes and learn from them.

Dr. E. would often ask me to go to the mall with him. Curiously, we would wander around while he browsed but never purchased a single item. At the end of the summer, he asked me why I thought he had wanted me to go with him on those "shopping trips."

I was embarrassed, but said: "Because you wanted to be with me."

"Exactly," Dr. E. replied, "A low-content shared experience is one of the best ways to communicate to someone that they are important – not because of what they have, not because of what they do, but because of who they are."

Because Dr. E. had built a bridge to my heart in that simple way, he was therefore able to minister to me later during one of the great crisis points of my life. He gave me an understanding of the gospel that has never left me.

We like that phrase: "low-content shared experience." At its root, it means inviting students into a safe space where they can learn and grow, not because of what you say, but because of who you are. Your willingness to be that kind of presence is the essence of life-on-life mentoring.

For ideas on how to have low-content shared experiences, see p. 241.

Step Three: Invite Conversation

The simplest and best way to initiate mentoring relationships is to make it known that you are available for conversation. In our experience there are plenty of people who are asking, or who want to ask, some version of the question: "Will you be my mentor?" And many parents are asking that question on behalf of their child: "Can you meet with my son/daughter?"

Make sure to avoid the six types of unhelpful questions found on p. 82.

However, don't feel you have to wait for the other person to initiate the relationship. You can invite someone into life-on-life relationships with simple conversations:

- "I'm interested in knowing more about you. What's your story?"
- "How are things going with _____?"
- "Tell me a little about yourself – how you see yourself, your likes and dislikes, your dreams."

If you see someone you think you could influence in a positive way, feel free to invite them into relationship. Here are some sample conversation openers:

- "I understand that you have recently accepted Christ as your savior. Would you like to get together over coffee and talk about what it means to live as a Christian?"

- "I hear that you've just taken a leadership position in the school. I was involved in student leadership and would be glad to meet with you. Would you be interested in talking about some things that helped me be more successful as a student leader?"
- "I'm sorry to hear you're going through this rough spot. If you'd like to have someone to talk with about it, I would enjoy meeting with you. Would you like to set a time to get together?"

The key concept here is *invitation*. You're not so much inviting someone to submit to your influence as you are inviting them into a relational space where they can be changed. The difference is crucial: it's not about you and what you can provide; it is a belief that only through relationships will we blossom into our full potential.

Step Four: Lay the Groundwork

Let's be honest: it usually doesn't work to just walk up to a student and offer your mentoring services. It seems kind of strange, and you wouldn't blame the student for being suspicious. Instead, try having a brief conversation that can plant a seed which may grow into a full-blown mentoring relationship later on. Here are some ways to plant conversational seeds of this nature:
- "May I tell you about a personal experience that might make the way clearer for you?"
- "Please listen very carefully for a moment. I have something I'd like to tell you that could have a big influence on your life."
- "I'd love to bring you along with me on this project so that we can get to know each other. Would you be willing to help?"
- "What is your greatest hope and your greatest concern in that area?"
- "I've had an experience that might shed some light on your current situation, and I'd be happy to share it if you're interested."
- "So much depends on what I'm about to share with you. Please give me your full attention."

Many effective mentoring relationships we've seen started from a larger group setting in which the leader expressed interest in being a mentor. So,

It's not about you and what you can provide; it is a belief that only through relationships will we blossom into our full potential.

151

find ways to be around students outside your role as teacher. Volunteer to be a small group leader, coach, sponsor, or club advisor, and use these opportunities to establish rapport. *Begin acting as a mentor even before mentoring opportunities arise.*

Nathan Magnuson, a life coach we've known for many years, tells the story of how his high school football coach began influencing him even before their mentoring conversation began.

Try some of the mentoring moves on p. 159.

Begin acting as a mentor even before mentoring opportunities arise.

> In high school my mentor was Coach Burton. When Coach Burton became our coach, our team had never won more than three games in a season. The first day of practice we ran enough sprints to keep us sore the entire season. "It's perfectly normal for your bodies to ache," he said. "They'll adjust to the grind if you have the courage to remain in control."
>
> He demanded mental and physical toughness, yet in a spirit of fair play. "Football is *not* a contact sport," he would say. "*Dancing* is a contact sport. Football is a *collision* sport." The Christian approach to this, he said, was to knock our opponents on their backsides, help them up, say, "Jesus loves you and so do I," and then knock them over again on the next play.
>
> During one game, we got whipped 48-0 by a contending state champ. Though only a bench-warmer at the time, I can still hear the silence in the locker room when Coach asked if *any* of us had played with 100% effort. He said, "Anybody not willing to give 100% for the rest of the season, don't bother showing up." My teeth were clenched, but I showed up – along with all the other guys – ready to give 100%.
>
> Coach Burton combined spirituality and sport. He ended each practice with scriptural encouragement. He reminded us of Olympian Eric Liddell who spoke of enjoying God's pleasure through sports. He told us that if we honored God with our attitude and work ethic, the ground we played on became holy.
>
> Coach told us, "Don't leave the field with any regrets, gentlemen, either in football or in life." We took it to heart and became a championship

team. Winning was fun, but the biggest blessing is what Coach Burton did to help me become a man. Even today I want to live in a way that would make Coach Burton proud.

Nathan's relationship with Coach Burton became more of a mentoring relationship later on, and even a friendship. But it was the coach's willingness to engage with his players life-on-life that created a strong platform for influence.

Step Five: Clarify Relationship

It's crucial that you and your mentoree are on the same page as you enter into your mentoring relationship. Here are some questions that may help you clarify expectations in a way that facilitates, rather than hinders, genuine personal interactions:

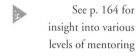 See p. 164 for insight into various levels of mentoring intensity.

- "What is the goal of our time together?"
- "What do we agree to do in preparation for each meeting?"
- "How many times do we plan to meet?"
- "How often will we meet?"
- "How long will each meeting be?"
- "Who is responsible for rescheduling if the meeting time must be changed?"
- "What steps will we take to evaluate the effectiveness of our time together?"

Lois Zachary, author of *The Mentor's Guide*, suggests eight simple ground rules for mentoring sessions:

- Our meetings will begin and end on time.
- Each of us actively participates in the relationship.
- Our communication is open, candid, and direct.
- We will respect our differences and learn from them.
- We will honor each other's expertise and experience.
- We will safeguard confidentiality.
- We will manage our time well.
- We will put interruptions aside.[117]

From Hallway Conversations to Pondering Tough Questions

Mr. R. was a history teacher at my Christian school who taught in such a way that students knew he was extremely interested in our lives. One afternoon, after a particularly good class discussion, he stopped a group of us out in the hallway and asked if we would be interested in starting a book club to discuss important issues in more depth. Needless to say, we loved the idea.

The book club began in eighth grade and we kept with it through high school. At first we met over lunch, but eventually we met in teachers' homes. Soon we grew from five or six students to twelve. Mr. R. opened up great literature to us; we read books like *Grapes of Wrath* and *Five Smooth Stones*. He thought that even as middle-schoolers we could handle big ideas – and we proved him right.

But we didn't just talk about literature – our discussions would delve into issues about growing up in the 70s, the everyday problems of life, and how we should live out our faith. I learned how to ask critical questions – not just of others (which young people were good at in the 70s), but of myself as well. I'm grateful to God for teachers like Mr. R., who went above and beyond the call of duty to make an impact in kids' lives.

– Bill V.

For each of the first few sessions, revisit the ground rules and ask, "How are we doing?" It may seem awkward at first, but it increases respect for the process and one another, making the relationship significantly more productive.

One concern we often hear expressed in a school setting is that a more intensive mentoring relationship between a teacher and student might change the nature of the relationship. Do student mentorees begin expecting preferential treatment?

We asked Sean Bevier this question. For 17 years Sean was a teacher and dean in a Christian school during which time he mentored literally hundreds of students. Sean said,

You would assume that there would be a dynamic change between the teacher and student when they enter a mentoring relationship, but that didn't happen in my experience. The students understood the student role, and I understood my teacher role. The boundaries were clear with behavior and grading expectations. The students didn't want to be perceived as "teacher's pets," and in many cases their performance actually rose because they didn't want to let me down.[118]

In these mentoring scenarios, Sean was dealing with student leaders who had applied to participate in a leader development program. It might be different with at-risk students or others who don't have a clear understanding of what relationships with authority figures should be like. In these situations, it would be good to have a conversation about it: "I am going to be your mentor, but I am also your teacher. I know you'll still put forth your best effort in class, and my expectations of you will not change just because I am also your mentor."

There's another side of being a "teacher's pet," though: that other students might resent the special attention you give to your mentoree. At school, you can explain (or help your mentoree explain) that you are "working with your mentoree on extra assignments that focus on learning leadership skills" (or whatever your specific focus may be). This may actually lead to the opportunity to mentor other students who would like to achieve more.

Knocking Down the Biggest Barrier: Finding the Time

Over and over again, people tell us that the biggest barrier to beginning to mentor is a lack of time. Our friend Wolfgang Seibler knows exactly what that feels like. He's a full time pastor and elder in charge of junior high through college-age ministries at his church. He teaches 12- to 15-year-olds on Wednesday nights, teaches 16- to 23-year-olds on Thursday nights, teaches parents and youth together on Sunday mornings, and, at the time of this writing, he and his wife are about to start up a Friday night group for young adults to discuss relationships. Wolf also owns a Quiznos Sub restaurant and helps his wife homeschool three of their sons.

But in spite of Wolf's busy schedule, this is what he says about life-on-life mentoring:

Wolf is a great
example of a mentor
whose heart is in
it. See p. 146.

For me, there is no other way to fulfill the biblical mandate of sharpening the next generation. How can we help the next generation become skillful in the things God has called them to without spending time with them? For me, this is a legacy question. It's what's important to me. That's why it's not hard to turn off a football game or miss a meal to invest life-on-life. I say "invest," not "spend," because this really doesn't cost me anything.[119]

Honestly, sometimes we find ourselves intimidated by those who seem to get so much more done in a day than we do. It makes us feel like slackers. That's precisely why this discussion about finding the time is so important. The goal is not to try to ramp up our energy, but to honestly evaluate the way we invest time to make sure it is in accord with what we really believe to be true – that the cultivation of young adults is essential to their flourishing and fruitfulness.

The goal is not to try to ramp up our energy, but to invest time to make sure it is in accord with what we really believe to be true.

Lynn Harold Houg says, "The tragedy of the world is that men have given first class loyalty to second class causes, and these causes have betrayed them."[120] The problem with a lack of time isn't so much a lack of minutes, but misaligned priorities. Wrong priorities don't usually begin as a conscious choice – "I don't think I get enough entertainment. Maybe I should watch more movies and play more video games." Rather, looking back, it's easy to see a seemingly innocent pattern of slowly giving greater and greater place to things that have no eternal value. As Dwight D. Eisenhower said: "We succeed only as we identify in life, or in war, or in anything else, a single overriding objective, and make all other considerations bend to that one objective."[121]

To that end, here are some ideas for you as you seek to reorder your priorities and make time for life-on-life relationships:

1. **Submit the issue to God in prayer.** Everything we do ultimately comes down to forming a dependence on God's power. Pray that God will give you confidence, energy, and inspiration to begin mentoring. Ask Him to point out specific areas in your life where your priorities need to be reordered.

2. Reflect on your priorities. Consider these thought-provoking questions:

- Think back on the people who made sacrifices for you and the difference they made in your life. What were their priorities that made it possible for them to invest in that way?
- What are some *good* things you could give up in order to do *great* things?
- What activities, priorities or belongings, if you got rid of them, would free you up to be more effective?

3. Start with your current life circumstances. Rather than adding mentoring as an item on your schedule, make it the means of accomplishing a few of the other items. Ask yourself, "What are some ways I could expand my life-on-life influence through things that already happen every day?"

One way to do this is to invite conversation with young adults you already interact with. See p. 150.

4. Focus on mentoring moments. Could you be more intentional about using well the mentoring moments that arise naturally, in which you can speak a word of encouragement or give a blessing? In our research, we find that people almost never remember the specific *content* of mentoring relationships they've had. What they do recall are the specific challenges and words of encouragement.

5. Expand your definition of mentoring. Consider the following strategies as ways to take advantage of life-on-life mentoring opportunities:

- **Use meal times.** We all have to eat sometime, right? We've found that having lunch with a small group of students at a favorite deli is a great way to carve out time for mentoring. It's a nice break, not too expensive, and a treat for both parties to look forward to. Why not share life while you share a meal?
- **Take people with you.** Proverbs 13:20 says that we grow wise by walking with the wise. A thoughtful mentoree will understand the value of fitting into your existing activities. If you're taking your kids to sports practice, for example, ask your mentoree to meet you at the sports field and visit while you wait and watch.

For more on this, see p. 132.

- **Work together.** Jeff is forever doing projects at his house. Often he'll say to the guys in his college classes, "I'll be doing yard work all day

Saturday. If you don't mind pitching in, come on over and we'll have lots of time to talk as we work."

- **Invite people into your messy life.** Some people make hospitality far too complex. The thought of planning out an impressive meal and getting the whole house straightened up discourages many people from extending a dinner invitation. However, hospitality (rightly understood) is about inviting someone into your life, not just into your house. If you've thought that hospitality requires you to clean everything and prepare an elaborate meal, you aren't welcoming people into your life – you're trying to impress them. True hospitality means inviting people into your mess. Try sharing a simple, everyday dinner with them.

6. **Get the key people on board.** Embracing life-on-life mentoring will involve changes to your schedule and priorities that affect those around you. It's crucial that you have the support of key people as you make these changes.

- **Boss.** As a teacher, this is especially important. You'll want it to be understood that mentoring is part of your vocation, so bring it up with your boss: "I have been reading a book about life-on-life mentoring and I'm excited about the opportunity to have a greater influence as a mentor. Can we talk about what that might look like in the context of our organization?"
- **Spiritual leader.** Talk with your pastor and say, "I've become convicted that I need to be investing in people more as a mentor. Can we meet together and talk about what that would involve, and how it could serve the church?" Having your pastor's support will help solidify your new priorities.
- **Spouse.** If you're married, your first priority is to your family. We asked Mr. Busy (Wolfgang Seibler) about how his wife, Maureen, feels about all of this mentoring activity. He said simply, "It's not hard to get your wife on board when she realizes that her life message is valuable – as valuable as yours."[122] In other words, it's not just about her getting on board with *his* priorities – they've found that

True hospitality means inviting people into your life, not just into your house.

mentoring has become her priority as well, as she has realized the equal value of her life message and legacy-leaving capacity.

- **Children.** If you have been blessed with children it is important to go ahead and verbally reassure them that you aren't replacing them with your mentorees. As Donna Otto put it in *Finding a Mentor, Being a Mentor:*

> Your own daughter needs to know that she is not being usurped, replaced, pushed aside, demoted, or slighted. She needs to know that you love her as much as always and that absolutely no other relationship with anyone else will ever change your love for her.[123]

Our biggest point here is that mentoring can happen in the midst of a busy day. If you are feeling overwhelmed, be encouraged that you can begin with what you already have.

Everyday Influence: Eleven Simple Mentoring Moves

Many Christian teachers excuse themselves from mentoring by saying: "I can be a friend to young people, but I've never been to Bible College or seminary, so I don't know enough to engage in more intensive Christian mentoring."

Similarly, claiming to not know enough is the main excuse given by most of the leaders God chose in scripture. Moses said, "I'm no good as a public speaker." Gideon said, "I'm the least man in the least tribe of Israel." Isaiah said, "I am a man of unclean lips."

God didn't sympathize with these men. He knew their limitations; He made them that way! Their self-abasement seemed like humility, but it was actually sin because it diminished the significance of God's design and work in their lives.

Regardless of your level of training, here are some mentoring moves you can make right now:

- **Listen:** "Tell me about what's important to you."
- **Give a blessing:** "Has anyone ever told you that you have the gift of _____?"

- **Affirm:** "Here's something about you that makes a great deal of difference to me..."
- **Be transparent:** "I've made mistakes in my life and I'd hate to see you go down that same path..."
- **Pray:** "I'm not sure what to do either. Can I pray with you about it?"
- **Encourage:** "I know it's tough, but I believe you can do it."
- **Share:** "May I share with you a scripture verse that has been important to me?"
- **Connect:** "I know someone who can help. Would you be interested in my putting you in touch with them?"
- **Admonish:** "You were running a good race. Who/what cut in on you?"
- **Love:** "No matter what, I'll be here."
- **Walk alongside:** "Let's go together."

Going In for the Long Haul

If you're the kind of person who tackles new tasks with enthusiasm only to realize that you've taken on too much responsibility, you run the risk of disappointing mentorees who've come to rely on you. It's like going to the gym on New Year's Day, working out for hours, and then becoming so sore that you never go back. This would not only be discouraging for you, but could seriously damage a mentoree's trust in you and in future mentors. Before you jump in feet first, here are some things to consider:

1. Start with what you know. Dan Egeler says, "My breakthrough was recognizing that, because young adults were watching me, I was a mentor whether I wanted to be or not."[124] Dan started mentoring by taking advantage of his current opportunities. As he describes in *Mentoring Millennials*, Dan was coaching soccer in Ecuador and decided to share some of his personal stories as "sermonettes" with the team throughout the season. He started with what he knew and eventually mentoring became more natural.

2. Consider your capacity. Be realistic about what you can actually do. Jesus built margin into his life, not to be "balanced," but to live a life close to God. Make sure short-term busyness doesn't turn into a long-term burden. If you get in over your head, fulfill your responsibilities but then ask, "How should I do this differently next time?" As you answer the question, consider your physical and emotional needs as well as the needs of your job and family. Our friend and Christian school teacher Kris Berger said it this way:

> I constantly have to move toward keeping balance in priorities because I am an over-achiever and can get carried away by causes or guilt – to the detriment of family. I think one has to be careful of the season. If someone is not in a *season* to mentor heavily they need to choose wisely. Each season's priorities should be carefully managed.[125]

3. Learn as you go. Our motto is, "Ready, Fire, Aim." You won't be a better mentor tomorrow than you are today unless you step out and get started. Jeff once met a man who employed an individual who seemed to be an excellent planner – he made detailed plans for everything. Jeff asked, "Are you happy with him?" "Actually, no," came the reply, "I'm frustrated because he spends so much time saddling up that he never has time to ride." Whatever you do, don't get so caught up in your preparation to mentor that you fail to actually mentor. Find the ways to get started now and learn along the way. One great way to jump right in is to invite a student to read a book with you: "I've found a book that I think we could both benefit from. I haven't read it yet but it comes highly recommended. How about if we read it and come together to talk about it?"

By this point, the "how" of life-on-life mentoring should be getting clearer. Now it's time to turn our attention toward the "who" and focus on choosing mentorees who can be good stewards of your investment.

Jesus built margin into his life, not to be "balanced," but to live a life close to God.

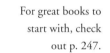

For great books to start with, check out p. 247.

CHAPTER 9:
Finding a Mentoree

What To Expect

- Guidelines for deciding what level of mentoring intensity is best for you based on your amount of experience, your gifts, and your life situation.
- Guidelines for determining what to do when someone asks: "Will you mentor me?"
- Guidelines for discerning *who* to mentor and *how* to make the most of mentoring opportunities.
- Guidelines for letting go of your "messiah complex."

You've caught the vision for cultivating young adults. You've seen the need and the opportunity. You understand the importance of discussing purpose, truth, and influence. You know the first steps to take to get started. But at this point, if you're like us, you probably still have a host of practical questions:

- "What kind of mentoring relationship should I look for?"
- "If someone asks, 'Will you mentor me?' what should I do?"
- "Should I look for someone to mentor who is struggling, or someone who I think shows a lot of potential?"
- "What if I have a person in mind that I want to mentor, but he or she doesn't seem interested?"
- "Wow, there are so many people who need encouragement from an older person, but if I say 'Yes' to everyone, I'll be overwhelmed. I feel so guilty for turning some away. What should I do?"

We've asked these tough questions of many of the wise counselors who have taught us a great deal about mentoring. We'll share their counsel and add some advice from our own experience so you're prepared to respond with an enthusiastic "Yes!" to the right kinds of opportunities.

Mentoring Formats: Passive, Occasional, & Intensive

In their book, *Connecting*, Paul Stanley and Robert Clinton developed a constellation model of mentoring which has helped tens of thousands of people establish a system of mentoring that works best for the particular situation.[126] Stanley and Clinton's model distinguishes between passive, occasional, and intensive mentoring types. Passive mentoring doesn't mean that the mentor doesn't do anything, just that the agenda for the relationship isn't driven by what the mentor *knows*. In passive mentoring relationships, the mentor walks alongside the mentoree as they read a book, listen to a teaching, or watch a video together and discuss how to apply what was learned. Occasional mentoring is intermittent. It may require weekly meetings for a while, and then monthly, and then quarterly, as the mentoree gains skills and calls for less input. Intensive mentoring requires regular meetings, usually weekly, with well-focused goals, and generally last for at

A Lifelong Mentor

I attended our small church school for four years. One of my teachers, Ms. V. also attended my church and led a weekly prayer group for teen girls. There we would share not only the mundane things of life (like boy/girl relationships) but also some of the more difficult things. Ms. V. used this rich time to build significant relationships with us.

When I turned 13, I was going through some difficult family issues. Ms. V. noticed that it was a hard time for me and asked if we could meet one-on-one. She gently encouraged me to share my struggles, and she brought me back to the truth of scripture time and time again.

At the age of 19 I went to a junior college where, lo and behold, Ms. V. was on staff. She continued to get together with me and helped me process a very challenging spiritual time in my life. Rather than let my doubts and questions fester, she encouraged me to really talk them out and take a good look at them. Through our conversations, she helped me come to grips with my faith and begin to find more direction for my life. To this day we still keep in touch. She is one of those people that I go to in order to share my dreams and my relationship with God. I am so thankful for how God has used her in my life!

– Estalee M.

least three to six months. Here are some guidelines for deciding where to start with mentoring.

1. If you see yourself as a novice mentor, start with passive mentoring. Choose a book or teaching series and invite a mentoree or several mentorees to join you:

- "For the next six weeks, I'd like to get together once a week to look at a DVD set about how to understand God's design for our lives. I think this could be of great benefit to you as you decide on a career, and I'd like to invite you to be involved."

For ideas on this, check out p. 247.

2. If you have something specific to offer, start with occasional mentoring. Invite a mentoree to walk alongside you in a context that you believe would be helpful:

- "Way to go in signing up for debate! I've had some experience in public speaking, and I'd like to get together for coffee to share some things I believe would be helpful to you. If the meeting goes well and you'd like to keep getting together, I'd be open to that."

3. **If you're willing to commit to meeting weekly one-on-one with a person for a period of several months, then intensive mentoring might be just the thing for you.** Initiate the conversation in a way that explains your rationale to the potential mentoree:
   - "I'm so glad to hear that you've trusted Christ as your Savior. You know, as a new Christian, there are a lot of things that would be helpful to know – how to get to know God better, how to understand and apply the Bible to life, how to share your faith, and how to practice the spiritual disciplines. If you're willing, I'd like to get together with you once a week for three months to go over these principles."

Don't worry if you don't yet feel equipped to mentor intensively. Just start exercising your mentoring muscles and you'll be able to move toward more intensive forms of mentoring relatively quickly. If it becomes clear that both you and the mentoree are ready for greater intensity, talk about it: "I think we may be ready to move to a more intensive level of mentoring, maybe a regular weekly commitment. What do you think? What expectations and goals would we have for a more intensive mentoring relationship?" Use discernment to navigate between organic growth and structure as seems best.

Group vs. One-on-One: Benefits and Drawbacks

Mentoring groups have developed over the years because there are so many young people who need mentoring and so few mentors available. Mentoring groups do have some distinct advantages though they aren't usually as focused or as helpful as one-on-one mentoring. As you decide whether group mentoring or one-on-one mentoring would be best for you, here are some advantages and disadvantages to consider, based on a report prepared by Public/Private Venture[127]:

Advantages of one-on-one mentoring relationships:

- They work well if the main goal is developing a personal relationship with a young adult.
- They offer more opportunities for understanding, vulnerability, and goal-setting.
- They enable the mentor to focus on the specific growth needs of the mentoree.

Disadvantages of one-on-one mentoring relationships:

- Some people may be uncomfortable with one-on-one meetings.
- The time commitment can be hard to maintain in busy seasons of your life.

Advantages of mentoring groups:

- They work well if the main goal is helping young adults learn to interact positively with one another.
- They provide a positive community focused on common interests.
- More people can be reached with the same time commitment.

Disadvantages of mentoring groups:

- Group dynamics can be difficult to manage.
- It is more difficult to get to know individual mentorees well.
- It may be difficult to keep young adults interested.

If your goal is intensive growth, then one-on-one relationships are probably the way you should go. If having quality time with several young adults is the main goal, though, mentoring groups could be for you.

Of the experts we asked, Paul Stanley prefers one-on-one relationships. He seems to be geared that way, and likes the opportunity to work intensively with a person to pursue dramatic growth.[128] Andy Crumpler, on the other hand, prefers group mentoring: "In groups, people are able to bring issues to the table and get input from several people at once."[129]

What is the ideal size of a mentoring group? The average group size in the Public/Private Venture study was ten. Yet, Andy thinks three is best, and his reasons are compelling: "The group is small enough to focus on individual growth or needs and big enough that one person missing doesn't leave

If your goal is intensive growth, then one-on-one relationships are probably the way you should go. If having quality time with several young adults is the main goal, though, mentoring groups could be for you.

you in a one-on-one session." In his experience, bigger groups are distracting and it is hard for members to get the attention they need. Also, larger groups of students may tend to develop a peer pressure dynamic which discourages serious engagement and growth.[130]

Gender Differences

Be aware that there are physiological differences as well as different God-given designs between boys and girls that will affect your mentoring relationships. We considered writing a whole chapter on gender differences, but instead we decided it would be better to simply recommend the resources we have found helpful. If you are interested in reading more about physiological differences, we recommend Leonard Sax's book, *Why Gender Matters*. With the exception of his chapter on homosexuality (which is oddly speculative in a book that is otherwise meticulously researched), his book substantiates the physiological basis of differences between men and women and what that means for working with boys and girls. If you're interested in reading more about the different God-given designs of men and women, we've found Bill and Barbara Mouser's *Five Aspects* studies to be enlightening.

Handling Mentoring Requests

Because mentoring is a common idea these days, it's probably more likely than ever that someone will approach you and ask, "Will you be my mentor?" This can be a bit disconcerting. Jeff remembers the first time one of his students asked that question:

> I was a new professor at Bryan College and had just spoken for the first time in chapel. A student came into my office and asked me to mentor him. Because I was unfamiliar with the idea of mentoring at the time, I had a mental picture of him sitting there with a pair of handcuffs, one cuff around his wrist, waiting for me to put my hand in the other cuff so that I could never escape! I made some excuse as to why I couldn't mentor him, and he left my office disappointed. I wish I could replay that scene from my life, knowing what I know now.

Because potential mentorees often don't know what they're looking for, it's unwise to rush into the relationship before determining what it is they are actually requesting.

Part of the problem in knowing how to handle requests is that when people ask for mentoring, they may mean a number of different things, such as:

- "I need a friend."
- "I think you're cool and I want you to rub off on me."
- "You seem to have a lot of answers and I want you to tell me what to do."
- "I need a father figure (or mother figure)."
- "People have told me I need a mentor, and I think you could fill that role for me."

These are all valid reasons to seek a mentor - because they touch on different mentoring gestures. See p. 61.

And so on.

Because potential mentorees often don't know what they're looking for, it's unwise to rush into the relationship before determining what it is they are actually requesting. Pause to consider a few things before answering a mentoring request.

1. **Ask some questions of the other person.** You'll want to find out what they perceive their need to be and why they've come to you with that need.
   - "I'm curious, what would you like to know or be able to do that makes you want to have a mentor?"
   - "I'm sure you know a lot of people who would make good mentors. May I ask why you thought to approach me in particular?"

2. **Ask some questions of yourself.** You'll want to take a look at whether or not there's a good fit and if the relationship would be appropriate.
   - "Is there a fit?" As you talk about potential mentoree's goals, you may realize that there isn't a natural fit between the two of you. If this happens, see Chapter Eleven on how to sponsor a student to another mentor.
   - "Is it appropriate?" Some time ago a male teacher who had attended our training said, "I have a female student who is hanging around my room a lot outside of class. Today she confided that she has an eating disorder and wants me to mentor her. What should I

For more on safety issues, see Chapter 12.

Conversations about expectations should take place at the beginning of the relationship.

do?" We replied, "We strongly recommend that you find a mature woman in the school to mentor this girl. From your description of the situation it sounds like this is not a healthy mentoring situation. There are too many complications – male mentor/female student, over-attachment, dealing with an issue that has psychological ramifications, etc. It's best to find a female teacher to help out, or to refer the girl to a counselor."

3. **Clarify expectations.** Paul Stanley, co-author of *Connecting*, says that conversations about expectations should take place at the beginning of the relationship and should be revisited often. Here are some questions dealing with expectations:

- "What would you expect to gain by the time we finish?"
- "If we were to study a subject together, what subject would interest you?"
- "How much time are you willing to put into this?"
- "Mentoring involves work. Are you willing to prepare for our times together?"[131]

4. **Give an assignment.** If someone is asking you to invest precious time, you want to make sure that person is serious. Paul Stanley says, "Always give a potential mentoree a little bit of a test to see how eager and faithful they will be." When we asked why that is so important, he said, "Often there's more enthusiasm than commitment. In my experience, probably only four out of ten people will get back to me." Paul suggests statements such as the following:

Like you the young adult might be hesitant to commit to a mentoring relationship. See p. 51.

- "Here's a little book to read or a CD to listen to. Get back with me to let me know what you think and we'll go from there."
- "I'd like for you to take some time to write down your expectations of what a mentoring relationship would be like. When you're done, let me know and we'll have breakfast together."[132]

5. **Establish a trial period.** Strong mentoring relationships take time, chemistry and thoughtfulness. But some mentoring relationships simply just aren't a good fit and "forcing it" can be frustrating to both parties. Because this is so, we recommend that you plan to meet for a pre-set

period of time and then re-evaluate. This will give you the opportunity to turn down a mentoring request graciously and honestly if it looks like it won't be helpful for either of you. Here's how you could bring that up:

- "How about if we get together a couple of times to talk about your goals and expectations? It would give us a chance to see what it might be like to commit to this relationship for a longer period of time, whether we're willing to put the work into it and how well we interact together. After a couple of meetings we can evaluate how things are going. If it works out, we can meet some more. If not, we'll always be friends, but we'll brainstorm together to see if there might be other people who could serve you in a mentoring capacity more effectively."

6. Pray about it. Our Heavenly Father knows the extent of your resources as well as the needs of your students. If you're reticent, He can help you discern whether you're holding back out of irrational fear or whether you genuinely believe the other person can be better helped elsewhere. If you're eager, He can help you see the connection between your desire to help and the needs of the other person.

Potential Mentorees: Deciding Who to Pursue

Some people believe that mentoring should be about serving at-risk youth because so many are neglected and without role models. However, there are others who make the case for focusing mentoring efforts on students who demonstrate high potential. They, like us, have seen many unfortunate situations where so much attention was placed on rescuing at-risk youth that relatively stable, healthy young people – who, with a small investment of time, could have gone far – didn't get the life-on-life attention they needed to really soar. So which is more vital?

Keep in mind those who are growing up in a broken family. See p. 33.

Keith Anderson and Randy Reese in their book, *Spiritual Mentoring*, actually make a case that the strong, as well as the weak, need special attention:

Richard Baxter, writing to other Puritans in 1656, listed four groups of people who needed special attention: the immature, those with a particular corruption, declining Christians and the strong. The last group, he declared, need the greatest care.[133]

Ultimately, determining what kind of student to mentor is a matter of calling. All mentoring relationships seek growth and transformation, and all our students – regardless of their risk level or life circumstances – are uniquely designed as image-bearers of God. Are you called to be the encourager of the athlete who is already running the race, or the handler of "weaker vessels" who may be called to build God's kingdom in ways unimaginable to those who are "stronger vessels"?

Remember: all young adults are both dignified and depraved. See p. 26.

Choosing a Mentoree Who Shows Great Potential

If your particular focus is going to be on relatively healthy, stable mentorees, Paul Stanley suggests five factors to consider.

- **Readiness.** Is the person ready to put some work into the mentoring relationship?
- **Responsiveness.** Is the person teachable and open to counsel?
- **Faithfulness.** Is the person able to follow-through on assignments and honor the meeting times?
- **Attraction.** Are the mentor and mentoree compatible – not necessarily in personality, but in wanting to spend time with and learn from one another?
- **Potential.** Ask questions that help you discern the person's potential to learn and grow: "What do you see in your future?" "What are some plans you have?" "What would you like to be?" "What do you already know about your gifts and potential?"[134]

Choosing A Mentoree Who is Struggling

Perhaps you have a particular calling to those who are struggling – whether spiritually, socially, academically, or otherwise. This is a tremendous calling, and there are many thousands of active, involved Christians who can point to someone who invested in their lives at a point when they were struggling.

Being an Advocate For a Shipwrecked Teen

I met my mentor and his wife when I was 13 at one of their many seminars for teens, and we wrote letters back and forth to stay in touch. My home situation was emotionally bankrupt because my parents fought constantly and were so unpredictable and detached that I never confided in them.

When I sent a particularly distressed or sad-sounding letter, he and his wife would call and cheer me up by telling me how special they thought I was and recalling encouraging scriptures they'd read that morning during devotions. It sounds simple, but it meant so much. He was an anchor and bouncing-wall for my ideas and troubles. The best thing he did was listen.

I felt like my mentor and his wife were my personal advocates – occasionally to other people or to my parents, but mostly to myself. Throughout the years they continually replied to my letters and checked in with phone calls – and I can hardly describe how these small gestures reassured me through many desperate hours. It was like clinging to driftwood after a shipwreck, staring disoriented into the darkness, and hearing someone call through the wind and fog, "Paddle this way! You can make the shore."

– Joy P.

Here's an incredible story from nature that illustrates the power of adult influence on struggling adolescents. Several years ago, a program called Operation Genesis was formed to populate a South African national park with thousands of animals. With government control and laws against poaching, park rangers assumed that the animals would be fully safe from harm. However, they began finding a startlingly high number of mutilated rhinoceros carcasses. They would soon come to learn that these mutilated rhinos had been gored to death by young bull elephants on a rampage.

It is normal for adolescent bull elephants to enter musth – an intense, intermittent period of aggressive behavior associated with reproduction. Upon close observation, it became apparent that these aggressive young bull elephants had entered musth far earlier than normal, and for unusually intense and prolonged periods. Because the onset of musth they were experiencing was abnormal, these young elephants went berserk and became a danger to all those around.

Why was this happening? As researchers looked for an explanation, more rhinos turned up dead and many of the raging elephants had to be destroyed. Meanwhile other national parks began discovering similar rhino deaths as well. A plausible theory finally emerged: perhaps these young bulls, orphaned from their families and relocated to the new parks, lacked the "socializing influence" of the older elephants in the herd.

The solution became evident: introduce mature bull elephants from other parks into the Operation Genesis herds. As park managers prepared to take this step, they invited scientists from the University of Natal to study the results. What the scientists soon found was truly astounding: the young bulls began "submitting" to the older bulls, trailing them all over the park. As this happened, the periods of musth began to shorten and eventually returned to normal patterns. As a result, no additional rhino deaths occurred.[135]

It seems that God has built into the elephant species a natural "mentoring" cycle in which the presence of the elders helps usher the youth into maturity. When this influence is absent, the youths enter into adulthood in a rapid and intense fashion. Unable to properly guide their impulses, these youth are prone to irrational, risky and even hurtful behavior.

We wonder if something similar is true for humans. Perhaps the struggling young adults you are considering mentoring have been devoid of the socializing influence of mature adults. Perhaps they have never had a good model. Perhaps their anger, immaturity, and poor choices are due in part to a great relational lack. And perhaps, with the help of your guiding influence, they can begin to find normalcy, stability, and eventually maturity.

How should you discern whether or not to mentor a struggling young adult? Here are some suggestions:

• **Ask God to give you His perspective.** Andy Crumpler, Paige's high school youth pastor, said: "I usually didn't choose people based on the need I saw in their lives. The few times I did, it didn't go well." Instead,

Andy asked God, "Who is it you have given me a special vision for?" He says, "This gave me the internal drive to see them become who God wanted them to become, and honestly gave me the energy to endure through the seasons when I felt that it was a waste of time."[136] In other words, don't just look at who has a need – look for who God is connecting you to. If you are mentoring struggling young adults solely because you feel bad for them, you may want to reconsider.

- **Search your own calling.** Mentoring a struggling young adult is not for everybody. Don't be "guilted" into it. Matt Benson says that he has tended to gravitate toward mature students, but he admires one of the residence hall directors he knew who was strongly called to immature students.[137] These are both vitally necessary, but distinct, callings.

- **Look for a person who is willing to grow.** If invited into a relationship, plenty of struggling young adults will express a strong desire to grow. Invest in them. Don't spend your time mentoring those who don't want to be mentored or don't want to grow. Be friendly and available if they have a change of heart, but focus on those who are willing to grow.

- **Remember that a mentor is not a counselor.** Mentoring is forward-focused, not healing-focused. As Paul Stanley says:

> Your mission is to help a person go forward, not to settle their psychological issues. If the person is preoccupied with a problem or struggle, I would try to get him to someone who could help. Once he's made progress, we could resume the mentoring relationship.[138]

Rejection: Handling an Uninterested Response

Would it surprise you to know that Jesus Himself was rejected by many of those whom He desired to influence? In Matthew 23:37, Jesus looked over the city of Jerusalem and said:

> O Jerusalem, Jerusalem, the city that kills the prophets and stones those who are sent to it! How often would I have gathered your children together as a hen gathers her brood under her wings, and you would not!

"Your mission is to help a person go forward, not to settle their psychological issues."

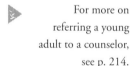

For more on referring a young adult to a counselor, see p. 214.

The sooner

you realize

that you

don't have

the power to

make people

change, the

better off

you'll be.

Jesus did not force himself onto people who were not interested, or who were not ready to believe in Him. This is actually counter to a tendency we have observed in the church today – the tendency toward powerful, persuasive communication that attempts to move people to respond against their will. Most of this so-called persuasion is actually manipulation, and it is almost always counterproductive in the long run.

Just as you cannot force someone to respond to the truth of the gospel, you cannot force someone to submit to mentoring. Tony Stoltzfus, an authority on Christian coaching, says "coaching is based on the person's internal motivation." Likewise, we believe that successful mentoring requires a willing mentoree, and Tony's wise advice about not pushing coaching onto someone applies to mentoring as well: "Let it be. It's a losing proposition to try to force them into it."[139]

The sooner you realize that you don't have the power to make people change, the better off you'll be. Don't fret about being able to manipulate the right outcome. Pass the baton as best you can. If mentorees drop it, then help them pick it up, but don't blame yourself. Relax.

If we can't force students to be mentored, how can we influence them? Consider these two points:

1. **Let God speak to them.** Andy Crumpler talked with many parents who wanted him to mentor their children, even though the child was not interested. He told the parents, "This has to be your child's decision." He then would go to the student and explain what a mentoring relationship would be like. He told them to wait at least 24 hours to make the decision, and think and pray about it. According to Andy, God often spoke to those students in a special way; ninety-five percent of them would come back and say yes.[140]

2. **Leave the door open.** Paul Stanley suggests saying something along these lines:
   - "How about if we just meet together and talk about your interests and plans. Would that be helpful?"

- "Well listen, this mentoring idea is new. Why don't you just think and pray about it. If you become interested, let me know."
- "I certainly see a lot in you and would love to help you reach your full maturity and strength. If you'd like to do that, give me a call."
- "I'll be praying for you. If you need anything or would like to get together sometime, let me know."[141]

Guilt: Letting Go of Your Messiah Complex

Have you ever had the experience of feeling overwhelmed with all of the needs in the world? Jesus certainly did. And yet he did not attempt to minister to everyone. In fact, a shocking passage in Matthew 8:18 says, "Now when Jesus saw a crowd around him, he gave orders to go over to the other side." Jesus actually abandoned the needy crowd!

We are not suggesting here that just because Jesus chose to not preach on one occasion we are free to ignore the needs he puts before us. On the contrary, scripture clearly indicates that we have responsibility for the needs God brings to our attention. But the fact of the matter is, we only have so much time and energy – how can we meet the countless needs?

Gregg Harris, a pastor in Oregon, says in regard to fulfilling our spiritual responsibilities: "If it is in God's will, then a reasonable amount of time each day will be sufficient. If it is not in God's will, then no amount of time will be sufficient." We have found this to be a helpful perspective. In fact, it's actually the perspective Jesus had – He did everything his heavenly Father wanted him to do *and nothing else*.

How was this possible for Jesus, and how might it be possible for us? In his book, *Handoff*, Jeff explains that Jesus was able to minister effectively in the midst of much pressure by surrendering the outcome to God. Here's Jeff's insight on how we can do the same:

> To surrender the outcome to God means acting faithfully through the *process*, but relinquishing control of the *results*...As long as I feel responsible for the outcome of the lives of others, I live in worry...But when I surrender the outcome to God, fear melts away. If I'm confident that God will bring about the outcome that pleases him, I'm free to stop

This is at the heart of being a cultivator rather than a boss. See p. 27.

wheedling and manipulating and cajoling. I'm free to let God open the floodgates of blessing if he chooses to do so.[142]

An important caveat is in order here: surrender is not the same thing as passivity. Surrender is an *active* trust that God is in charge and that he will bring about the result that glorifies himself. Here are some ways to actively surrender the outcome to God:

- **Surrender constantly.** As missionary Frank Laubach wrote, pray that God will give you a minute-by-minute ability to ask, "What do You want me to do right now?"[143]
- **Seek connections made by the Holy Spirit.** Dan Egeler says it is best to acknowledge that "I can't be a mentor to everybody."[144] This acknowledgement allows you to look for the natural connections that present themselves. What natural, daily interactions create opportunities to influence others?
- **Just keep multiplying.** One of the obvious solutions to the lack of mentors is for you to invest a lot of your time training other mentors, in addition to mentoring young adults yourself. Andy Crumpler says, "Let your understanding of the need shape your heart to train others. Multiplying yourself is one of the greatest investments of your time."[145]

As you have seen throughout this chapter, deciding who to mentor is a spiritual decision, one requiring prayer, discernment, and even some trial and error. Now let's turn our attention to how you can build relationship with your mentoree once you've entered into mentoring.

Surrender is an active trust that God is in charge and that He will bring about the result that glorifies Himself.

CHAPTER 10:
Deepening Relationship with Your Mentoree

What To Expect

- How to develop a higher level of understanding with mentorees.
- Ten questions you can use to get into more serious conversations.
- Ways to share your life story – tactfully and truthfully.
- How to have hard conversations and provide accountability.

A friend of Jeff's went on a swordfishing expedition and described the event with great enthusiasm. With expert guidance from the boat captain, it wasn't long before Jeff's friend snagged the first bite. After the initial surge of adrenalin, though, he quickly realized that the heart of a swordfish expedition is not in *hooking* the fish but *landing* it. Jeff's friend buckled into a seat and alternately let the line out and reeled it in, being sensitive to the fish's movements. He had to be careful; if he pulled too hard, too soon, the line would break and the fish would escape. This kind of fishing experience certainly isn't for everyone. It took about an hour and left Jeff's friend exhausted. Those who care only about hooking as many fish as possible and dropping them in a bucket will find it to be taxing and unrewarding. But those who are patient enough to persevere are rewarded with a tremendous sense of accomplishment.

It's not a perfect analogy, but, in many ways, life-on-life mentoring is like that swordfish expedition. It takes patience, perseverance, and a willingness to pay attention to what God is doing in your own life as well as that of your mentoree. In Chapter Nine we discussed how to initiate a mentoring relationship. In this chapter we'll examine how to progress to higher levels of understanding in the pursuit of mentoring success.

Taking the Lead

Regardless of who initiates the relationship, the most successful mentoring relationships are those in which the mentor takes the lead – at least at first. The mentoree expects and usually desires this. Roger Erdvig says,

> Initially I want to shape the goals of our time together so I can focus on specific, important things. Through time, though, I want to encourage the mentoree to shape our time together more and more, but based on what I've already framed.[146]

Admittedly, taking the lead is a balancing act. On the one hand, some folks hold back when it comes to imposing a meaningful structure only to find that unstructured meetings quickly become boring and unfulfilling ("What do you want to talk about?" "I don't know. What do *you* want to talk about?"). On the other hand, some folks grasp the rudder all too firmly,

Be careful not to fall into "boss mentality." See p. 27.

making blueprints for the other person's life. When mentors are over-eager in giving direction, they risk creating a sense that mentorees are just projects. Such relationships miss the heart of the word "relationship" and feel confining rather than freeing.

We've put lots of tools in this book to help you maintain this delicate, structured balance. For example, in Appendix A we'll suggest a plan for your first five meetings together. Please, do not take this as a "do this or die trying" command. Rather, recognize with us that successful mentoring is a form of cooperation with what God is doing in the mentoree's life. This stance humbly recognizes that God is the initiator and we are the responders. Anderson and Reese explain:

> God's heart has already felt and loved and hoped before we ever arrived. The songs of our soul have already been whispered and sung into our souls. *If this notion is true, and we believe passionately that it is, then the work of the mentor is not to create but to notice, not to invent but to discern* (emphasis ours).[147]

Whatever relational gestures you choose to employ as you mentor life-on-life, or whatever plans you hope to implement, regularly ask, "What is God doing in this relationship?" and allow Him to focus your attention on what He wants to have happen.

One of the most profound needs of the human heart is for someone to really know and understand you. Developing such understanding is hard, but once it is developed, everything else about the relationship becomes much simpler. This kind of understanding involves being advocates of our mentorees and creating space for them to succeed. We say, in essence, "I see what God is doing in your life and I want to cooperate with Him in helping you become all you were designed to be."

Inviting Their Story through Powerful Questions

Research shows that "strong bonds depend on the ability to understand and respond empathetically to others' experiences."[148] Thus, understanding arises from empathy, and the starting place for empathy is de-centering, which means moving away from seeing the world from a self-centered

Successful mentoring is a form of cooperation with what God is doing in the mentoree's life. God is the initiator and we are the responders.

Noticing and discerning are rooted in good listening. See p. 80.

Coaching is about the other person. If you're hogging the conversational space, it's starting to become about you . . .

viewpoint. Tony Stoltzfus says: "coaching is about the other person, so you shouldn't be talking half of the time." We believe this also applies to mentoring: if you're hogging the conversational space, as he says, "it's starting to become about you."[149] Fortunately, if you use the conversational space to ask good questions and listen well, you can develop trust and rapport in a very short period of time. Here are a few basic get-to-know-you questions, along with follow-up questions:

1. "I'm interested in knowing more about you."
   - "What's your story?"
   - "Can you tell me a little about your family?"
   - "What were some of the shaping experiences of your life so far?"
   - "How do you see yourself in terms of your gifts and potential?"
   - "What is it you dream about being or doing someday?"

2. "I'd like to know more about your interests."
   - "What are some of your likes and dislikes?"
   - "What kinds of activities (extracurricular activities, hobbies, etc.) interest you?"
   - "What is it about those things that you find interesting?"
   - "What sorts of activities are you involved in at the present time?"
   - "What have you done that you've gotten really good feedback on from others?"
   - "What context are you in when you feel most like yourself?"
   - "What kinds of activities sound interesting to you, but you haven't tried yet?"

3. "I'm interested in spiritual things and would like to know where you are spiritually."
   - "Have you come to the point of trusting Jesus Christ for your salvation? Can you tell me a little about how that happened?"
   - "How would you describe your spiritual growth at the present time?"
   - "In what ways would you most like to grow spiritually?"
   - "How do you see God working in your life?"
   - "If you haven't trusted Jesus Christ to be your Savior, can you tell me a little about your beliefs regarding spiritual matters?"

In asking thoughtful questions, we're imitating how Jesus interacted with people. Paul Stanley points out:

> Jesus asked 288 questions in the gospels. He already knew the answers to all of these questions, but He asked them anyway. It just shows how important questions are in the relationship to spark thinking, involvement, and responsibility.[150]

Ten Conversation Starters for Developing Greater Understanding

As mentoring relationships develop, there may be opportunities to ask questions that lead to more serious conversation. Mentoring guru, Bobb Biehl, is the go-to guy on asking questions. In fact, he's written a helpful booklet called *Asking to Win*.[151] Here are ten questions Bobb suggests that you ask in getting to know someone:

This is a great question for a stressed-out generation. See p. 52.

- "If you could do anything you wanted, if God told you that you were free to choose, and you had all the time, money, education, etc. you needed, and you knew for certain that you couldn't fail, what would you do?"
- "Is something heavy on your shoulders today? What transitions (stressful) are you experiencing? If I could remove one burden from your shoulders today, what would it be?"
- "What three principles would you say are most responsible for your success?"
- "What surprised you most about _____? What do you like best about _____?"
- "What five milestones/turning points have most shaped your life at this point?"
- "What three people do you admire most? Why?"
- "Where do you see yourself ten years from now?"
- "What causes 80% of your frustration, tension, and pressure? Why? What brings you 80% of your pleasure, joy, fun? Why?"
- "What is the key to understanding the real you that most people miss?"
- "What have been the three highlights and three hurts of your life? What are your three main hopes for your future?"

Vulnerability: Sharing Your Own Story

The Center for Coaching Excellence calls the first meeting between a coach and a client the "Intake Session." A significant part of this first meeting is the opportunity to share life stories. We think this is also a great idea when carried over into the realm of mentoring. You can say to your mentoree: "Since we're going to be meeting together, I'd like to know a little about your life story and I'd like to tell you a little about mine. Let's take ten minutes to share our stories. Would it be okay if I go first?" Consider including some of the following in your story:

- A little about your life history (your family, where you've lived, etc.).
- How you have seen God working in your life.
- Points of success that helped you advance on your current path.

- Points of failure you've seen God redeem.
- A snapshot of your hopes and dreams.

How you tell your story will cue mentorees on how to tell their stories, so take care to be open and appropriately vulnerable. At the same time, keep it general and not overly detailed, so as not to blow your time frame or make your mentoree uncomfortable.

Anderson and Reese note that telling life stories is a test of the depth of a relationship. The only way to inspire a genuinely honest relationship is to model vulnerability. Here's how they phrase it:

> We want to tell our life stories, but we wonder if the stories are too common, too confused, too carnal or just plain too complicated. It is the ongoing role of the mentor to create and nurture a safe place in which the mentoree can disclose his or her interior self to the mentor. For a relationship to grow into one of intimate trust, both mentor and mentoree must become vulnerable with sin, pain and questions related to living a life of holiness and service.[152]

In many ways, it is that simple: if you want the relationship to go deep and effect profound change, model for your mentoree what vulnerability looks like. Don't underestimate the life-changing impact of honest openness.

Discernment: Knowing What to Share and What Not to Share

We are often asked, "How much vulnerability is appropriate?" It's tricky: if you disclose too little, the other person may see you as cold and distant. On the other hand, if you disclose too much, the other person may feel uncomfortable. As Irwin Altman and Dalmas Taylor explain in their theory of social penetration, the goal is to "scaffold" the level of self-disclosure: you take the lead by being a little vulnerable and others usually reciprocate. When they do, you can disclose a little more. This helps you develop trust with the mentoree over time, as both of you become more comfortable with the relationship.[153]

The only way to inspire a genuinely honest relationship is to model vulnerability.

The emerging generation's lack of inhibition makes this a natural step of trust for them. See p. 56.

Walking Through the Valleys

My freshman year at Christian college, I was still adjusting to life in the U.S. after my family fled the civil war in Zimbabwe. I was grieving the loss of friends and was very unsure of my own identity. A college professor, Dr. D., and his wife, reached out to me - they believed in me and spoke blessings to me. I will never forget their words. But the greater lesson would be learned as we witnessed the D. family face their greatest trial.

Dr. and Mrs. D. and their four children lived near the dorms and truly felt like family. When their beautiful 12 year old daughter was diagnosed with cancer, the entire campus was affected. Rather than withdraw, Dr. and Mrs. D. allowed us to walk beside them through their valley, crying and praying together. They showed us their love and trust in God in the midst of deep, dark pain. They invited us to sit at the bedside of a young girl who knew she would soon be with Jesus. They taught us to celebrate the good days, even baking her last birthday cake. They shared with us the harsh finality of death as we took turns standing watch by her casket for the wake. And amidst their tears they shared our glorious hope in Christ as they led the entire student body in the song "It Is Well With My Soul".

The willingness of Dr. and Mrs. D. to reach out to hurting young people, and to allow us to share in their darkest time, made a profound impact on my life in ways that only God truly knows.

- Carolyn S.

However, there is another question here. Does what constitutes appropriate disclosure between two adults constitute appropriate disclosure between an older adult and younger adult? Andy Crumpler says,

> I tend to be very vulnerable with my struggles. I share about the times I've doubted God, but I also exercise wisdom when sharing such things and examine my motives for sharing. It's important for mentors to examine *how* they are sharing, so as not to glorify sin.[154]

We're not aware of any academic studies having been done specifically related to the level of self-disclosure in older adult/younger adult mentoring relationships. However, studies of mentoring in the workplace show that protégés typically disclose more than mentors. Interestingly, those protégés assess the value of the relationship based on how much they are able to disclose, not on how much the mentor discloses.[155] In other words, you don't have to "let it all hang out" in order to develop the kind of trust necessary for a good mentoring relationship.

Because it is important to arrive at the right level of vulnerability, especially in teacher/student mentoring relationships, we've devised some questions you can use for self-assessment:

- Am I talking too much?
- Is this level of sharing appropriate for this stage of the relationship?
- Is it wise to share this?
- Does this burden the mentoree with information he or she shouldn't have to shoulder?
- What are my motives for sharing this information in this way?
- Will sharing this information lead the mentoree into temptation?
- Does the way I am sharing my past glorify sin?
- Am I clearly communicating my trust in God?

Wisdom: Making Your Mess Your Message

Guilt is a big reason the established generation doesn't want to mentor the emerging generation. Many adults look back over a past that is marred by self-centeredness, premarital sexual activity, drug or alcohol abuse, and divorce. Even if they have renounced these things, many feel disqualified to have a positive influence on students. Again, as we said in Chapter Eight, if your struggles are ongoing, it is probably wisest to not seek more intensive mentoring relationships. That being said, however, there is a strong biblical precedent for continuing to exert a godly influence on the emerging generation in spite of past sin. Consider for a moment the testimony of Solomon:

> Listen, my sons, to a father's discipline, and pay attention so that you may gain understanding, for I am giving you good instruction. Don't abandon my teaching. When I was a son with my father, tender and precious to my mother, he taught me and said: 'Your heart must hold on to my words. Keep my commands and live.' (Proverbs 4:1-4)

You don't have to "let it all hang out" in order to develop the kind of trust necessary for a good mentoring relationship.

Your mess, and how God redeemed you in the midst of it, **is** your message!

But wait a minute! Wasn't Solomon's father King David, the man who committed adultery with Bathsheba (Solomon's mother) and even had Bathsheba's innocent, honorable husband killed to cover up his sin? If living a blameless life was a criterion for giving wise counsel, David certainly would have been disqualified. Yet David did not use his sin as an excuse to avoid giving wise counsel to his son. In Psalm 51, David recorded a prayer of confession, that he would be made clean and steadfast *so that* he could use his life as an example to those who had gone astray:

> God, create a clean heart for me and renew a steadfast spirit within me. Do not banish me from Your presence or take Your Holy Spirit from me. Restore the joy of Your salvation to me, and give me a willing spirit. *Then I will teach the rebellious Your ways, and sinners will return to you.* (Psalm 51:10-13) [Emphasis ours]

If you believe you've been disqualified to give wise counsel to young adults because of your past sins, pray Psalm 51 – as David did – asking God to make you clean and steadfast so that you can impart wisdom to the next generation. Author, teacher, and champion of mentoring, Susan Hunt, puts it this way: "Many would-be mentors will say 'But you don't know the failures in my life.' God is the Redeemer of those failures. Those failures are part of God's story in you."[156] Remember: your mess, and how God redeemed you in the midst of it, *is* your message! Here are some examples of what to say to your mentoree to explain how this is so:

- "I wish I could mentor you based on having lived a perfect life, but that won't be the case. I've made many tragic errors that have hurt a lot of people and brought dishonor to God."
- "Because of my past I must rely completely on God's grace and His offer of forgiveness."
- "It's embarrassing to have to admit my sins, but I need for you to know that my counsel to you is based on the wisdom God has revealed, not on my having lived a blameless life."
- "My point in telling you this is not to make excuses for myself or to give you an excuse for acting like I did, but to display the calamitous effects of sin and the magnitude of God's grace."

- "I understand if you're thinking: 'Why should I listen to you?' I don't blame you, and I'm sorry that my example has led you to think that way. What I'm asking you to do, though, is not to follow my example but to learn from my mistakes and do what God has revealed is right."

How to Have Hard Conversations with Your Mentoree

So far in this chapter we've focused on intensifying relationships and developing understanding. At this point, you might be wondering: "Is there ever a time and place for flat-out confrontation?" Absolutely. Dan Egeler explains:

> There is this idea that friendship trumps all. This is particularly difficult with younger mentors who worry that the relationship will be sabotaged if they try to speak confrontational truth. Most adolescents have plenty of buddies – what they need is an adult in their lives. Yes, you need a foundation of friendship, but you also want the relationship to grow to the point where you can really speak truth.[157]

Sometimes hard conversations are necessary because, as we dealt with in Chapter One, young adults – like all of us – are fallen.

In a recent workshop, a teacher challenged Jeff's training about coaching and asked:

> I have a student who confided in me that he intends to deceive his parents by dating a girl they don't want him to date and meeting her at the mall without telling them about it. I obviously need to go beyond just listening if I am to speak truth into his life. How should I do it?

The student's deception definitely needed to be confronted, yet Jeff recommended starting that confrontation with questions. Why? Because the goal is not to live this mentoree's life for him, but to walk with him as he learns how to live his own life in a way that glorifies God. If you *tell* him what to do, it can create defensiveness (recall how you felt as a young person when someone said, "Now you listen to me. What you need to do is…").

Avoid asking the types of questions described on p. 82 so you don't create defensiveness.

189

The Impact of Accountability

My senior year of high school was very difficult. I really hoped to go to Bible College and then Nursing school, but my school's guidance counselors had basically written me off as not being "college material." On top of that, I developed an infection that turned into a tumor. At the beginning of the year I underwent a supposedly easy surgery that turned into a nine day hospital stay. I ended up missing about two months of school in all.

The class I was struggling the most to catch up in was College Prep English. The teacher, Mrs. S., was known to be tough, and I had always been overwhelmed by writing. But Mrs. S. refused to give up on me like other teachers had. She began taking time after school to meet with me. She helped me choose a topic for my major paper. She challenged me to develop my own goals, and to give myself small, doable deadlines so that I could catch up in the class. She would even call me at home to keep me accountable for the goals I had set, refusing to let me give up. Most importantly, she told me that I could succeed – not just in her class, but in college as well.

And she was right. Imagine my elation when I was able to pull a "B" for the class that I had dreaded so much – and started so far behind in. The time that Mrs. S. invested in me made a significant difference – not just in one class but in my entire life.

– Jeannie R.

At the same time, Proverbs 27:17 says that we should sharpen one another as "iron sharpens iron." Iron can only sharpen iron by striking against it; clearly, there's a place for direct challenging. Although many people fear (and avoid) confrontation because it can damage relationships, properly handled confrontation can actually build relationships by creating greater trust and respect. Here are a few guidelines for helpful confrontation:

1. **Ask permission.** Once others have given you permission to tell them something, they will likely be far less defensive toward, and simultaneously more responsive to, your words. Paul Stanley suggests saying something like this: "I've observed a couple of things. Could I have your permission to just shoot straight with you?"[158]

2. **Make an observation.** After asking permission, state your observation clearly: "Here's what I've noticed. It seems that..."

3. **Inquire before concluding.** After asking permission and stating your observation, Paul Stanley recommends following-through with inquisitiveness (rather than stating your own conclusions): "Tell me a little about that. How do you feel about it? How do you see it? Have you ever seen it before? When does it happen? What seems to prompt it?"[159] Tony Stoltzfus gives a whole workshop on confrontation, and his advice was fascinatingly similar: name the issue and then ask about it. Tony suggests saying: "Here's a problem I observe. Talk to me about that." This will cause much less defensiveness than most confrontational strategies, which are often perceived as personal attacks.[160]

4. **Speak the truth in love.** If you make it all the way through these questions and the mentoree still doesn't get it, it's time to lay it on the line: "Can I share something with you in a spirit of love? It seems clear to me that what you're doing is wrong. I wouldn't be sincerely caring for you if I didn't tell you what I saw and try to persuade you to change." After sharing the truth, engage in dialogue about what should be done:
   - "In this situation, how are you acting on what you know to be true – and how are you not?"
   - "How do you think God intends for you to handle this situation?"
   - "Who benefits most from this course of action?"
   - "How does this line up with scripture?"
   - "Where is this decision going to take you? Is that where you want to go in life?"

5. **Challenge forward.** Tony points out that most people focus on the past in an attempt to motivate better behavior: "You did this, it was wrong, and you're bad." Instead, inspire your mentoree by focusing on the future: "You could do this great thing – rise up!"[161]

Providing Accountability for Your Mentoree

As your mentoring relationships intensify, you'll find yourself moving past the occasional hard conversation to the point where you provide accountability for your mentoree's goals and struggles. We've learned a great

Properly handled confrontation can actually build relationships by creating greater trust and respect.

Paint the big picture for them. See p. 114.

deal about accountability from Tony Stoltzfus. Here are his three principles for crafting expert accountability questions as they apply to mentoring[162]:

1. **Make sure your question is both direct and closed.** Now, you may be picking up on a seeming contradiction in what we're saying about questions. In Chapter Four we said closed questions are bad and open-ended questions are good. However, the accountability conversation is the exception to this rule. In this context, closed questions are the best questions because they remove the opportunity to avoid the question or fudge on an answer. Honest, bold questions are best. Example: "How did you do at accomplishing your goal of reading the Bible for 15 minutes each morning last week?"

2. **Allow your mentoree to develop the question.** One great way to remove that nagging feeling from accountability conversations is to let mentorees develop accountability questions themselves. Example: "Tell me what you want me to ask you next time we meet." Having been invited to ask the question, you'll both know what's coming.

3. **Phrase the question positively.** Asking "Did you do such-and-such last week?" communicates an assumption that mentorees may *not* have done such-and-such, which can quickly put them on the defensive. Instead of interrogating, phrase the question in a way that reflects your belief in their capacity to succeed. Example: "How'd such-and-such go last week?"

Changing Direction

Often a mentor and mentoree will begin with a particular goal in mind only to realize that the real issue is something else. This should be welcomed. The shifting from one goal to another may be a sign that the relationship is really working the way it should. Tony Stoltzfus explains:

This may be hard for those who struggle with "boss mentality." See p. 27.

> I almost always let people change goals. First of all, people often start out with goals that aren't the real goal, and they may not even know this. Once they get into the relationship they feel they can be more authentic and get to the real issues. A person ought to be working on what they're most motivated to work on. The only time when I put the

brakes on is when the person bounces from goal to goal without really attempting to reach them.[163]

However, if you're concerned that the relationship is losing focus because of unrelated, but real, issues that are popping up, Paul Stanley recommends saying something like this:

- "I want to talk with you about that. Can we finish what we're working on here and then dedicate some time to really dig in to it?"
- "How about if we finish our session here and then stay a little longer. I'd really like to hear about what you're struggling with."
- "It sounds like this is really important to you. Can we set up another time to get together to talk about it? That way we can deal with what is really important to you and also keep making progress toward our goals."[164]

The basic question is, "What is God's agenda for this mentoree, for this time?" Openly and honestly address this with your mentoree:

- "I am discerning that it might be a good idea to change direction to deal with some issues that are coming up."
- "I am discerning that if we continue on our present course and are patient, we'll be able to resolve some of the side issues that are coming up. Let's try to stay focused on our plan."

When our priority is on what God wants, rather than what we want, it's easier to figure out the balance between focus and flexibility. That said, starting off on the right foot with a properly structured mentoring relationship will make it easier to figure out the balance between focus and flexibility, and evaluating along the way will help you keep an eye on God's aims for the relationship. We'll look at structuring and evaluating in the next chapter.

The basic question is, "What is God's agenda for this mentoree, for this time?"

CHAPTER 11:
Evaluating and Closing a Mentoring Relationship

What To Expect

- How to evaluate the success of a mentoring relationship.
- How to deal with over-dependent/clingy mentorees.
- When and how to bring a mentoring relationship to an appropriate, satisfying close.
- What to do if your mentoring relationship doesn't work out.

One of the most dangerous assumptions people can make about relationships is that they exist only within the vague realm of feelings and therefore cannot be evaluated thoughtfully. Quite the opposite is true; even the most successful and deeply committed relationships thrive with evaluation.

Paul Gutacker's great aunt, Bernadine Gutacker, joined the School Sisters of Notre Dame in 1949 when she was twenty years old. Over the last sixty years, she has served the poor in Chile, taught children in Puerto Rico, and ministered to battered women in Connecticut. Paul recently had the privilege of sitting down with her and asking what she had learned during her life of dedicated service lived side-by-side with others.

> When I talked with Aunt Bernadine about sixty years of life lived in community, she told me that prayer and sharing life together – especially meals – were the two cornerstones of communal life. She went on to stress how evaluation is absolutely crucial to a thriving community. Although the School Sisters have set guidelines that they live by, they are constantly evaluating themselves through asking questions such as: "What are we doing well?" "What could we be doing better?" and "What needs are going unmet?"
>
> Aunt Bernadine told me that living in an unevaluated community is a significantly less valuable experience because of the adjustments that go unmade and the lessons that go unlearned. Evaluation provides an opportunity to reflect on what truly matters, encourages honesty between persons, makes room for celebrating successes, and promotes making adjustments where needed. It truly caught me off guard to learn that these women of the faith in their golden years continue to evaluate how they might better do life together and fulfill their kingdom mission.

Aunt Bernadine's wise reflection demonstrates a powerful principle: the more you value your relationships, the more you'll evaluate them. Whether for a whole community of like-minded believers or for a mentor and mentoree, relationships thrive when they are reflected upon. This intentional reflection is the fertile soil for the tremendous growth that relationships can bring about in our lives.

Evaluating a Mentoring Relationship

People don't often like to reflect on what is happening in a relationship – they would rather just talk about other things and let the relationship take care of itself. Because mentoring, by its nature, is more intensive than some other relationships, it's healthy from the beginning to build in the expectation that the relationship itself is one of the topics to be discussed. Because of his immense experience, we asked Paul Stanley how to go about evaluating a mentoring relationship. Here's what he said:

1. **Introduce the evaluation at the front end.** "It's important for both of us to grow in this relationship, so let's pause throughout our time together to see how our time is working for you and for me. We'll take a look at the schedule, the pace, and how well we're doing in meeting our goals."

2. **Evaluate after about six to nine meetings.** "We made an agreement at the beginning that every once in a while we'd pause to evaluate. How are we doing? What has been helpful about our time together? Are we hitting the nail on the head here?"

3. **Focus the evaluation on both the growth goals as well as the format.** "How is the schedule working for you? Are we going too fast or too slow? Have we met our goals and expectations? Would you like to go deeper? Faster?"

4. **Build in natural stopping points.** "How about if we meet every week for two months, and then we'll take a look at how we're doing. Maybe we could then still meet every week, or we might decide to meet once a month, or eventually just check in once every three months or so."[165]

There's also a personal aspect to the evaluation. Here are some questions to ask yourself:

- Does my mentoree seem to be learning and growing?
- How challenging is it for my mentoree? Am I confronting the real issues and helping him/her grow?
- How are our discussions? Am I teaching/talking too much?
- Am I being more directive than I should be?

In mentoring relationships it's healthy from the beginning to build in the expectation that the relationship itself is one of the topics to be discussed.

For more on setting worthy goals, see p. 86.

As part of the evaluation process, it is important to constantly discern whether or not the mentoring relationship is a genuine partnership. Paul Stanley points out:

> The picture of mentoring is *not* the mentor saying, 'Do this' or 'Do that.' The picture is of the mentor coming around from his side of the table and facing the issue side-by-side. Mentoring is two-way, not one way. The more we share that value, the more we're both going to learn.[166]

For more on the two-way nature of mentoring, see p. 223.

When it comes to evaluation, the ideal is to get to the point where you can speak openly and honestly about the relationship itself. This type of aerial view analysis of the relationship can serve to confirm if you're on the right track, can bring to light areas where change is called for, and can assist you in determining when it's the right time to conclude the mentoring relationship.

Obsession: Responding to an Over-Dependent Mentoree

Sometimes mentors face the problem of a mentoree who is so hungry for attention that he or she wants all of their time: stopping by, calling, and texting. It can be draining. Here are some steps you can take to help an over-dependent mentoree:

Keep in mind that many young adults are very lonely. See p. 57.

1. **Ask yourself: "Am I dominating the relationship?"** Paul Stanley points out that a dominant mentor can cause a mentoree to stop taking initiative and become overly reliant.[167] Tony Stoltzfus agrees: "If I have an answer for everything and the person feels more secure getting answers, he or she will just keep coming back for answers." Rather than always offering your ideas, Tony suggests giving mentorees room to think of what actions they need to take.[168]

2. **Assure the mentoree that your relationship is secure.** The emerging generation has grown up in a time when relationships are aborted when they become inconvenient. A third of Millennials have been abandoned by at least one parent. As we discussed in Chapter Four, many are lonely and without secure friendships. Understandably, they may become frantic that their relationship with a mentor will also end. Paul Stanley says,

When my mentorees become over-dependent, I tell them: 'It seems like you're doing these things just to keep our relationship going. Our relationship will remain. We're okay. I would like to see a little more of your initiative in growing stronger so you can be a blessing to others.'[169]

3. Help your mentoree develop dependence on God. Say, "I've noticed that you have been calling and stopping by a lot, and it seems that you are depending on me to fill needs that nobody can fill except for God. I'd like to spend some time working through a Bible study about putting your hope in God."

4. Be prepared to ask for help. Dan Egeler says, "Those wearing a mantle of mentoring need to have some back-up."[170] Mentorees who are overly needy may need professional help. See Chapter Twelve for information on when to refer a mentoree to a counselor.

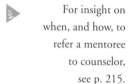

For insight on when, and how, to refer a mentoree to counselor, see p. 215.

Seasons: Bringing Closure to a Mentoring Relationship

Sometimes mentoring relationships get into a rut and seem like they're winding down. Other times they reach the goals the mentor and mentoree had set forth and neither person can discern a natural next step to take together. Each of these is an important phase in the relationship, and neither necessarily means the relationship is over – maybe it just means that it is time to evaluate the relationship. Whatever you do, be proactive; As Dan Egeler says, "There can be hurt feelings if a relationship just peters out."[171] Be prayerful and prepared. Paul Stanley says, "It's easy to fall into a rut if I'm not praying for the other person and preparing for the time (coming up with questions, thinking it through, etc.)."[172]

Even in the best circumstances, though, mentoring relationships are not supposed to last forever. As we've stated earlier in the book, the goal is to pull mentorees up to where we are, then push them on ahead of us. Sending the mentoree out is ultimately desirable, and something that should be clearly communicated and celebrated throughout. Lois Zachary, author of *The Mentor's Guide*, says:

Closure involves evaluating, acknowledging, and celebrating achievement of learning outcomes. Mentors, as well as mentees [*sic*], can benefit from closure. When closure is seen as an opportunity to evaluate personal learning and apply that learning to other relationships and situations, mentors leverage their own learning and growth and reap the full harvest of the relationship.[173]

How will you know when it is time to bring closure to the relationship? Here are some positive and negative indicators:

- When you've accomplished the goal you set out to accomplish.
- When the student is ready to move on to be mentored by someone at a higher level and/or to begin mentoring others.
- When you reach the agreed upon end point.
- When the relationship would naturally come to an end, such as at the end of a school term, upon moving away, or upon graduation.
- When the mentoree stops being interested in putting effort into the relationship. The usual indicators are that he/she has become distracted, doesn't make the meetings a priority, or is uncommunicative.
- When it doesn't seem that the goals of the relationship are being met.

Some people dread this stage in the relationship because it seems hard to avoid hurt feelings. It doesn't have to be that way, though. As you conclude, express your genuine thoughts about the relationship and offer a blessing to the mentoree: "Here is what I see God doing in your life with the gifts He's given to you." If the situation is ending on a sour note, be honest but affirming:

Words of blessing can be enormously influential. See p. 126.

- "It seems to me that the effectiveness of our time together has tapered off. That's okay – life is dynamic; things change. I want you to know that even though we won't be meeting regularly, I'm available anytime you want to connect."

Be careful to define closure as a new phase of the relationship. Stephen E. Olsen explains, in a quote from Bobb Biehl's book, *Mentoring: Confidence in Finding a Mentor and Becoming One:*

When a relationship comes to closure (due to a move or some other life circumstance), I have found it very helpful to verbally define it simply as a new phase of our relationship. It doesn't mean an end; it simply means a continuation under different circumstances. This keeps it open for a variety of ways of relating. This is especially helpful when the relationship has been exceptionally intimate.[174]

If both people recognize in advance that mentoring relationships swell and recede just like the tide, it helps avoid the hurt feelings that could make both the mentor and mentoree wary of engaging in future mentoring relationships.

Connection: Sponsoring Your Mentoree to a New Mentor

Part of the natural conclusion of a mentoring relationship is to serve as a bridge to connect your mentoree to the next stage of life. This is called sponsoring, which Paul Stanley defines as leveraging your status for the benefit of your mentoree.[175] Sponsoring can either be a reason to end your mentoring relationship or a natural step as you're already finding closure. It involves at least three things:

1. Introducing your mentoree to people he or she needs to know.
2. Enabling your mentoree to move more easily into an area of giftedness.
3. Standing behind your mentoree with your reputation.

Here are some example sentences:

- "I know someone who is really good at this. Could I introduce you to her?"[176]
- "I think I know someone who could help you get to where you need to go from here. Can we meet together, the three of us, next time? If things click you could carry on by being mentored by this person."

Make sure your mentoree knows that this is a positive step in the relationship. Paul Stanley suggests saying: "It's time for me to bridge you into other relationships you need to succeed. We'll always be friends and maybe we can get together for breakfast and pray together and catch up. I would enjoy that."[177]

Mentoring relationships swell and recede just like the tide. Recognizing this helps avoid the hurt feelings

You may want your mentoree to work through the questions on p. 105.

The Impact of an Introduction

Mr. E. was my high school machine shop teacher for two years, and taught me metalworking and how to run machines. He took a personal interest in us, and in our success as productive contributors to society. He emphasized that what we were doing in class had a very direct influence on life beyond high school.

Mr. E. not only prodded us to be our best, he took it upon himself to give us every opportunity possible. He introduced a number of us to companies and men that we would eventually work for. The way in which he sponsored us showed how he cared about our success. I'll never forget his influence and the ways in which he taught me to be excellent and diligent at my work.

- Tom J.

With students, it may also be important to explain exactly what is happening at this stage of the relationship so they take it seriously. We suggest you say something like,

- "I believe in you, and I'd like to use my reputation and status to help you advance. I'll be connecting you with someone who will take the relationship seriously because of his relationship with me. Over time, though, as you put effort into that relationship, you'll develop a strong relational basis with him on your own."

Again, be sure to communicate that sponsoring is a sign that the relationship has succeeded, not that it has failed.

Some mentoring relationships do fail, though. What happens if the relationship doesn't go as planned?

Failure: Responding Well When Things Go Badly

Failure is a distinct possibility in a mentoring relationship due to many factors, some of which are outside of your control. The most significant reason for failure is that relationships involve sinners and are, therefore, inherently messy and unpredictable. Sometimes relationships just fall apart. Other times they never really get off the ground in the first place. Although there is a lot to be said for the powerful relationality that comes through implementing the six relational gestures (remember M-FACTS: modeling, friendship, advising, coaching, teaching, and sponsoring), sometimes even the most valiant attempts to connect with another person don't work out. You can't force or guarantee relationship.

Even though failure should not be all that surprising, it's easy to allow a tanked relationship to cause us to sink into apathy – which, ironically, perpetuates a sinful cycle of inaction. So, how do you avoid letting a mentoring failure sour you on the value of life-on-life mentoring?

F. W. Robertson's perspective on perseverance serves as a bracing antidote to failure and its consequences. Robertson was a brilliant preacher and the pastor of the famous Trinity Church at Brighton in Great Britain. Though he died in his late 30's more than a century and a half ago, Robertson's eloquence and insight are celebrated to this day. Recognizing his own frailty, he once sermonized on Philippians 3:13-14 ("forgetting those things which are behind…") and said this about mistakes:

> Life, like war, is a series of mistakes, and he is not the best Christian nor the best general who makes the fewest false steps. Poor mediocrity may secure that; but he is the best who wins the most splendid victories by the retrieval of mistakes. Forget mistakes: organize victory out of mistakes.[178]

"Organize victories out of mistakes." That's the perspective we need for successful life-on-life mentoring relationships. Rather than give up, we should evaluate what *worked well* and what we should *do differently* next time, trusting God's providence to guide us – and our mentorees – into purposes that bring Him glory. We've always found it helpful to ask those two evaluation questions at the end of every process, including the conclusion of a mentoring relationship:

- *WW:* What **W**orked **W**ell?
- *DD:* What should we **D**o **D**ifferently next time?

In some ways, mentors are like inventors – they continue to try things, experiment, and adapt until they succeed. Dean Kamen, creator of inven-

Sponsoring is a sign that the relationship has succeeded, not that it has failed.

▶ Remember that you can make your mess your message. See p. 187.

tions as diverse as the Segway, the first insulin pump, and an electronic motor for cars, said it this way:

> I think the public has this perception that inventors run around with great ideas, get the parts, and make the product. But the process of inventing couldn't be further from that – it's not a linear, straightforward process. You have to be willing to adapt your ideas quickly, no matter how passionate you are about them, and just keep chipping away.[179]

If Kamen is correct, taking risks that *will* most likely fail is the only way to really succeed in the long run. So be inventive, open yourself to learning from what happens, and trust God for the results.

If relationships are inherently risky and if failure is a distinct possibility, how can we set ourselves up to deal well with failure when it comes? Here's what a number of our wise counselors said:

- **Recognize from the beginning that mentoring is a risk.** Matt Benson says: "If we acknowledge that mentoring is a risk up front, we won't be shocked by thinking, 'This was supposed to work!'"[180]
- **Recall that a failure is an opportunity to learn.** Paul Stanley says, "Admit that something went wrong, but don't immediately blame yourself. Analyze it. Was it timing? Chemistry? What can I learn? What do I need to do differently?"[181]
- **Remember that it's not always about you.** Dan Egeler says, "You have to go back to the realization that you can't be a mentor to everybody. Often what we call 'failure' is just the inability to connect with someone. Learn from it, but understand that you can't relate to everyone."[182]

However, there is one area in which we must strongly guard against failure: the safety of the mentoree and mentor. What safeguards can be put into place to protect students and keep mentors' reputations from being called into question? We'll examine this question in detail in the next chapter.

Taking risks that will most likely fail is the only way to really succeed in the long run.

204

CHAPTER 12:
Safe and Secure:
Protecting Yourself and Your Mentoree

What To Expect
- An introduction to the biblical standard of safety.
- Establishing trustworthiness through common sense safeguards.
- Gaining parents' permission for mentoring adolescents.
- Handling tough issues and learning the place of confidentiality and counseling referrals.

Our friend Juergen Kneifel knows first-hand the awesome power of mentoring. Tragically, when Juergen was only ten years old, his father died. It was then that many caring adults in his church reached out to him. Men in the church took him to ballgames and on camping trips. It was this experience with men obeying the scriptural injunction to be fathers to the fatherless (James 1:27) that motivated Juergen to want to be a mentor. In fact, he's started a wonderful mentoring organization, Mission2Mentor, and is a respected leader in the community of people who advocate youth mentoring. But Juergen tells us that things have changed since he was a boy:

> What happened to me – respected men taking me under their wing – was a natural thing in churches back then. The distinct difference today is that there have been so many abuses. It is because of this that there is a great benefit for churches or schools that adopt mentoring programs to make them as safe as possible.[183]

If you aren't sure if your past disqualifies you from mentoring, see p. 148.

These days, parents are rightly suspicious of anyone who wants to spend extra time with their child. Newspaper stories are rife with examples of pedophiles who have joined youth-serving organizations with the specific purpose of finding children who would be vulnerable to sexual abuse. Sadly, there have also been many instances of false accusations of molestation, often from disturbed, angry, or manipulative young people who don't realize the chain of devastation they set in motion through such accusations.

We understand that some people, after considering the implications of safety issues, might conclude that mentoring is not worth the bother. However, our goal in discussing safety is actually the opposite of turning you off to mentoring. Rather, we want to equip you with a strong sense of how to be wise, so you can confidently mentor and glorify God in doing so.

Being Above Reproach: The Biblical Standard

Scripture outlines fearsome consequences for adults who harm children. The words of Jesus about this matter are stated simply in *The Message*:

> But if you give them a hard time, bullying or taking advantage of their simple trust, you'll soon wish you hadn't. You'd be better off dropped in the middle of the lake with a millstone around your neck. Doom to the

world for giving these God-believing children a hard time! Hard times are inevitable, but you don't have to make it worse – and it's doomsday to you if you do. (Matthew 18:6, *The Message*)

Some translations use the phrase "cause them to fall into sin," but the reality of the Greek phrasing is much starker – it literally conveys the idea of causing them to fall away from the faith. How many young people have fallen away from the faith because their simple trust was abused by an adult claiming to be a Christian? There are no two ways about it. We must invest in the emerging generation, and it must be an absolute priority to ensure their physical, spiritual, and emotional safety.

We'll give a lot of suggestions in this chapter. The standard for all of these suggestions is to follow the scriptural injunction in 1 Timothy 3:2, that "an overseer must be above reproach." The Apostle Paul specifically uses the word "overseer" or "bishop" here, but the principle applies to anyone in spiritual authority. This would obviously include those who are mentoring young adults. Our question is, "What steps should we take so that we may be above reproach in all things?"

In many ways, being above reproach is simply a common sense standard. Andy Crumpler shares some of this common sense:

> Avoid one-on-one contact in isolated places. Even be careful when taking kids to their homes, especially if you're a man. We're living in a society where it is as much for your own protection as it is for the kids'. Be very careful of the subject matter you talk about. It's not appropriate for an adult to get too deep into the details of a kid's sin. If it gets too intimate, just stop the discussion.[184]

To be above reproach requires strong common sense, as well as proactive actions that reflect integrity in all things. If you're not sure what those actions should look like in your context, seek wise counsel from trustworthy individuals.

Notice that being above reproach is not a legal standard. Just to be sure that everyone understands the nature of the counsel we're offering, we put the following notice on the copyright page:

We must invest in the emerging generation, and it must be an absolute priority to ensure their physical, spiritual, and emotional safety.

We are not engaged in giving any professional, counseling, psychotherapeutic or legal services. If professional advice is needed, please seek out the proper professional. We disclaim any loss, either directly or indirectly, as a consequence of applying the information presented herein.

This doesn't mean that we have the right to give irresponsible advice. It just means that if you need legal advice, check with a lawyer. We're not lawyers. If you need counseling, seek out a licensed counselor. That's not us. Our goal is to present things that reasonable and prudent people do to ensure the safety of their students.

Some of our motivation for writing this chapter comes from an experience Jeff had years ago while working with a camp for youth. He took all of the organization's documents through a legal audit, including the counselor application. It was an eye-opening process:

> When we got our documents back from the lawyers, I was surprised at two things. First, that the lawyers had made so many suggestions, and second, that they hadn't done so in "legalese." One of the attorneys explained, "Jeff, if you are ever accused of wrong doing and taken to jury trial, the jury will be asked to use the standard of negligence. This means, in effect, that they are asking, "Did you take every reasonable precaution to ensure a safe outcome?" That's what they'll be debating when they are sequestered into the jury room. You can't guard against everything, but they will be trying to consider whether you did everything a reasonable and prudent person should have done in that circumstance.

Reasonable and prudent – that's what we're going for here.

Common Sense Safeguards that Build Trust

Trustworthiness is the basis of all mentoring relationships. Because this is so, we suggest the following guidelines of respect as a starting point for building trust.

Respect the goals of the relationship. Clarify the purpose of the relationship and have agreed-upon goals in view. This distinguishes a mentoring relationship from just hanging out. Isaiah 32:8 says, "But he who is noble plans noble things, and on noble things he stands."

Respect the dignity of the student. This brings confidentiality into play and means not revealing the nature of your discussions with others. Also keep in mind that, if your agreement is for one-on-one mentoring, you are not free to invite others to attend. (The exceptions here are when a mentoree shares information about a person getting hurt or being in danger. We'll discuss this exception in more detail later in the chapter.)

Respect parents. Seek parental permission if your mentoree is a juvenile. God has given the responsibility for rearing children to parents – not to teachers or mentors. Never do anything that contradicts or disrespects parental authority.

Respect gender differences. In almost every case, men should mentor males and women should mentor females. There are exceptions, of course, such as when mentoring is part of a job requirement. As we mentioned back in Chapter Three, Dr. Mary Rowland was Jeff's mentor when he was president of the student government at Washburn University, and it was her job to help him successfully carry out his leadership responsibilities. Still, respect was given for their gender difference. When they met in an office, they kept the door open. When they went for a meal off campus, Dr. Rowland would invite another student to go along. Similarly, when Paige was the student body president at Bryan College and was mentored by Matt Benson, they met during office hours when others were around, and there was a window in the office door. On nice weather days, they would even meet outside on a park bench in the center of campus, simultaneously exemplifying prudence and enjoying a sunny day. If cross-gender mentoring

Trustworthiness is the basis of all mentoring relationships.

When young
people
connect with
mentors,
their ability
to connect
with their
parents also
improves.

is unavoidable in intensive situations such as counseling, take great pains to avoid the appearance of compromise. For example, a man meeting with a female student should ask an older, respected woman to join the conversation. Let prudence be your guide.

Respect propriety. Even in same gender mentoring relationships, great care must be taken to avoid the appearance of impropriety. Avoid compromising situations by meeting in public places such as restaurants or parks. Jeff often meets with his students over lunch in the Bryan College cafeteria, a common gathering place for professors and students. If you meet in an office, leave the door open and curtains open, and make sure other people are in the building and aware of what you are doing. In most cases, respecting propriety means not driving alone with a juvenile mentoree (a car is not a public place). In addition, driving a mentoree puts you in the position of being liable if there is an accident. Organizations such as schools and churches may have, and should have, guidelines about driving youth. Most will want to check your driving record and insurance and will require parental permission to give a youth a ride.

Respect good moral character. Do not drink, smoke, swear or discuss questionable topics during your time with your mentoree. If questionable topics come up, don't be afraid to close the topic off right there by saying: "I'm uncomfortable with the direction this conversation is going. Let's talk about something else instead."

Respect the process. Especially when you are mentoring juveniles, it is an excellent idea to keep a record of what happens during your times together. For just such a purpose, we've included mentoring journals in Appendix B that you are free to reproduce.

Gaining Parents' Permission and Supporting Their Goals

As we mentioned in Chapter One, we live in a country where at least a quarter of young adults are at-risk, and at least one-third live in a home where there is no biological father present.[185] In the midst of this parenting crisis in our nation, we believe that our Christian responsibility to the fatherless (James 1:27) extends to today's young people who don't have a

Reconciling Fathers to Their Children

I was mentoring a young man who was a high school student of mine, and he was really struggling with some personal sin issues. It was the type of situation where he needed special support from his parents – but he was reluctant to talk to them, especially his father. With a bit of encouragement we finally agreed he would have a conversation with both of his parents within a certain timeframe so he'd be accountable to follow through.

Not only did his conversation with his father go great, but it broke through the ice and they were able to take their relationship to a deeper level. On graduation day, I watched with joy in my heart – and tears in my eyes – as this young man stopped at the end of the stage for a long embrace with his father.

Four years later, as he was about to finish college, I had an opportunity to sit down with this young man to talk about his future plans. He mentioned the primary person he was looking to for wisdom and counsel was his father. What a powerful turnaround!

– Name Withheld

positive father influence. Some people believe that mentoring wouldn't be necessary if parents were doing their jobs. We disagree.

Even when parents are involved, there is still great value in securing mentors for young adults who come from healthy families. As Proverbs 11:14 says, "in an abundance of counselors, there is safety." There are simply many areas in which a parent cannot advance a child's understanding or skill, and needs godly mentors to assist in the process. Moreover, researcher Jean E. Rhodes points out that when young people connect with mentors, their ability to connect with their parents also improves.[186]

In some ways, mentors get to have the "grandparent benefit," as Juergen Kneifel calls it. Because they aren't responsible for discipline, they can offer a perspective that is sometimes hard to hear from parents. Because of this added ease for mentors, it is possible for parents to become jealous or suspicious of the unique relationship the mentor has with their child.[187] All the more reason to ensure parental understanding upfront.

It is truly imperative, for numerous reasons, to gain parents' permission to mentor a young adult – especially if that young adult is a juvenile. In

America, age 18 is the age at which children are considered to be responsible for their own actions, so our primary concern in this chapter is with those under the age of 18. That said, honoring the parents by explaining the nature of the mentoring relationship is important regardless of the age of the young adult mentoree. Here are some suggestions for a phone call or visit:

- "My name is _____ and I am a teacher at _____. I was visiting with (student's name) the other day and believe he/she has significant potential in _____. I would like to mentor him/her. Here's what that would look like (times, duration, topics, etc.)."
- "I want you to know that I will be employing the following safeguards (review the list of respect guidelines from earlier in this chapter, for example) to ensure that this is a safe, comfortable experience for your child."
- "As we get started I'd like you to know that I want to honor you and your authority. Can you share with me some of your goals for your child?"

The National Mentoring Partnership suggests that when you initiate a mentoring relationship with a young adult, you get the parents on board right away through a letter. We'd go a step further to suggest a letter followed by a telephone call to answer any questions. Here's a sample letter from the National Mentoring Partnership, along with a sample parental permission form.[188] These examples are from a school-based mentoring program, but the basic format can be adjusted for a variety of situations:

Dear Parent/Guardian:

Your child has been chosen to participate in the (name of program) offered through his/her school. In the program, your child will be matched with an adult volunteer mentor who will meet him/her at the school. The volunteer will act as a tutor on subjects specified by your child's teachers, as well as act as an adult role model and source of friendship and encouragement. The activities between your child and the mentor will be closely monitored and structured by the Program Manager in charge of the relationship. The school feels that your child will greatly benefit from having another positive adult role model in his/her life and hopes that the relationship will lead to increased academic performance, self-esteem, and emotional development.

The mentors who have volunteered for our program have been thoroughly screened and investigated by (name of screening company). We respect your role as a parent/guardian and will provide every opportunity for you to meet with the mentor and be involved in the development of their relationship.

As your child goes through the program, his/her teachers will monitor academic performance. All information gathered about the effect of the relationship on your child's school performance is strictly for the purposes of evaluating the program and will be kept confidential.

We feel that these caring adult volunteers will be making an excellent contribution to the quality of education in our school. If you would like your child to participate in the program, talk about it with him/her. If he/she is comfortable with the idea of having a mentor, please grant your permission by signing below. One of our Program Managers will soon be in contact with you about your child's new mentor.

Thank you for your time. We hope this program will be of great benefit to everyone involved.

Sincerely,

_____

And the parental permission form:

I give permission for my child, _____, to participate in the mentoring program at his/her school. I understand the nature and rules of the school's mentoring efforts and reserve the right to withdraw my child from the program at any time. I give permission for my child's school records to be released to the Mentoring Program Coordinator and mentor in order to best support my child's achievement.

_____   _____
Parent/Guardian Signature   Date

If mentorees reveal information about abuse or behavior that could be harmful to them or to others, you are obligated to report it to the authorities.

This letter mentions a screening company. If you're an individual not associated with a particular program or organization, you might ask your church to take you through an application process, finger-printing and criminal background check, just as it would do, or should be doing, for anyone working with children in church programs. If you are an individual wanting to be screened, Christianmentors.org can meet your needs. If you are part of a school-based mentoring program, your entire school can be screened through http://apps.mentoring.org/safetynet/. See Appendix C for more information on screening organizations.

Confidentiality

Sometimes tough situations arise in mentoring relationships. They're more rare than people think, but knowing what to do in these situations can give you confidence that – should they arise – you can handle them in an appropriate fashion. It all begins with confidentiality. Bobb Biehl states the bottom line:

> The rule of thumb for confidentiality is that anything that the protégé has *not* said in public is assumed to be confidential until that person says it's okay to share it.[189]

We typically think of confidentiality as not sharing hard or negative information about a mentoree, but it actually includes repeating any kind of personal information or illustration. Even sharing poignant or humorous statements made by your mentoree could be considered disrespectful gossip. Bobb goes on to say:

> In other words, in the mentoring relationship, it's critical to assume confidentiality of everything the protégé says until the protégé gives you specific permission not to be confidential in a given area.[190]

There is one significant exception to this rule of thumb, however. If mentorees reveal information about abuse or behavior that could be harmful to them or to others, you are obligated to report it to the authorities. Check with your state laws to make sure you are in compliance, but as an example, if a student says to you, "I need to tell you something, but you must promise not to tell anyone else," you must reply, "Only if what you share does not involve someone being hurt or in danger."

Because of this significant exception to the promise of confidentiality, we recommend that you distinguish between respecting the *dignity* of mentorees and respecting their *confidentiality*. Tell your mentoree:

> "As part of this relationship we need to agree to respect one another's dignity. This means that we both agree not to pass along information from our times together without each other's permission unless it reveals issues of abuse or behavior that could be harmful to either of us, or to others."

Referring a Mentoree to a Counselor

Occasionally, you may be in a situation where you realize that your mentoree is dealing with issues that may require counseling. Often informal counseling (what some people call "pastoral counseling," along with Bible study, prayer, and personal concern) can bring healing. But unless you are a trained, licensed counselor, there may be situations in which a counseling referral is appropriate:

- When a student's past experience is so burdensome that he or she is finding it difficult to move ahead.
- When you realize that something isn't right with the person; when what he or she is dealing with isn't normal.
- When the issues the young person is dealing with are beyond your understanding or skill level.

To refer someone to a counselor sounds like a scary thing. It doesn't have to be, though. Consider articulating it to a mentoree as follows:

- "Some of the things you're dealing with seem to go pretty deep, and I am not sure that our mentoring relationship will be able to progress until you have the opportunity to grapple with those issues. There is someone I would like to recommend that you see. This person is a professional counselor, which just means that he or she has developed skills in helping people heal from emotional and spiritual wounds."

To refer someone to a counselor sounds like a scary thing. It doesn't have to be, though.

- "As we've visited, I am beginning to see that what would be most helpful for you right now would be to deal with some things that go beyond my understanding. I would like to recommend someone for you to talk to who can meet with you regularly and help you more than I can in these areas." Always emphasize that this does not mean the end of your relationship together: "We will still be friends, and I will be praying for you and looking forward to getting together to see how things are going. After a period of time, we may agree that we are ready to start resuming regular meetings. How does that sound to you?"

Referring someone to a counselor does have many implications. For a juvenile this means having a conversation with a parent/guardian about the nature of the issue. Parental permission is required and usually there is some cost involved. Sometimes insurance covers some or all of the cost. If finances are a concern, many churches and non-profits offer free counseling services. If you don't know who to refer a mentoree to, ask a trusted Christian who knows your local ministry community, or call Focus on the Family at 1-800-A-FAMILY to obtain a list of licensed Christian counselors in your area.

Keep in mind that the ultimate goal is cultivating a young adult within an understanding relationship. The need to maintain safety shouldn't discourage you from this goal; in our personal experiences, prudent steps to stay above reproach have never impeded a mentoring relationship. In fact, they help both mentors and mentorees take the process seriously and develop healthy life habits of good communication and proactive precautions.

In the last five chapters, we've covered a wide range of the how-to's of mentoring. Now there's one crucial discussion left: how you can develop the emotional and spiritual reserves you need to exert an ongoing mentoring influence with the emerging generation.

CHAPTER 13:
Your Own Cultivation

What To Expect

- Why your personal spiritual growth is crucial to your mentoring effectiveness.
- Six probing questions to evaluate your life's trajectory.
- Finding your mentors: how to be poured into so you can pour out.
- How your mentoring relationship is about more than your mentoree's growth.

Why Your Growth Matters

As a cultivator it is absolutely essential that you yourself are growing. Your example is the main thing your mentoree will take away from the relationship. The question is not *if* you will be modeling, but *what* you will be modeling.

As we mentioned in Chapter Two, those in the emerging generation crave authenticity and do a fantastic job of sniffing out hypocrisy. If you are advocating growth in maturity, purpose, understanding, and influence for young adults, but you are perfectly content to personally remain stagnant, they will see right through you. If you talk to them about living out their faith with a vibrant sense of who God is and what His Kingdom is about, but you personally go through the motions on Sunday and live just like the world on Monday – they will find your words empty and your message dissuasive. At best you will turn them off from wanting to be like you; at worst you will foster deadly apathy and cynicism towards life and the gospel. Jesus had strong words for those who led youth astray in this way.

Don't let this be discouraging. We aren't saying that you must arrive at a certain point of maturity or spiritual vitality before you're ready to mentor. There is no universal standard for mentoring readiness. However, there is a certain trajectory that you should be on if you want to cultivate young adults to truly grow and bear fruit. In other words, although your readiness to mentor is influenced by where you are now, it is very much more determined by where you are heading.

Your Trajectory as a Mentor

Throughout scripture and church history, a favorite metaphor for the Christian life has been pilgrimage: a walk up to the holy hill of God, a procession of worshippers on their way to festival, or a long journey home that takes the pilgrim through foreign lands. These images remind us of the forward motion of our spiritual lives; we are en route and have not yet arrived – at least not until our redemption is completed in eternity. A similar movement is true of mentoring. It is a sort of pilgrimage where those involved are en route. The mentor is not, as some assume, the one who has

As a cultivator it is absolutely essential that you yourself are growing.

arrived but rather is the one who comes alongside a fellow traveler heading in the same direction.

Instead of trying to determine whether or not you have arrived, reflect on where you are headed. Here are a number of questions that we hope will serve as compass readings by which you can reorient yourself, if necessary:

- **What does your relationship with God look like?** Do you know Him? In what ways are you intentional about growing in your faith – knowing and loving Christ more? What spiritual disciplines are part of the fabric of your day-to-day life? What are some disciplines that you would like to enter more fully into?
- **Where do you see God at work in your life?** Ask this question of yourself and also ask others to reflect on what they see in you: Where do they see God shaping you? How is your understanding of what it means to be redeemed growing?
- **What kind of community do you have?** Who are the people who truly know you? What voices speak into your life and draw you deeper into your spiritual journey? When your communities (friends, church, office, family) come together, what is it that they are about? What are they centered on?
- **What is the big story that you find yourself believing?** Most of us spend our lives only believing in fragments of the true story God is telling. What do you believe God about? What are you staking your life on? Here's another way to get at this question: What are some things that you truly value? How is your life congruent with those values? How is it incongruent?
- **Where do you find yourself struggling?** What unanswered questions are you wrestling with? What pain points do you feel in your life or faith journey? In what ways are your beliefs about God, the church, yourself, and culture inadequate? What areas of your life, if any, are incongruent with what you say you believe?
- **What do you find yourself longing for?** What truly makes you tick? What is it that you daydream of? What captivates your imagination? What do you find yourself thinking about every day?

Mentors need
to be filled up
by God and
also poured
into by other
believers.
Mentors need
mentors.

Your answers to these questions indicate your trajectory and they may inspire prayers for growth or conversations with a friend or mentor.

Mentors Need Mentors

Jeff tells a story about one of Passing the Baton's international partners who was training Christian school teachers to become mentors in his own country, the Philippines.

> I had the pleasure of mentoring Julius Tajale and watching him present sessions in our workshop on how discipleship should flow naturally from our lives. He held up a glass of water and asked, "Imagine that the water in this glass represents your potential for influencing your students for Christ. How can you get the water to flow out of this glass?" "By pouring it out," replied the audience.
>
> Julius poured most of the water out and held up the nearly empty glass. The teachers became hushed as they realized the implication: how many times had they been "poured out" and left feeling empty?
>
> Then Julius took a pitcher and poured water into the glass until it overflowed. "Look," he said, "it is flowing out – yet it remains full because there is a greater source of water pouring into it." Julius told the audience, "We need to be 'poured into' so that we can remain full while overflowing into the lives of others."

This eye-opening illustration affirms the idea that mentors need to be invested in if they are to invest well in others. Mentors need to be filled up by God and also poured into by the community of believers surrounding them. Bottom line: mentors need mentors.

Susan Hunt has written in-depth about Titus 2, the portion of scripture which teaches that the older women should be training up the younger women and so forth. When Susan was asked "Who *is* the older and who *is* the younger?" she gave a simple, profound reply: "The reality is: every one of us is both."[191] The biblical model – indeed the biblical command – is that we are to both seek to cultivate younger adults and seek to be cultivated ourselves.

We've all heard John Donne's famous assertion that no man is an island. We are not isolated from one another. Scripture teaches that, as part of the body of Christ, we are interdependent and are part of something much bigger than our own personal spheres. We must walk side-by-side; We cannot make this pilgrimage alone. We all need someone to understand us, to ask good questions, to encourage, and champion our own growth and fruitfulness.

If you already have some people in your life who are voices of encouragement, insight and challenge, you may want to ask them to cultivate you in some new ways. Perhaps you can begin meeting intentionally with someone to have conversations about your spiritual life. You may want to do a book study together or talk through some of the questions listed above. If you ever start to feel guilty asking someone to invest in you, pause and remember that you are giving them an opportunity to participate in kingdom work, and on a very practical level, mentoring you may serve to meet some of their own needs for knowing they make a difference.

Perhaps you don't know who to pursue for mentoring. In *Connecting*, Stanley and Clinton speak to this issue and give advice on locating the right mentor for you:

> You may be seeking an ideal mentor who can fulfill the whole range of mentoring functions. You will rarely find one. But if you narrow your mentoring needs to a specific area, you will usually find someone available to mentor you in relation to that need.[192]

It may be helpful to stop looking for an all-around mentor and look for certain people to fill certain needs. Successful companies have an entire board of directors to give them wise counsel. So we've learned to ask (as we mentioned back in Chapter Five): "Who's on your board of directors?" In other words, who are the people with which you are intentionally cultivating relationships, who want to invest in you?

Here are some simple steps to finding your "board members" and asking them to invest in you:

1. **Clarify your challenge/task and the skills you need.** We recommend that you make a list of things you know you need to know, but that you currently do not know, to be successful in this season of your life.

2. **Search for someone with experience, success and favor in each of the areas you identify.** Remember, experience is not the best teacher – *evaluated* experience is. Look for the kind of people who are continuing to learn and grow themselves.

3. **Set out to establish a relationship.** As we've mentioned, Proverbs 13:20 says that we grow wise by walking with the wise. Get to know one another; their journeys may be better because you're along as an encouragement!

4. **Arrange a meeting.** Be bold! "I admire you because of _____. I would like to grow in that area myself. Could I take you to (name a meal) at (time) on (date) and ask you ten questions about how you found success?" (Be sure to be prompt, be well-prepared, and always, always pick up the check.)

5. **Ask for advice, not answers.** "Here's what I'm working through. I don't want to pressure you to solve the problem for me. I know that's my responsibility. But can I ask you for a few pointers about it?"

6. **Follow through.** If you really want to gain favor with someone, show them that you've been a good steward of their counsel: "Can I contact you next week to give you an update on how I've followed through with what we've discussed?"

7. **Look for opportunities to keep it going.** "I've really enjoyed and benefited from hearing your story. Would you be open to getting together again sometime?" After the meeting, keep your mentor in mind. Send birthday and Christmas cards. If you find a book you really like, buy an extra copy and send it to them with a note. The constant refrain should be, "Thank you for your wise counsel and investment in my life; I want to be a blessing to you the way you've been a blessing to me."

You can ask some of the 18 questions for wise counselors found in Appendix E.

The greater point is that you need people to invest in you if you want to be growing. And your growth becomes exponentially important when you are cultivating others. To put it bluntly, if you are not being cultivated, you can expect a high rate of failure when it comes to cultivating younger adults. Being mentored increases the likelihood that you'll be a good mentor.

Expanding the *Cultivate* Metaphor

Throughout this book, we have used the metaphor of gardening to describe the mentoring relationship: the mentor cultivates a young adult's growth much like a gardener cultivates a seedling, with a goal of flourishing and fruitfulness. While we love the imagery contained in this metaphor, we also recognize its limitations to portray the scope of the mentoring relationship.

Here's what we mean: *You* are also growing. *You* need cultivation. *You* must be bearing fruit. If we were to pan way out and look down on that garden from above, in many ways you are side-by-side with your mentoree. You share the same soil as part of the body of Christ. You share the same makeup as marvelously designed, image-bearing humans. You share the same struggles as fallen, broken, sinful people. And you are both being carefully cultivated by the Master Gardener to grow and bear glorious fruit for His kingdom according to His plan for you.

One of the many implications of life-on-life mentoring is that it goes both ways; both mentoree and mentor will grow through the relationship. As you share your stories and your lives, have honest conversations, ask hard questions, and listen deeply to another human being, you, too, will be formed. That said, here are three great questions to ask yourself as the mentor-recipient of life-on-life mentoring:

- **What is God trying to teach both of us?** It is often easy to recognize areas of your mentoree's life that are deficient or weak. As you spend time working through those areas together, make sure to reflect on how you can grow as well. It may be that the two of you will share common struggles, failures, or questions. You may also share common passions, gifts, and dreams. Recognizing and

If you are not being cultivated, you can expect a high rate of failure when it comes to cultivating younger adults. Being mentored increases the likelihood that you'll be a good mentor.

articulating these shared realities can not only build great trust and understanding, it can allow for greater growth for you as a mentor.

- **What does my mentoree have to offer me?** It is no accident when God brings you into a relationship with certain young adults. God will bring your lives together for the benefit of both of you. Because your mentoree bears God's image, and because God has brought you together, it's a safe assumption that your mentoree has something significant to offer you. How might his or her example or unique gifts deepen your understanding of who God is, who you are, and how you can live this life well?

- **How is God present in this relationship?** Be mindful of the hand of God in your mentoring relationship, and spend time developing (and helping your mentoree develop) a sense of how He is working. Reflect together on what you are both learning. Spend time in prayer together. Sacralize the everyday gifts from God that you share – a beautiful day, a good cup of good coffee, or an enjoyable book. Both of you will grow as your awareness of God's presence in your relationship deepens.

When you begin to reflect on these questions, expect your mentoring relationship to be a place where God transforms not only your mentoree, but you as well. You will serve; you will be served. You will be a blessing; you will be blessed.

Epilogue

You are embarking on a journey that is intimately linked to the work of the triune God. It is a theme of his kingdom.

What you will do is rooted in the work of God from the beginning of time. Mentoring finds its source in creation; God made man and woman in His image, in the image of the triune God. Just as God is in relationship with Himself – Father, Son, and Holy Spirit from eternity past – we were designed for relationship with each other and with Him for now and for eternity future. Thus, part of what it means to bear the *imago Dei* is that we are relational persons. Mentoring is an outworking of what it actually means to be a person – one who is face-to-face with another image-bearer.

What you will do is part of the work of God throughout human history. He is forming his bride, the church. The mentor's desired outcome is not to produce a young adult who is independent, but rather one who is actually more interdependent within the community of believers. Success occurs when young adults become flourishing members of the body of Christ. In this way, the mentor is emboldened to be part of what Christ has promised he will accomplish: the building of his church.

Finally, what you will do points to the culmination of the work of God in eternity. It mirrors the deep, loving, honest, and rich relationships we will share in the new heaven and new earth. When we are part of a formative mentoring relationship, we point to both what ought to be and what will be. In this way, mentoring actually gives us a taste of the already-but-not-yet kingdom that Christ proclaimed.

This is the goal of all of your efforts to cultivate. It is the high purpose for which you will talk over coffee, listen to stories in the cafeteria, and pray quietly in a crowded hallway. We must remember that the end goal is the kingdom of God. As you put down this book and begin cultivating young adults to the glory of God, you partake in the work of the His kingdom. And it is this kingdom, Jesus said, that is like a pearl of great price or a treasure hidden in a field. Those with eyes to see will sell all they have to buy.

Appendices

APPENDIX A:
The First 5 Sessions

Trying to decide how to get started? With the help of our friend and mentoring expert, Paul Stanley, we've put together a plan for what to talk about in your first five meetings together.

Session One: Understand needs.

Goal: To clarify what the mentoree wants to get out of the mentoring relationship.

Approach:
- "Tell me a little about yourself. Where do you see yourself going in the future?"
- "Imagine that it is three years in the future and you can look back on this year. What things do you hope to have accomplished? What kind of life do you want to have led?"
- "Where do you feel you are in those areas?"
- "What do you think the next steps are in getting there?"
- "How can I support you?"

Tip: Use the words "expectations" and "desires" instead of "goals." Goal-setting can be intimidating to people, but contemplating "desires" gives the mentoree room to freely think out loud.

Session Two: Set expectations.

Goal: To make sure you and your mentoree both understand how to make the mentoring relationship successful.

Approach:
- "Let's talk a little bit about what we'd like to get out of these meetings."
- "Can I explain what I look for in a mentoring relationship?"
  Readiness. A willingness to put some work into the relationship.
  Responsiveness. A teachable spirit that is open to counsel.

Faithfulness. The ability to follow-through on assignments and honor the meeting times.

Attraction. Compatibility – a desire to spend time together and learn from one another.

Potential. A willingness to dig down to search out gifts and make future plans.

- "Let's talk about the structure of our relationship. How often should we get together? How long will the meetings be? Will we have assignments to work on?"

Tip: Keep in mind that your mentoree may not know how to answer these questions. You have the freedom to say, "Here's what I suggest..." and then outline a plan.

Session Three: Share life stories.

Goal: To get to know one another better.

Approach:

- "Since we're going to be meeting together, I'd like to know a little about your life story and I'd like to tell you a little about mine. Let's take ten minutes to share our stories. Would it be okay if I go first?"
- Things to consider sharing:
  ○ A little about your life history (your family, where you've lived, etc.).
  ○ How you have seen God working in your life.
  ○ Points of success that helped you advance on your current path.
  ○ Points of failure you've seen God redeem.
  ○ A snapshot of your hopes and dreams.

Tip: How you tell your story will cue the other person on how to tell his or her story, so take care to be open and appropriately vulnerable. At the same time, keep it general and not overly detailed, so as not to blow your time frame or make the other person uncomfortable.

Session Four: Determine growth areas.

Goal: To help your mentoree get a sense of the areas in which he or she would like to grow.

Approach:
- Photocopy the 'Wheel of Life' form at the end of this appendix and give it to your mentoree.
- "The Wheel of Life helps you figure out the areas of your life with which you are satisfied. Rank your satisfaction in each area of life with '5' being 'very satisfied' and '1' being 'not at all satisfied.' Then shade in each section of the wheel. If you gave yourself an '4' in 'Extracurricular activities' shade in 4/5 of that wedge. When you're finished you'll have a visual picture of some areas of your life you might want to work on."

Tip: Consider filling out a copy the wheel for yourself as well. It's not that you expect your mentoree to give you the same kind of guidance you are offering him or her; it's more of a way to show that you're continuing to grow as well.

Session Five: Focus on spiritual journey.

Goal: To focus on the foundational principles of a spiritual journey.

Approach:
- "I'm interested in spiritual things and would like to know where you are spiritually at this point in your life."
- "Have you come to the point of trusting Jesus Christ for your salvation? Can you tell me a little about how that happened?"
- "How would you describe your spiritual growth at the present time?"
- "In what ways would you most like to grow spiritually?"
- "How do you see God working in your life?"
- "If you haven't trusted Jesus Christ to be your Savior, can you tell me a little about your beliefs regarding spiritual matters?"
- "One of the things I'd like to do as we meet together is to encourage your spiritual growth – and mine as well."
- "I'd like to include at least 4 or 5 times a week of you reading the Bible and praying in the mornings and journaling on it a little. Why don't we start in the book of John?"

- "When we come together we'll spend the first 15 minutes sharing what God is showing about Himself and about how we should live."

Tip: Doing a study of scripture is a simple, foundational aspect of any mentoring relationship. It doesn't have to be too theologically deep – it just needs to open a spiritual door in the relationship and draw the mentoree closer to God.

What Next?

These five sessions can get you started. As you can see, these sessions are a compilation of questions, thoughts and ideas from the text of the book. As we put forth in PART TWO: GROWING SEASONS, at some point in every mentoring relationship with a student, we believe that at least three subjects must be discussed and acted upon:
- Design: Living with purpose
- Wisdom: Knowing and living the truth
- Leadership: Influencing others and creating change

How you move toward these goals could go a number of different directions depending on the leading of the Holy Spirit in your life, the life experiences you feel compelled to share, what God is teaching you at the present time. And the path you take could be a study of scripture, the chapter-by-chapter study of a book, a course provided by a Christian publishing company, or something else entirely. Your goal is to bring your *encouragement* and experience to bear in a way that enables your mentoree to more successfully move toward the goals God has given him or her to pursue.

Wheel of Life Exercise (For Session Four)

The Wheel of Life exercise helps you think about how satisfied you are within various areas of your life. In the list below, circle the number that best represents your level of satisfaction with that area, with "5" being "very satisfied" and "1" being "not at all satisfied." Then shade in each pie slice for that category. For example, if you gave yourself an "4" in "Extracurricular activities," shade in 4/5 of that slice.

When the pie is complete, take a close look:
- What areas would you like to work on?
- What desires or expectations do you have for those areas?
- What would a "5" look like on those areas?

Think of the Wheel of Life as an actual wheel. If you were on a bicycle with wheels shaped like your filled-out Wheel of Life, how bumpy or smooth would the ride be? What would it feel like? Look like? How far/fast could you go? The picture of the Wheel of Life on the bicycle demonstrates that if a couple areas of your life aren't going well, they affect all the others. What's giving your life a bumpy ride? What would you like to do about it?

Friends	1 2 3 4 5
Family	1 2 3 4 5
Relationships with opposite sex	1 2 3 4 5
Spiritual life	1 2 3 4 5
Academic growth	1 2 3 4 5
Extracurricular activities	1 2 3 4 5
Job	1 2 3 4 5
Fitness/health	1 2 3 4 5

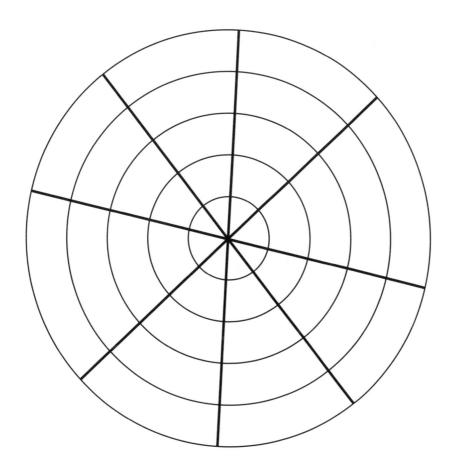

APPENDIX B:
Mentoring Journals

Keeping a journal of your mentoring interactions allows you to have a permanent record of every meeting and track the progress of your mentoree over time. Note that mentorees who also take notes are likely to be more engaged. The following pages feature photocopy-permitted Mentoring Journal forms. Here are some tips on getting the most out of these forms:

1. **Be organized from the start.** Get two notebooks, one for you as the mentor and the other for your mentoree. Make enough copies of the forms to cover the number of meetings you hope to have together.

2. **Explain note-taking to your mentoree.** "I would like for us to use this form to keep track of what we talk about in our meetings. Before each meeting, take a moment to review the notes from our last meeting and write down a goal for the meeting. Toward the end of each meeting we can write down the actions we will take based on the meeting. By doing this we'll be able to stay focused and track our growth through time."

3. **Don't let note-taking get in the way of learning.** These forms are to help keep mentoring meetings on track. Keep in mind, though, that the goal of the mentoring meetings is *conversation*, not *completion* of the forms.

4. **Be careful about taking notes during the meeting itself.** This can make some mentorees feel that they are being "psycho-analyzed." If you need to take notes during the meeting, ask permission: "That's an important thought and I want to be sure to remember it. Do you mind if I jot it down?"

MENTORING JOURNAL – MENTOR

Date: _____   Mentoree: _____

Goal of the meeting:

Questions to ask:

1.

2.

3.

Action: What I will do by the next meeting

1.

2.

Action: What my mentoree(s) will do by the next meeting

1.

2.

Date and time of next meeting:

MENTORING JOURNAL – MENTOREE

Date: _____   Mentor: _____

Goal of the meeting:

Questions to think about:

1.

2.

3.

Action: What I will do by the next meeting

1.

2.

Action: What my mentor will do by the next meeting

1.

2.

Date and time of next meeting:

APPENDIX C:
Safety Resources

Background checks:. Those working with minors should be pre-screened, both for the safety of the mentorees as well as for their own safety. Fortunately, organizations exist that take the confusion out of this process:

1. **Organization-wide background checks.** An organization called *Mentor* offers the "Mentor SafetyNET program" which, in partnership with the FBI, makes fingerprint-based background checks available to any mentoring program, including those that are school-based. Each background check costs $18 and the turnaround time is approximately five business days. You can read more here: http://apps.mentoring.org/safetynet/

2. **Individual safety certification.** *Christian Mentors* enables adults who are interested in mentoring youth to do so under the guidance, legitimacy, and support of a non-profit 501(c)3 Christian mentoring organization. Participants go through a 30-minute online course and send in an application along with fingerprint cards and references. *Christian Mentors* then completes a background check, reference checks and a personal interview. Once you've been selected as a safe, effective mentor you'll be sent a certificate stating that you've been trained and screened by *Christian Mentors*. A parent training program is also provided, and all mentors in this program are included in a liability insurance policy to provide added protection against claims of abuse. Go to http://www.christianmentors.org for more information.

Policies. Most organizations that encourage personal relationships with minors develop a set of policies that people in the organization must abide by. Such policies protect against organizational neglect of the unfortunate realities of our day. They also protect students' safety, and protect teachers from false accusations of molestation or other charges. If your school doesn't already have an effective, written policy about activities with students, you'll need to craft one for the administration and board to formally adopt. Below is a list of sample policies. It is important to note that these policies may need to be modified to account for the nature of your mentoring program. It is also important to note that these policies have not been tested in a court of law. Be sure to submit all written policy statements to a qualified attorney for review.

1. *Mentoring.* Research shows that interpersonal relationship skills of school personnel are significantly related to student engagement, motivation, academic goal achievement and a positive social environment. To this end school teachers may engage students in one-on-one conversations for the purpose of encouraging students in spiritual growth, academic achievement, and life purpose planning.

   a. *Mentoring defined.* A mentoring interaction is a purposefully scheduled one-on-one or small group conversation that has a primary goal of personal growth, and that goes beyond normally occurring teacher-student interactions, such as classroom or athletic instruction.

   b. *The goal of mentoring is to minister.* The purpose of mentoring in the context of our school is to walk with students as they grow spiritually and become more like Christ. Teachers and staff are admonished to not use mentoring interactions to implement a personal agenda in the lives of students (for example, having a primary purpose of persuading students to a particular political or doctrinal viewpoint).

   c. *Mentoring does not take the place of parenting or counseling.* Our goal in mentoring interactions is not to supplant parental authority or to solve any emotional or psychological problems students may have. Teachers and staff are admonished to communicate with parents and be aware of situations in which professional counseling may be a desired course of action.

2. *Safeguards to protect students, faculty and staff.* The following safeguards are for two purposes: protecting the safety of students and protecting

teachers and staff from false accusations of molestation or other related charges.

a. *Right to socialize.* As individuals, school teachers have the right to socialize with anyone they choose, but if it involves a student at our school, then the school as employer has the right to set procedures.

b. *Written notification.* The school office is to be notified, in writing, beforehand, of any off-campus activities involving students.

c. *Electronic communication.* Students are accustomed to communicating with one another and with adults through electronic communication tools (for example, interaction through instant messaging, social networking sites, personal e-mail, phone calls or text messages). Electronic communication with students that goes beyond the scope of the teacher's defined job responsibilities should be reported in writing to the school office.

d. *Parental permission.* Prior written permission must be given by the parent, acknowledging that he/she understands that activities that go beyond the normal scope of daily interaction are not school activities. Teachers must explain specific goals of the mentoring interaction and the safeguards that are being used to protect the child.

e. *Gender relationships.* In mentoring interactions about personal issues that extend beyond teachers' defined job responsibilities, male students should be mentored by men and female students should be mentored by women.

f. *Moral character.* Teachers must exhibit good moral character in mentoring interactions with students, including not engaging in alcohol or tobacco use, profanity, sexual talk, gambling, or questionable topics and practices.

g. *Public space.* One-on-one meetings with students must take place in a public space, defined as a space in which the interaction is visible to others. This could mean classrooms as long as the door is open, or other public spaces within the school. In private offices, the conversation must be visible to others through either an open door or a window in the door.

h. *Transportation.* Teachers who intend to drive students in a private vehicle must provide a copy of their driving record and insurance policy to the school office. A car is not a public space and teachers should avoid being alone with a student in a car. Such activities should be done with two or more students at a time, including dropping-off or picking-up students.

i. *Background checks.* Everyone participating with students in any overnight activity/trip must pass a fingerprinting and criminal background check. This includes parents and/or volunteers.

j. *Psychological counseling.* No teacher or staff person is to be considered a psychological counselor unless that person possesses the educational training and proper licensing. However, "pastoral" guidance and prayer with a student may be done under the following conditions:

   i.   *Check with your local and state laws, but generally information is not confidential if it involves any report of illegal activity or a threat to harm himself/herself or others, or an expressed intent to engage in harmful activities such as running away from home. This information must be promptly reported.*

   ii. The students' parent has given prior permission and the school office has been notified of the particulars (student involved, date, location, time, approximate duration).

   iii. The classroom door or draperies have been opened, giving those who might walk by a clear view of the teacher and student.

   iv. The counseling session be recorded on a calendar or log, noting the students' name, date, location, time, and approximate duration, along with a brief description of what was discussed.

APPENDIX D:
50 Ideas For Spending Time with Your Mentoree

Need some ideas to jump-start mentoring interactions or add creativity to your times together with your mentoree? These 50 ideas should offer something for everyone. (Note: Use good judgment about the appropriateness of each activity if the relationship in question is a teacher/student relationship.) These 50 ideas are compiled from the following sources:

- Mentor Consulting Group's 82 ideas entitled, "What Will We Do Each Week?"[193]
- MENTORific Women!'s "75 Cool Activities for Mentors & Mentees!"[194]
- Connie Witt and Cathi Workman's 36 item list, "Things to Do... Together."[195]

Things to Do: As you'll see most of the activities are for women/girls, but we've thrown in some "guy" activities as well.

- Play a game of cards together.
- Go for a walk on a nice day; sit at a park and talk.
- Take your dog for a walk together.
- Go for a bike ride or go skating.
- Listen to music and talk about it.
- Give your car a wash on a sunny afternoon.
- Find something you can buy or sell on eBay together.
- Learn how to use a map or GPS together. Do some orienteering.
- Teach your mentoree life skills: laundry, easy sewing fixes, changing a flat tire, changing your car's oil.

- Collect items from around the house to donate to the Salvation Army.
- Cook a favorite meal together or grill out.
- Take a group to a sporting event, concert or movie.
- Discover and learn a new hobby.
- Ask your mentoree to teach you something he/she knows how to do well.
- Plan and carry out a random act of kindness for someone else.
- Volunteer for community service together.
- Read your favorite books out loud together.
- Organize a game of "mentors vs. mentorees" basketball, soccer, football, or volleyball.
- Prepare for job hunting: stage a mock job interview, go through the want ads together, research dress codes, and fill out a practice job application.

Places to Go:
- Search the newspapers for a listing of local events, festivals, lectures, book signings, etc.
- Make up a picnic lunch and go to a park for an afternoon.
- Take your mentoree along while you run errands.
- Visit a home for senior citizens and read books to the residents.
- Make a grocery list and go shopping together.
- Conquer the local putt-putt course.
- Spend an afternoon visiting local museums.
- Research a new restaurant you've never been to and try it out together.
- Wander through a pet store or bookstore together.
- Check out some books at the local library.
- Invite your mentoree to spend a day at work with you.
- Make plans to shadow executives on "National Groundhog Job Shadow Day" in February.

Things to Talk About:

- Have a conversation about your heroes and then do research together about their lives.
- Buy a newspaper or news magazine and discuss what's going on in the world.
- Watch a TV show as a group – then turn it off and talk about it.
- Have a group movie-discussion night.
- Study proper etiquette for fine dining together, then make a reservation at a fine restaurant as a reward for learning (make this a group activity, remember to get parental permission, and bring a chaperone if necessary).
- Work on a personal budget for and with your mentoree.
- Have a "big dreams" conversation about your mentoree's hopes for the future, and turn them into a personal mission statement.
- Craft a resume for and with your mentoree based on past experience, accomplishments, and involvement.

Things to Create:

- Make something delicious (cookies, popsicles, or cupcakes) and surprise a mutual friend with a gift of sweets.
- Buy and construct a model together.
- Research how to make a homemade kite – then build it and fly it.
- Build a rocket and invite your mentoree's friends to a launch party.
- Plot out and plant a garden together.
- Sponsor a trip to a rock climbing gym or paintball course.
- Decorate T-shirts together and then proudly wear them on the same day.
- Make a time capsule, pick a date for it to be opened, and then bury it somewhere secret.
- Write and illustrate a children's story together, and then arrange for a reading at a day care, school, or library in town.
- Work together to brainstorm and design a special night for one of your mentoree's loved ones.
- Buy a disposable camera and use it to capture moments with your mentoree throughout the year – then make a scrapbook together.

APPENDIX E:
18 Questions To Ask Of Wise Counselors

Here's a list of questions Jeff has developed over the years for when he meets people he'd like to seek counsel from. Use these to get the mentoring you need and to teach to your mentoree so he/she can seek wise counsel.

Get started well:
- "I'd like to hear the story about how you got into _____."

Success in your field:
- "You've been successful at this field when so many others have failed. What made the difference for you?"
- "What are the essential principles for success in this field?"
- "Who are some of the people who personally influenced you toward success?"
- "Have you ever coached anyone else to be successful in this field?"

The big lessons:
- "What are the most important lessons you've learned along the way?"
- "If you had it to do over again, what would you do differently?"
- "What advice would you give to someone getting into this field today?"
- "What are some of the obstacles along the way that I'll need to be aware of?"

The big questions:
- "What are your goals at the present time?"
- "How do you manage your time successfully?"
- "Do you have a yearly planning process? If so, how does it work?"
- "Time and money aside, what would you rather be doing?"

Direction for further learning:

- "What are some ways I can learn more about this field?"
- "Who are the key leaders in this field that I should be paying attention to?"
- "What are the five books you have found most helpful in this field?"
- "Are there any magazines or publications I need to be reading on a regular basis?"

Wrap it up well:

- "What questions have I not asked that I should be asking?"

APPENDIX F:
12 Distinctives of the Emerging Generation at a Glance

How they think:
- The emerging generation lives in complexity.
- The emerging generation is overly self-confident.
- The emerging generation wants to change the world.

What they believe:
- The emerging generation has a negative view of church.
- The emerging generation wants what works.
- The emerging generation embraces moral relativism.

How they live:
- The emerging generation multitasks.
- The emerging generation is slow to make decisions.
- The emerging generation is overwhelmingly stressed out.

How they relate:
- The emerging generation is extremely connected.
- The emerging generation is uninhibited.
- The emerging generation is lonely.

APPENDIX G:
DVD & Book Studies to Use with Your Mentoree

A study can provide a great context for learning together – discovering new perspectives, wrestling with questions, and forming opinions and plans. For each recommendation, we've outlined a simple synopsis of the content/format, the reasons we think it's a great resource, and the level of intensity required (on a scale of Light, Fairly in-depth, and Very in-depth).

First, here's a list of "Dos" and "Don'ts" for using study materials in mentoring relationships:

Do:

- Make sure both the mentor and mentoree have an attitude of learning
- Choose resources you are sincerely interested in
- Select resources that provide a platform for articulating and discussing new thoughts
- Study the resource ahead of time
- Carve out time to ponder, question and explore the ideas being presented
- Focus on mutual understanding and growth

Don't:

- Use video or book content to avoid dialogue and connection
- Stubbornly insist on completing the course if the material isn't stimulating growth
- Treat a book study as a magic formula for learning
- Use a book or video as a syllabus that must be followed down to the letter

Resources to Use with Your Mentoree

The Summit Curriculum Series: Building on the Rock (elementary +), *Lightbearers* (8th grade +), and *Understanding The Times* (10th grade +) *by David Noebel.* More information at www.summit.org.

- **What it is:** The Summit curriculum series is the definitive worldview resource available today. *Building on the Rock* is designed to help elementary students begin to formulate and relate learned Bible facts to a genuine Christian worldview, while laying the groundwork for later comparative worldview studies. *Lightbearers* is designed to help 8th grade students clearly understand the tenets of the Christian worldview and how these tenets compare to the tenets of the leading humanistic worldviews of our day. *Understanding the Times* is designed to help older high school students understand all the major worldview systems: Biblical Christianity, Secular Humanism, Marxism/Leninism, Islam, Cosmic Humanism (New Age) and Postmodernism in ten key areas (theology, philosophy, ethics, biology, psychology, sociology, politics, economics, history, and law).

- **Why it matters:** If you want to radically open up the world of ideas to mentorees, there's simply no better way to start. These courses will give mentorees a lens through which they can understand the major worldviews that are battling for supremacy in today's media, pop-culture, and universities. They'll be able to discern the assumptions that these worldviews bring and compare them to a biblical worldview.

- **Level of intensity:** Very in-depth. These courses involve a lot of preparation and study, and could easily last for more than a year's worth of weekly meetings. One option is to treat the components of the course as a "buffet," working through units that seem most relevant to what your mentorees are facing (for example, answering common attacks on Christian beliefs).

Five Aspects of Man: A Biblical Theology of Masculinity / Five Aspects of Woman: A Biblical Theology of Femininity by *William & Barbara Mouser.* More information at www.fiveaspects.org.

- **What it is:** The *Five Aspects* courses provide a framework within which young people can rightly understand themselves as the masculine or feminine creatures God created them to be. The aspects of man/woman are drawn from five Bible passages which say something basic about males and females and how they relate to one another. Each course contains 20 lessons and a workbook.
- **Why it matters:** It is becoming increasingly difficult in our society for young men and women to understand what their gender means. These studies give a phenomenal foundation for true manhood and womanhood which can completely change the way mentorees view their identity.
- **Level of intensity:** Very in-depth. The course will involve a minimum of 15 weekly meetings if you allot 45 minutes for each meeting.

Secrets of World Changers by *Jeff Myers.* More information at www.TheCultivateProject.org.

- **What it is:** SWC examines the lives of world-changing leaders to see how, when faced with great obstacles, they broke through personal and societal barriers and lived out their God-given gifts. SWC walks students (middle school age and older) through an easy process to discover how God has uniquely designed them to achieve a world-changing mission. This identity-building course offers six DVD lessons by Jeff Myers, a study guide, and a CD-ROM with teacher's guide, role plays, and case studies.
- **Why it matters:** This course will equip mentorees to see the eternal impact they could have by discovering their God-inspired purpose. In a culture and generation that struggles to identify any personal sense of direction, mentorees can learn to discover and articulate a clear vision for their lives. It offers a great context for a mentoring

relationship to explore self-understanding and forward motion for mentorees.

- **Level of intensity:** Fairly in-depth. The mentor has the flexibility to move through the six sessions weekly for 6 weeks or to intersperse sessions of watching the 20 minute video segments with sessions of working on components – such as writing vision and mission statements.

Secrets of Great Communicators by Jeff Myers. More information at www.TheCultivateProject.org.

- **What it is:** SGC looks at some of history's most compelling communicators and derives simple lessons, taking students (age 12 and up) and adults through a step-by-step process to design and deliver a great speech. The student will learn to overcome fear, organize a credible talk, reach the heart of an audience, and deliver a message with poise. This course offers six DVD lessons by Jeff Myers, a study guide, and a CD-ROM with teacher's guide, role plays, and case studies.
- **Why it matters:** Studies show that young people who learn effective public speaking skills rise to the top 5% and are selected for advancement by teachers, employers, and communities. They're better equipped to live with confidence and grace, to reach their goals, and to make an eternal impact.
- **Level of intensity:** Fairly in-depth. This is a hands-on course – six 20 minute DVD sessions as well as assignments. Mentorees will craft and give speeches, which will involve an hour or two of "homework" outside of the mentoring time.

Secrets of Everyday Leaders by Jeff Myers. More information at www.TheCultivateProject.org.

- **What it is:** SEL teaches emerging leaders how they can instill confidence and inspire dedication in their team. Mentorees (seniors in high school and up) will learn how to break down the barriers to leadership and be motivated to do great things for God. This course includes 12 DVD lessons by Jeff Myers, a study guide, and a CD-ROM with teacher's guide, role plays, and case studies.

- **Why it matters:** As young people develop as leaders, it is crucial that they learn how to inspire others on their team – whether that may be on student government, sports, ministry/missions, or even at work. Your mentoree's ability to lead people to enthusiastic participation will determine how influential a leader he or she becomes.
- **Level of intensity:** Fairly in-depth. Each of the 12 unites contains personal reflection worksheets that take about an hour to complete.

Do Hard Things: A Teenage Rebellion Against Low Expectations by Alex & Brett Harris. More information at www.therebelution.com.
- **What it is:** Written by teens for teens, *Do Hard Things* is a clarion call to reject the cultural expectation of adolescence in favor of a purposeful, missional young life for God's kingdom. The book looks at biblical teaching, history, and contemporary examples for turning the teenage years into a launching pad for life.
- **Why it matters:** The potential of the teenage years is enormous, but, tragically, our culture considers it to be normal to waste them on trivial pursuits. This book radically redefines what it means to be a teenager, and can inspire mentorees to discover a new way to think and live.
- **Level of intensity:** Light. *Do Hard Things* is an easy read with lots of practical suggestions that can be implemented right away.

Let Me Be a Woman by Elisabeth Elliot. Available online or in many Christian bookstores.
- **What it is:** *Let Me Be a Woman* is a collection of 49 short letters Elisabeth Elliot wrote to her engaged daughter. Sprinkled with deep theological truths discussed in easy-to-understand ways, this

collection of timeless wisdom from a mother to her soon-to-be-married daughter is sure to spark discussion on topics such as the life of faith, self-discipline, the single life, masculinity vs. femininity, what makes a good marriage, and more.

- **Why it matters:** Identity is a universally significant question, but it is perhaps *the* most significant worldview question being asked today by the emerging generation. Women of all ages – especially teenagers – struggle to live out their femininity well. *Let Me Be A Woman* is a conversational approach to the topics of identity and femininity that is full of selflessness, humility, and joy.
- **Level of intensity:** Light. Although its topics are weighty and significant, it is a conversational read. Formatted in tiny chapters that could stand alone, there is great flexibility offered in terms of pace and duration of a study based on this book. We recommend it for women from high-school-age on up, and suggest it as a great book for the female mentor and mentoree to read and discuss together.

Apologetics for a New Generation by Sean McDowell. Available online or in many Christian bookstores.

- **What it is:** *Apologetics for a New Generation* is a resource for those who want to interact with the emerging generation about the claims of Christ. It includes contributions from Dan Kimball, Brian Godawa, and Josh McDowell to carefully explain a proper approach to apologetics for this new generation.
- **Why it matters:** Many teenagers leave home for college without taking their faith with them. This book offers a solution to the problem: a radically humble and relational way of approaching faith that addresses the questions asked by the emerging generation.
- **Level of intensity:** Light. Great for discussions over a cup of coffee.

Mere Christianity by *C.S. Lewis*. Available online or in many Christian bookstores.

- **What it is:** A clear, compelling defense of the basic tenets of orthodox faith, *Mere Christianity* presents logical arguments in an eloquent fashion.
- **Why it matters:** This book is considered to be a true classic of the last century. Many Christian leaders point to this book as pivotal to their understanding of the faith and development as a believer.
- **Level of intensity:** Fairly in-depth. Because of its apologetic and philosophical nature, this is not a light read. It can lead into deep conversations and many weeks of further discussion.

StrengthsFinder 2.0 by *Tom Rath*. Available online or in many Christian bookstores.

- **What it is:** The *StrengthsFinder 2.0* assessment is an understandable, affordable, and accessible strength-discovering resource. Each copy of the book contains a code for an online evaluation that generates a customized report. This tool can be the basis for a great conversation between mentor and mentoree.
- **Why it matters:** Understanding one's own unique design is a key step to crafting purpose and finding fulfillment in work. For mentorees who are about to embark on life-defining journeys (such as college or a new career), *StrengthsFinder 2.0* could serve to clarify their own identity and design.
- **Level of intensity:** Fairly in-depth. After the initial 45 minute online evaluation, the report can serve as a launching point for discussions on the mentoree's strengths and how he/she sees them playing out in life.

The Call: Finding and Fulfilling the Central Purpose of Your Life by *Os Guinness*. Available online or in many Christian bookstores.

- **What it is:** Guinness outlines a Christian understanding of vocation in a profound and applicable way. He teaches that God has a unique, specific calling for each of us – and it is there that we can truly find purpose and fulfillment.
- **Why it matters:** Young adults are asking the question: "Why am I here?" *The Call* helps them to understand that God has a call on their life that will affect their plans for the future, and reshape their ideas of what success is.
- **Level of intensity:** Fairly in-depth. There is plenty of material for discussion in the book. Both mentor and mentoree will want to spend time reflecting on and discussing how the book informs their understanding of God's call for their lives.

How to be Your Own Selfish Pig by *Susan Schaeffer Macaulay*. Available online at www.Summit.org.
- **What it is:** *How to be Your Own Selfish Pig* is a humorous, easy-to-read look at what it means to live with purpose outside yourself. It is a down-to-earth explanation of significant worldview ideas on a level that teenagers can both understand and enjoy.
- **Why it matters:** Many young people may be uninterested in worldview ideas or intimidated by deep, dense books. This book breaks through the stereotype and offers profound ideas in a fun, accessible way.
- **Level of intensity:** Fairly in-depth. Enough material to discuss for a number of weeks.

Habitudes by *Tim Elmore*. Available online or in many Christian book-stores.
- **What it is:** Creatively crafted around visual images of leadership, this series of short books outlines various habits that form character and develop leadership skills. Clever and meaningful.

- **Why it matters:** *Habitudes* engages young adults in the crucial issues of character such as time management, self discipline, mental toughness, responsibility, and more.
- **Level of intensity:** Light. Great jumping point for discussions on character and leadership.

TruthQuest Survival Guide: The Quest Begins *by Steve Keels and Dan Vorm*. Available online or in many Christian bookstores.
- **What it is:** This series would be a good introduction to theological truths for any young person. It looks at basic attributes of God as found in scripture.
- **Why it matters:** Many young adults – even those raised in the church – do not have a concrete understanding of basic truths about God and the Bible. This series opens the door to conversations about theological truth.
- **Level of intensity:** Light.

Of Knights and Fair Maidens *by Jeff and Danielle Myers*. Available online at www.TheCultivateProject.org.
- **What it is:** Thirteen years ago Jeff and Danielle Myers wrote a book entitled *Of Knights and Fair Maidens* to help singles of all ages break through the uncertainty of the dating culture. It contains three simple, biblical principles of true romance that the Myers' learned and applied during their courtship.
- **Why it matters:** This book offers fresh, relevant insight on dating, courtship, and marriage. Along the way, readers will get a biblical, balanced antidote to both the heartbreak of the popular dating culture and the frantic legalism that often characterizes Christian literature on the subject.
- **Level of intensity:** Light.

We are discovering new resources all the time, and new ones are being written every year. Check www.TheCultivateProject.org for additional resources.

APPENDIX H:
Recommended Reading for the Mentor

We believe in the accuracy of the old saying, "If you want to be a leader, you've got to be a reader." To increase your influence on the emerging generation, you need to be a student – willing to learn, hungry for new ideas and insight, and well-grounded in your thinking.

We've organized our favorite books on a variety of issues: generational trends and youth issues, biblical worldview, theology and Christian growth, mentoring and leadership development, culture and ideas, design and purpose, character.

Here's our challenge to you as a mentor: pick one category and buy three of the books listed. Read one a month for the next three months. If you do that, you'll be well on your way to expanding your knowledge and increasing your influence.

1. Generational Trends & Youth Issues

unChristian: What a New Generation Really Thinks about Christianity by *David Kinnaman & Gabe Lyons*

> This eye-opening book takes an honest look at how young teens through 30-year-olds perceive church.

Youth Culture 101 by *Walt Mueller*

> Widely considered one of the most in-depth looks into youth culture today, this book provides a biblical perspective on popular culture in an easy-to-read style.

The Death of the Grown-Up by *Diana West*

This book offers a scathing critique of the "perpetual adolescence" phenomenon in our culture today. An insightful and alarming read.

The Fabric of Faithfulness: Weaving Together Belief And Behavior *by Steve Garber*

This is the book that educators need to read regarding the emerging generation's faith. Absolutely essential.

Soul Searching and ***Souls in Transition*** *by Christian Smith*

Soul Searching is a ground-breaking study of the spirituality of the emerging generation. *Souls in Transition* continues their excellent research by following up with the same youth a number of years later to see how their faith had developed.

Counseling Youth in Crisis *by Josh McDowell*

This massive resource offers an in-depth look into each of the most critical issues young people face today, including anorexia, parental divorce, sexuality, drug abuse, and more.

2. Biblical Worldview

Understanding the Times *by David Noebel*

An essential text for every Christian, *Understanding the Times* summaries the worldviews of our day – what they believe, and how Christians can engage the culture in theology, philosophy, ethics, biology, psychology, sociology, politics, economics, history, and law.

Total Truth *by Nancy Pearcey*

Thorough, yet surprisingly readable, this book looks at our culture's misunderstanding of truth and how Christians can break down the sacred/secular divide.

Relativism: Feet Firmly Planted in Mid-Air *by Frank Beckwith and Greg Koukl*

This book critiques moral relativism and offers ways that Christians can defend against it.

The Creation Hypothesis *by J.P. Moreland*

> This book offers a persuasive argument for intelligent design from astronomy, physics, bio-chemistry, paleontology, and linguistics.

Bioethics: A Primer for Christians *by Gilbert Meilaender*

> An insightful look into the bioethical issues of our day: abortion, euthanasia, and stem-cell research.

Money, Greed, and God *by Jay Richards*

> Richards offers a fresh look at capitalism, demonstrating how it is consistent both with the teachings of Christ and the Christian tradition. He then shows that this system is our best hope for economic growth.

3. Theology & Christian Growth

A Long Obedience in the Same Direction *by Eugene Peterson*

> One of the best articulations of true discipleship, this book is a must read for any Christian.

Engaging God's World: A Christian Vision of Faith, Learning and Living *by Cornelius Plantinga*

> A stimulating approach to understanding the world and our role as humans and as Christians in it. Plantinga is one of the most highly regarded Christian thinkers of our time.

Good News About Injustice *by Gary A. Haugen*

> Written by the president of the International Justice Mission (IJM), this book is a clarion call to Christians to be about the kingdom work of justice – not in a humanistic way, but rather in a biblical way.

The Politically Incorrect Guide to the Bible *by Robert Hutchinson*

> This book challenges many common views of the Bible and defends its truth and importance to a democratic, free society.

4. Mentoring & Leadership Development

Leadership Coaching: The Disciplines, Skills, and Heart of a Christian Coach by Tony Stoltzfus

> This book provides a comprehensive approach to coaching. It introduces coaching and provides a very practical outline for how to begin practicing coaching skills.

Connecting: The Mentoring Relationships You Need To Succeed by Paul Stanley and Robert Clinton

> The gold standard of books on Christian mentoring. Stanley and Clinton carefully outline how to become a mentor and be mentored – and the importance of both for the Christian leader.

Spiritual Mentoring: A Guide for Seeking and Giving Direction by Randy D. Reese and Keith R. Anderson

> A profound yet accessible book that looks at great spiritual influencers throughout church history and applies lessons to us today.

Handoff: The Only Way to Win the Race of Life by Jeff Myers

> Written with a deep understanding of human tendencies and fears, this book uses humorous and poignant stories and practical strategies to help you invest in the next generation in a natural and stress-free way.

That Makes Two of Us: Lifestyle Mentoring for Women by Connie Witt and Cathi Workman

> The authors, a mentor and mentoree, bring insight as two women of different generations who have connected in a thriving mentoring relationship. Short, sweet, and humor-filled, this non-program-based book offers a breath-of-fresh-air flexibility and encourages women to connect with other women *as they go*. We recommend it as an excellent book for use in a women's small group.

As Iron Sharpens Iron by Howard Hendricks and William Hendricks

> A simple collection of thoughts and helps on mentoring recommended to us by Paul Stanley.

The Power of Mentoring *by John W. Kirkpatrick*

> This book is simple, clear, and full of good ideas. An easy read.

5. Culture & Ideas

Culture Making: Recovering Our Creative Calling *by Andy Crouch*

> This book looks at typical Christian approaches to the issue of culture and offers an alternative based on God's design and image in humanity.

All God's Children and Blue Suede Shoes: Christians and Popular Culture *by Ken Myers*

> Considered one of the best Christians treatments of popular culture, this book evaluates the effect of pop culture on its consumers and explores what the church's response should be.

Eyes Wide Open: Looking for God in Popular Culture *by William Romanowski*

> An excellent perspective on popular culture (particularly movies) and what a Christian interaction with it should be. Romanowski challenges us to look deeper at the messages of movies in discerning which ones we should avoid and which we should laud.

Amusing Ourselves to Death *by Neil Postman*

> Postman's critique of the media-driven culture isn't just a polemic against television – it analyzes how our society has moved from a print-based society to an image-driven society and explores the implications of that shift for education, politics, and religion.

Art and the Bible *by Francis Schaeffer*

> Written by one of the most revered Christian thinkers of the 20th Century, this quick, easy read articulates a biblical worldview of art.

Books & Culture: A Christian Review published *by Christianity Today International.*

> This bimonthly Christian magazine covers theology, art, poetry, history, and social issues in a particularly thoughtful way. A great way to

engage contemporary society and expand your knowledge of current ideas and books.

6. Design & Purpose

Overload Syndrome by Dr. Richard Swenson

Dr. Swensen is a medical doctor who articulated what everyone sensed in their hearts – that too many of us were living without margin, and thus were being robbed of joy and meaning in life – and gave practical solutions to the overload problem.

Finding a Job You Can Love by Ralph T. Mattson and Arthur F. Miller

The authors articulate a biblical view of work, and show how God intends for us to find satisfaction and joy in our calling. It includes a coaching tool that helps you outline your motivated abilities and understand your God-given design.

Mere Humanity: Chesterton, Lewis, and Tolkien on the Human Condition by Donald Williams

A great book on one of the most pressing questions of our age: "What does it mean to be human?" Williams looks at some of the great Christian thoughts on the issue.

7. Character

The Young Peacemaker by Corlette Sande

An excellent resource for conflict resolution. It takes the principles of biblical conflict resolution practiced by Peacemaker Ministries and teaches them to young people from the 3rd to 8th grades.

Say Goodbye to Whining, Complaining, and Bad Attitudes by Scott Turansky and Joanne Miller

Parents and teachers don't just want obedient behavior – they want obedient hearts. The authors show how learning the character quality of honor solves the problem.

Leading Little Ones to God: A Child's Book of Bible Teachings *by Marian M. Schoolland*

This wonderful family devotion tool teaches young children ages 3 and up the basics about God, creation, sin, redemption, and more.

APPENDIX I: Development Opportunities for the Mentor

Passing the Baton DVD Training Course

The *Passing the Baton DVD Training Course* equips mentors in three unique ways: First, it looks at the way Christ trained world changers and applies what He did to you as a mentor. Second, it looks at how your God-given design should be the source and shape of your mentoring. Third, it teaches basic coaching skills to center your mentoring around listening and asking powerful questions rather than advice giving. One year after he hosted the training at his school, Dr. S. L. Sherrill said: "We continue to see great enthusiasm for having a life-on-life influence on students. Our teachers are intentionally mentoring students and the students are being changed."

Check it out at: www.passingthebaton.org

Summit Adult Conference

Students today are bombarded with all kinds of worldview messages before they ever set foot in a classroom. If you want to learn how to train students in biblical worldview, then the Summit Adult Conference is for you. You will learn how to equip mentorees with worldview analysis tools so that they can survive the cultural battles of our day and champion the Christian faith. This conference is geared specifically for Christian educators who want to learn how to integrate a biblical worldview in both their classrooms and in student culture.

Check it out at: www.summit.org

Conversational Leadership

Coaching is a crucial relational gesture for the mentor. The 8-week Conversational Leadership course shows you how to apply coaching skills within your job, mentoring, and other relationships. It will help you increase your influence and ability to develop other leaders by using some of the best practices of professional coaches. The course equips you to:

- Listen carefully and intuitively to what others are saying,
- Ask effective questions which help others uncover new ideas and plans,
- Assist others to create and commit to specific action plans, which will move them toward reaching their goals.

Check it out at: www.alliantleadership.com

Acton University

Christian leaders ought to be able to intelligently engage issues of social justice, economics, and politics. The Acton University is a four-day conference with an international faculty that explores the intellectual foundations of a free society. Considering the unique characteristics of the emerging generation we discussed in Chapter 2, today's most effective mentors will seek to become articulate in these issues.

Check it out at: www.acton.org

Trinity Forum

The Trinity Forum is a leadership academy that seeks to cultivate networks of leaders whose integrity and vision will help renew culture and promote human freedom and flourishing. Their programs and publications offer contexts for leaders to consider together the big ideas that have shaped Western Civilization and the faith that has animated its highest achievements.

Check it out at: www.ttf.org

Veritas Forum

Veritas Forums are university events that engage students and faculty in discussions about life's hardest questions and the relevance of Jesus Christ to all of life. The forums are created by local university students, professors, and ministers and are shaped and guided by the Veritas team.

Check it out at: veritas.org/

APPENDIX J:
Sponsoring Opportunities for the Mentoree

One of the most important things you can do as a mentor is sponsor your mentoree into programs that will help him or her further develop transformational leadership skills. Here are some opportunities we're personally familiar with and excited about:

Summit Ministries Student Conferences

This is the most important event that you can sponsor your mentoree to. An intensive two-week conference, Summit trains students ages 16-24 in Christian worldview thinking. In our estimation, there is no better way for students to be prepared for the battle of ideas that they will face in college and culture at large. Summit brings in highly respected, biblically trustworthy, conservative Christian thinkers and speakers on topics ranging from bioethics, art, politics, abortion, homosexuality, economics, and more. Open up your student's mind to the issues of today and how a biblical worldview speaks to them.

Check it out at: http://www.summit.org

TeenPact Leadership Schools

TeenPact conferences seek to train young people to be world-changing leaders. Beginning with one-day meetings at the state capitol for children ages eight and up, TeenPact has a thoughtful program of leader development that prepares students with an understanding of public policy, public speaking and debate skills, and even opportunities to gain campaign experience.

Every year, TeenPact prepares hundreds of students to grow personally and spiritually, improving their ability to bring change.

Check it out at: www.teenpact.com

Worldview Academy

Worldview Academy is similar to Summit Ministries in that it seeks to train students to hold their faith as a total worldview. The difference is that it is one week program rather than a two week program, and it is geared toward somewhat younger students (ages 13-15). WVA offers Leadership Camps and Christianity/Culture Conferences for students, as well as podcasts and curriculum.

Check it out at: www.worldview.org

Institute for Cultural Communication (Communicators for Christ)

A young person who becomes a confident communicator will become more confident as a leader in other areas of life. ICC's fast-paced, fun programs will equip students ages eight and up (even those who are fearful of public speaking) with both the skills and character to become "cultural communicators" – ones who will influence culture for Christ.

Check it out at: www.instituteforculturalcommunicators.org

Student Leadership University

If your mentoree shows signs of budding leadership ability, you may want to consider sponsoring him or her to Student Leadership University. SLU challenges high school students to develop skills such as goal-setting, time management, interpersonal relationships, vision, conflict-resolution, and more. SLU's programs begin with a short course in Orlando, Florida. For those who are financially able, advanced courses take students to locations around the world, incorporating studies of great leaders from history, and creating a memorable context for developing as leaders.

Check it out: www.studentleadership.net

APPENDIX K:
Recommended Speakers

There's nothing like a live event to mobilize your group to enthusiastically invest in the next generation. Here are some speaker options for everything from banquets to retreats to teacher in-service workshops:

Dr. Jeff Myers

Jeff Myers, Ph.D. is the president of Passing the Baton International. For the last twenty years, he's been on the front lines of youth leadership development as a college professor, communicator, author, and curriculum developer. Jeff is the author of seven books, including *Handoff: The Only Way to Win the Race of Life,* and five video coaching systems, including *Understanding the Times* – the curriculum that introduced biblical worldview training to Christian schools around the world. More than two million people have used Jeff's training courses in worldview, leadership, and communication. Jeff is Associate Professor of Communication Studies at Bryan College where he teaches undergraduate and graduate leadership courses. He also serves as chairman of the board of Colorado-based Summit Ministries. Jeff and his family live in Tennessee.

Contact Jeff:

Email: jeff@passingthebaton.org

Phone: 423-570-1000

John Stonestreet

John is the Executive Director of Summit Ministries. A popular speaker at camps, conventions, and conferences, he works with thousands of parents, teachers, and students each year. His speaking topics include: developing a biblical worldview, understanding comparative worldviews, defending the Christian faith, applying a biblical worldview to education, and engaging important cultural issues. He holds a M.A. in Christian Thought from Trinity Evangelical Divinity School and is a Fellow of the Wilberforce Forum, a division of Breakpoint. John is the co-author with W. Gary Phillips and William E. Brown of *Making Sense of Your World: A Biblical Worldview*, 2nd. ed. (Sheffield, 2007), as well as numerous web and journal articles. John joined the Summit team in 1999, and has served in numerous roles including directing the Eastern Summit programs in Tennessee and Virginia. He, his wife Sarah, and their three daughters live in Colorado Springs, Colorado.

Contact John:

Email: johns@summit.org

Phone: 866-786-6483

Ben Williams

Ben is the Director of Worldview Formation at Bryan College in Dayton, Tennessee – his alma mater. An honors graduate from Bryan College in English Literature, Ben began his career teaching high school English at a large private Christian school in Orlando, Florida. Ben challenged students toward a biblical understanding of literature and humanity, and was honored as Educator of the Year and listed in *Who's Who Among American Teachers 2004-2005*. Ben is passionate about connecting students to the story of Christianity and equipping teachers to incorporate into their classes an understanding of how to view, and live in, the world as Christians. He lives in Dayton, Tennessee with his wife, Jess, and their son Neal.

Contact Ben:

E-mail: ben.williams@bryan.edu

Phone: 423-775-7191

Sean McDowell

Sean is an educator, speaker, and author who shares candid and compelling stories while challenging both young people and adults to defend their faith and deepen their walk with Christ. Sean was mentored by and is a co-author with his father, Josh McDowell, and has become a popular speaker at churches, conferences, camps, and schools around the nation. Sean has spoken for organizations including Focus on the Family, Campus Crusade for Christ, Youth Specialties, and the Association of Christian Schools International. His recent book, *Apologetics for a New Generation*, focuses on passing a biblical worldview to the next generation. Sean and his family live in Capistrano, California.

Contact Sean:

Email: sean@seanmcdowell.org

Phone: 866-400-2036

Endnotes

1. Most of this information comes from Jeffry H. Morrison, *John Witherspoon and the Founding of the American Republic* (Notre Dame, IN: University of Notre Dame Press, 2005), p. 4.

2. Mark A. Noll, *Princeton and the Republic 1768-1822* (Vancouver, BC: Regent College Press, 1989), p. 28.

3. http://www.princeton.edu/pr/facts/revolution.html

4. John Witherspoon, *The Works of the Rev. John Witherspoon To Which is Prefixed an Account of the Author's Life*, In a Sermon Occasioned By His Death, Vol. 3 (Boston: William W. Woodward, 1802), p. 563.

5. Ibid., p. 564.

6. Noll, p. 29.

7. Jason Lanker, *The Relationship Between Mid-Adolescent Natural Mentoring and the Christian Spirituality of North American First-Year Christian College Students.* May 2009, Unpublished. Talbot School of Theology, Biola University. pp. 141, 147.

8. Ibid.

9. Andrew J. Martin and Martin Dowson (2009), "Interpersonal Relationships, Motivation, Engagement, and Achievement: Yields for Theory, Current Issues and Educational Practice," *Review of Educational Research*, Vol. 79, No. 1, pp. 344.

10. Ibid.

11. Ibid.

12. Ibid.

13. Kathryn R. Wentzel (1999), "Social-Motivational Processes and interpersonal Relationships: Implications for Understanding Motivation at School," *Journal of Educational Psychology*, Vol. 91, No. 1, pp. 76-97.

14. Andrew J. Martin, Herbert W. Marsh, Dennis M. McInerney, Jasmine Green, and Martin Dowson (2007), "Getting Along with Teachers and Parents: The Yields of Good Relationships for Students' Achievement Motivation and Self-Esteem," *Australian Journal of Guidance and Counseling*, Vol. 17, No. 2, pp. 109-125.

15. Barbara Fresko and Cheruta Wertheim (2006), "Learning by Mentoring: Prospective Teachers as Mentors to Children at Risk," *Mentoring and Tutoring*, Vol. 14, No. 2, pp. 149-161.

16. Keith A. King, Rebecca A. Vidourek, Beth Davis, and Warren McClellan (2002), "Increasing Self-Esteem and School Connectedness Through a Multidimensional Mentoring Program," *Journal of School Health*, Vol. 72, No. 7, pp. 294-299; Rachel C. Vreeman and Aaron E. Carroll (2007), "A Systematic Review of School-Based Interventions to Prevent Bullying," Archives of Pediatric and Adolescent Medicine, Vol. 161, p, 86.

17. George Barna, "Twentysomethings struggle to find their place in Christian churches," http://www.barna.org/barna-update/article/5-barna-update/127-twentysomethings-struggle-to-find-their-place-in-christian-churches

18. Ken Ham and Britt Beemer, *Already Gone: Why Your Kids Will Quit Church and What You Can Do to Stop It* (Green Forest, AR: Master Books, 2009), p. 24.

19. Norman Willis, *The Ancient Path: A Return to the Kingdom Mandate of Generational Transfer* (Kirkland, WA: Christ Church Publishing, 1998), p. 17.

20. Wade F. Horn and Tom Sylvester, *Father Facts*, 4th ed. (Gaithersburg, MD: National Fatherhood Initiative, 2002), p. 15. Quoted in Walt Mueller, *Youth Culture 101* (El Cajon, CA: Youth Specialties, 2007), p. 45.

21. The Commission on Children at Risk, *Hardwired to Connect: The New Scientific Case for Authoritative Communities* (New York: Institute for American Values, 2003), p. 8.

22. At http://www.mentoryouth.com/ you can get involved as a mentor, learn about mentoring, and gather materials for beginning a mentoring program in your community.

23. http://www.charityguide.org/volunteer/fewhours/mentoring.htm

24. Kara Powell, Cheryl A. Crawford, and Cameron Lee, "High School Youth Group Seniors Transitioning to College: Risk Behavior, Social Support, Religiosity, and Attitude Toward Youth Group," *Christian Education Journal*, Series 3, Vol. 5, No. 1, pp. 47-59.

25. George Orwell, *In Front of Your Nose*, 1945-1950 (*Collected Essays Journalism and Letters of George Orwell*) (Boston: David R. Godine, 2000), p. 51.

26. These terms gained familiarity through Howe & Strauss' book *Generations* and *Generation X* by Douglas Coupland.

27. See the Beloit College Mindset list at http://www.beloit.edu/mindset/

28. Orwell, p. 51.

29. Ron Alsop, *The Trophy Kids Grow Up: How the Millennial Generation Is Shaking Up the Workplace* (San Francisco: Jossey-Bass, 2008).

30. David Kinnaman and Gabe Lyons, *UnChristian: What a New Generation Really Thinks About Christianity…and Why It Matters* (Grand Rapids, MI: Baker Books, 2007), p. 125.

31. Alsop, pp. 27, 4 and 7.

32. From a 2006 survey by Cone Inc., a communications agency, and Amp Insights, a marketing agency, reported in Alsop, p. 226.

33. Ibid., pp. 34, 28, and 25.

34. Ibid., p. 163.

35. Kinnaman and Lyons, p. 127.

36. Alsop, p. 21.

37. From a Kaiser Family Foundation study reported in Alsop, p. 136.

38. See, for example, http://www.apa.org/monitor/2009/02/multitaskers.html and http://www.thenewatlantis.com/publications/the-myth-of-multitasking

39. Alsop, p. 12 and 115.

40. Ibid., p. 14.

41. See "APA Survey Raises Concern about Parent Perceptions of Children's Stress." at http://www.apa.org/news/press/releases/2009/11/stress.aspx

42. Alsop, pp. 10, 11, and 120.

43. Kim Woody. Personal Interview. 25 March 2010.

44. Alsop, p. 12.

45. Ibid., p. 151.

46. Sean McDowell. Telephone Interview. 15 September 2009.

47. Shane Hipps, Lecture entitled *The Spirituality of the Cell Phone*, Q Conference, Austin, TX, April 28, 2009.

48. See "Still relevant after decades, the Beatles set to rock 9/9/09." http://www.cnn.com/2009/SHOWBIZ/Music/09/04/beatles.999/index.html?iref=newsearch

49. Albert Mehrabian, "Communication Without Words," from *Psychology Today Magazine,* 1968, reprinted in C. David Mortensen, ed., *Communication Theory* 2nd ed., (New Brunswick, NJ: Transaction, 2008), p. 193.

50. Jean E. Rhodes, *Stand By Me: The Risks and Rewards of Mentoring Today's Youth* (Cambridge, MA: Harvard University Press, 2002), p. 45.

51. Alan Loy McGinnis, *The Friendship Factor* (Minneapolis: Augsburg, 1979), p. 9.

52. Miller McPherson, Lynn Smith-Lovin and Matthew Brashears, "Social Isolation in America: Changes in Core Discussion Networks over Two Decades," *American Sociological Review*, 2006, V. 71, pp. 353–375.

53. Jeff Myers, *Handoff: The Only Way to Win the Race of Life* (Dayton, TN: Legacy Worldwide, 2008).

54. Interview with Parker Palmer, *Teaching By Heart: The Foxfire Interviews*, Sara Day Hatton (ed.) (New York: Teachers College Press, 2005), p. 74.

55. Elliot Aronson, *The Power of Self-Persuasion*. American Psychologist. Vol. 54, Issue 11. November 1999. p. 882.

56. Tony Stoltzfus, *Leadership Coaching: The disciplines, skills and heart of a coach* (Virginia Beach, VA: BookSurge, 2005), p. 291.

57. Olivero, G., Bane, K.D., & Kopelman, R.E. (1997). Executive coaching as a transfer of training tool: Effects on productivity in a public agency. Public Personnel Management, 26(4), pp. 461-469.

58. Tony Stoltzfus. Telephone Interview. 12 August 2009.

59. Roger Erdvig and Mary Verstraete, *Conversational Leadership For Today's Christian Leaders* (Patchogue, NY: Center for Coaching Excellence, 2008), pp. 46-47.

60. Ibid., p. 44.

61. This and similar models are widely used in professional coaching circles. It is unclear where G.R.O.W. originated.

62. William Damon, *The Path to Purpose* (New York: Free Press, 2008) p. 8.

63. Ibid, throughout text.

64. Kinnaman and Lyons, p. 45.

65. *Daily Mail*, December 18, 2006. http://www.dailymail.co.uk/news/article-423273/Being-celebrity-best-thing-world-say-children.html

66. Twenge and Campbell, p. 90.

67. Ibid., p. 206.

68. Harold J. Sala, *Heroes: People Who Made a Difference in Our World* (Uhrichsville, OH: Promise Press, 1998), pp. 21-22.

69. Diana West, *The Death of the Grown-Up*, (New York: St. Martins Press, 2007), pp. 1-2.

70. Alex and Brett Harris, *Do Hard Things: A Teenage Rebellion Against Low Expectations* (Colorado Springs: Multnomah, 2008), p. 41.

71. Ibid., p. 45.

72. Ibid., pp. 58-59.

73. Robert Epstein, *The Case Against Adolescence: Rediscovering the Adult in Every Teen* (Sanger, CA: Quill Driver, 2007), pp. 148-157.

74. See Chapter Three, "Living Like a Winner," in the study guide accompanying Jeff Myers, *Secrets of the World Changers* (Nashville: Broadman and Holman, 2006), p. 20.

75. Arthur F. Miller, *Designed for Life: Hard-Wired, Empowered, Purposed – The Birthright of Every Human Being* (Charlotte, NC: Life(n) Media, 2006), p. 42.

76. Ibid., p. 45.

77. Garry Friesen and J. Robin Maxson, *Decision-Making and the Will of God: A Biblical Alternative to the Traditional View* (Colorado Springs: Multnomah, 2004), p. 15.

78. This particular list was brought to the "Christian consciousness" by Bill Gothard. About these unchangeables Gothard said: "Since we cannot change these things, we have a choice. Either we choose to be grateful for God's purposes for these unchangeable features, or we will resent them and likely become bitter toward God and toward life in general. The basic principle is that true happiness does not come from our outward appearance or physical circumstances, but from the development of inward character, such as gratefulness, patience, compassion, and joyfulness." See "What I Teach" at http://billgothard.com/bill/about/whatiteach/

79. Matt Benson. Personal Interview. 11 August 2009.

80. Willis, p. 32.

81. Ripley, J., Garzon, F., Hall, E., and Mangis, M. "Pilgrim's Progress," *Journal of Psychology and Theology*, 2009, v. 37, n. 1, pp. 5-14.

82. John Stonestreet. Telephone Interview. 21 October 2009.

83. JR Kerr. Telephone Interview. 10 August 2009.

84. Stonestreet, Interview.

85. Dan Egeler. Telephone Interview. 10 August 2009.

86. Kinnaman and Lyons, p. 40.

87. David Noebel, *Thinking Like a Christian: Understanding and Living a Christian Worldview* (Nashville: Broadman and Holman, 2002), p. 6.

88. Nancy Pearcey, *Total Truth: Liberating Christianity from Its Cultural Captivity* (Wheaton, IL: Crossways, 2005), p. 20.

89. Stonestreet, Interview.

90. McDowell, Interview.

91. Ibid.

92. Steve Keels, *TruthQuest Survival Guide: The Quest Begins* (Nashville: Broadman and Holman, 2002), p. 34.

93. Ibid., p. 37.

94. Ibid., p. 47.

95. Ibid., p. 51.

96. Ibid., p. 59.

97. Ibid., p. 62.

98. Ibid., p. 71.

99. McDowell, Interview.

100. Ibid.

101. John Calvin, *Institutes of the Christian Religion* (New York: Westminster John Knox Press, 1960), p. 35.

102. Bonnie-Marie Yager. Personal Interview. 16 September 2009.

103. Andy Crouch, *Culture Making* (Downers Grove, IL: InterVarsity Press, 2008), pp. 65-77.

104. Myers, *Handoff*.

105. G. Curtis Jones, *1000 Illustrations for Preaching and Teaching* (Nashville: Broadman and Holman, 1986), p. 183.

106. Mary Verstraete, *PCT1: Professional Coach Training 1–Advanced Training For Distinctly Christian Coaches* (manual produced by the Center for Coaching Excellence for use in their Professional Coach Training 1 course), pp. 268-269.

107. See, for instance, Claudia M. Mueller and Carol S. Dweck (1998), "Praise for Intelligence Can Undermine Children's Motivation and Performance," *Journal of Personality and Social Psychology*, Vol. 75, No. 1, pp. 33-52.

108. Roger Erdvig. Telephone Interview. 12 August 2009.

109. Gunter Krallmann. *Mentoring For Mission*. Waynesboro, GA: Authentic Media, 2003.

110. Jeff's talk makes use of an outline that is part of a thorough and important study of biblical masculinity called *Five Aspects of Man* by Bill Mouser. You can get more information at www.fiveaspects.org

111. Jeff Myers, *Secrets of Everyday Leaders* (Nashville: Broadman and Holman, 2006).

112. Willis, pp. 21-22.

113. See "Mentoring: A Synthesis of P/PV's Research: 1988-1995," at http://www.ppv.org

114. Juergen Kneifel. Telephone Interview. 12 August 2009.

115. Ibid.

116. Shane Hipps, "Our Nomadic Existence: How Electronic Culture Shapes Community," http://www.qideas.org/essays/our-nomadic-existence-how-electronic-culture-shapes-community.aspx

117. Lois Zachary, *The Mentor's Guide: Facilitating Effective Learning Relationships*, (San Francisco: Jossey-Bass, 2000), p. 103.

118. Sean Bevier. Telephone Interview. 20 September 2009.

119. Wolfgang Seibler. Telephone Interview. 19 August 2009.

120. Lynn Harold Houg, quoted in Richard R. Wynn, Ex. Ed., Lead On: A Mentor's Guide (Englewood, CO: Emerging Young Leaders, Inc., 1998), p. 70.

121. Dwight David Eisenhower, quoted in *Lead On: A Mentor's Guide*, p. 71.

122. Seibler, Interview.

123. Donna Otto, *Finding a Mentor, Being a Mentor* (Eugene, OR: Harvest House Publishers, 2001), p. 83.

124. Egeler, Interview.

125. Kris Berger. Personal Interview. 18 March 2010.

126. Paul D. Stanley and J. Robert Clinton, *Connecting: The Mentoring Relationships You Need to Succeed in Life* (Colorado Springs: NavPress, 1992), p. 42.

127. Carla Herrer, Zoua Vang, Lisa Y. Gale, "Group Mentoring: A Study of Mentoring Groups in Three Programs," Prepared for the National Mentoring Partnership's Public Policy Council. http://www.ppv.org/ppv/publications/assets/153_publication.pdf

128. Stanley, Interview.

129. Crumpler, Interview.

130. Ibid.

131. Stanley, Interview.

132. Ibid.

133. Keith Anderson and Randy Reese, *Spiritual Mentoring: A Guide for Seeking and Giving Direction* (Downers Grove, IL: Intervarsity Press, 1999), p. 25.

134. Stanley, Interview.

135. For summaries of this story, see http://www.go2africa.com/africa-travel-articles/pilanesberg-national-park, or http://home.intekom.com/ecotravel/game-nature-reserves/pilanesberg-national-park/wildlife-fauna-flora.htm

136. Crumpler, Interview.

137. Benson, Interview.

138. Stanley, Interview.

139. Stoltzfus, Interview.

140. Crumpler, Interview.

141. Stanley, Interview.

142. Myers, *Handoff,* pp. 143-144.

143. Frank C. Laubach. *Letters By a Modern Mystic.* Syracuse, NY: New Readers Press, 1979.

144. Egeler, Interview.

145. Crumpler, Interview.

146. Erdvig, Interview.

147. Anderson and Reese, p. 44.

148. Rhodes, p. 37.

149. Stoltzfus, Interview.

150. Stanley, Interview.

151. Bobb Biehl, Asking to Win: *One hundred profound questions available to help you win twenty-four hours a day, seven days a week for the rest of your life* (Lake Mary, FL: Masterplanning Group, 1996), p. 7.

152. Anderson and Reese, p. 78.

153. If you'd like to look into this theory a little further, Altman and Taylor's book is called *Social Penetration: The Development of Interpersonal Relationships* (New York: Holt, Rinehart and Winston, 1973). A new study by Joseph P. Mazer, Richard E. Murphy, and Cheri J. Simonds looks specifically at self-disclosure theory of classroom teachers, reporting that teachers who use personal illustrations and self-disclosure in their teaching are perceived by students to be more effective in communicating course content. Further, the authors argue that teachers who use more self-disclosure on their Facebook pages have higher credibility with their students. You can find the study in *Learning, Media and Technology*, Vol. 34, No. 2. (2009), pp. 175-183.

154. Crumpler, Interview.

155. See, for example, Connie R. Wanberg, Elizabeth T. Welsh, and John Kammeyer-Mueller, "Protégé and mentor self-disclosure: Levels and outcomes within formal mentoring dyads in a corporate context," *Journal of Vocational Behavior*, 70 (2007), pp. 398-412. See also Chrystal Bartless, "Supervisory communication and subordinate job satisfaction: The relationship between superiors' self-disclosure, offers of help, offers of cooperation, frequency of contact, trust and subordinates' job satisfaction," *Public Library Quarterly*, 18(1), 2000, pp. 9-30.

156. Susan Hunt. "Spiritual Mothering: The Titus 2 Mandate for Women Mentoring Women." True Woman Conference. Chattanooga Convention Center, Chattanooga, TN. March 26, 2010.

157. Egeler, Interview.

158. Stanley, Interview.

159. Ibid.

160. Stoltzfus, Interview.

161. Ibid.

162. Stoltzfus, *Leadership Coaching*, p. 267.

163. Stoltzfus, Interview.

164. Stanley, Interview.

165. Ibid.

166. Ibid.

167. Ibid.

168. Stoltzfus, Interview.

169. Stanley, Interview.

170. Egeler, Interview.

171. Ibid.

172. Stanley, Interview.

173. Zachary, p. 52.

174. Stephen E. Olsen, quoted in Bobb Biehl, *Mentoring: Confidence in Finding a Mentor and Becoming One* (Nashville: Broadman and Holman, 1996), p. 54.

175. Stanley, Interview.

176. Ibid.

177. Ibid.

178. Frederick W. Robertson, "Christian Progress by Oblivion of the Past," in *Sermons Preached at Brighton* (New York: Harper and Brothers Publishers, 1857), p. 66.

179. Dean Kamen, *Saturday Evening Post*, September/October 2009, http://www.saturdayeveningpost.com/2009/08/24/lifestyle/features/profiles-creativity.html.

180. Benson, Interview.

181. Stanley, Interview.

182. Egeler, Interview.

183. Kneifel, Interview.

184. Crumpler, Interview.

185. See endnotes 12 and 13.

186. Rhodes, p. 38.

187. Kneifel, Interview.

188. This and other documents from the National Mentoring Partnership may be found at www.mentoring.org. The particular letter and permission form may be found at www.mentoring.org/downloads/mentoring_587.doc

189. Bobb Biehl, *Mentoring: Confidence in Finding a Mentor and Becoming One*, p. 161.

190. Ibid.

191. Hunt. "Spiritual Mothering."

192. Stanley and Clinton, p. 42.

193. Mentor Consulting Group's 82 ideas entitled "What Will We Do Each Week?" www.mentoring.org/downloads/mentoring_613.doc.

194. MENTORific Women!'s "75 Cool Activities for Mentors & Mentees!" available at www.mentoring.org/downloads/mentoring_1135.pdf.

195. Connie Witt and Cathi Workman, *That Makes Two of Us* (Loveland, CO: Group, 2008), pp. 92-93.